Sew Special Baby Gifts

Nothing says welcome into this world more than a personally sewn gift for the new baby. This book is packed with cute and useful gifts that you can stitch up in no time for the new parents.

Select one of the toy patterns filled with textured materials that will stimulate Baby's senses and awaken the curiosity in the little one. Or choose an organizer or diaper tote to help the new mom keep track of all those endless baby items. We've also included adorable hats, cute diaper covers, and a beautiful and easy jacket set, sure to get compliments and smiles from everyone who sees them.

So select your patterns, head to the fabric store, dig through your fabric stash, and sew up a fabulous personal baby gift that will truly be a one-of-a-kind gift from your heart!

Happy stitching,

Sharon Frank

Sewing Editor

Tidy Tot Bib, ***page 47***

Table of Contents

Sleepy-Time Giraffe, ***page 9***

Chic Beret, ***page 56***

General Instructions

Basic Tools & Supplies

Basic Sewing Supplies & Equipment

Besides a clean and fit sewing machine with a new needle in the appropriate size for your fabric and project, you will also need:

- Hand-sewing needles and thimble
- Pattern-tracing paper or transfer cloth
- Scissors
- Serger (optional)
- Straight pins and pincushion
- Seam ripper
- Machine needles: sharps
- Removable marking pens or tailor's chalk
- Measuring tools: tape measure and ruler
- Point turner
- Iron and ironing board
- Pressing tools: pressing hams and press cloths
- Rotary cutter, mat and straightedges
- Seam sealant
- Thread in appropriate color and weight

Fabric Selection

Refer to specific fabric instructions for list of recommended fabrics. Fabric amounts are listed based on the fabrics used.

Batting Selection

Batting provides loft and warmth to a project. Be sure to purchase the type of batting listed with each project.

Binding

Both straight-grain and bias binding are used. We suggest you use bias binding on projects with curved edges to take advantage of the natural stretch of bias.

Premade bias tape is available in a wide variety of colors and can be used; however, it is easy to make your own from coordinating fabrics that will really complement the design. Follow these simple steps to make bias binding:

1. Mark a 45-degree diagonal line on fabric along the selvage or lengthwise grain edge (Figure 1). ***Note:*** *You can also fold fabric diagonally so the crosswise grain straight edge is parallel to the selvage or lengthwise grain. Cut fabric along this fold line to mark the true bias.*

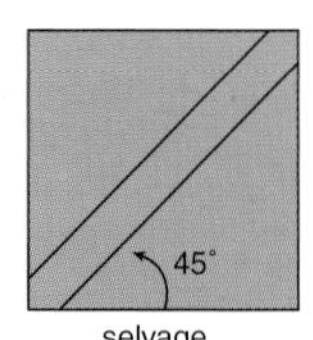

Figure 1

2. Using a clear ruler, mark successive bias lines the instructed width apart referring again to Figure 1. Carefully cut along lines. Handle edges carefully to avoid stretching.

3. Sew short ends of strips together diagonally; press seams open making one long bias strip (Figure 2).

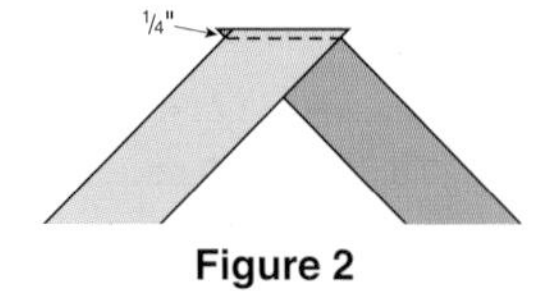

Figure 2

4. Fold and press bias strips as instructed in pattern to make bias binding.

To make straight-grain binding, cut fabric-width strips and refer to individual project instructions for joining strips and adding binding to the project.

Paper-Backed Fusible Web

You can purchase fusible web in sheets or by the yard from several manufacturers. Follow the manufacturer's directions included with the brand purchased. Always finish the edges of fused shapes with hand- or machine-stitched blanket or satin stitches to secure the shapes or as recommended with individual projects.

Safety First

We recommend using felt buttons wherever buttons are added to a project in this book. Felt buttons may be secured with stitching all around. Other types of buttons are a curiosity to a little one and can be pulled off becoming a choking hazard.

General Assembly Instructions

Seam allowances vary from project to project and pattern to pattern. If a pattern piece is given, the seam allowance is shown as a dashed line a particular distance away from the cutting line. Most projects use a ¼-inch seam allowance.

Cutting Without Patterns

Refer to the Cutting lists for each pattern and cut the pieces in the sizes listed. Label pieces as necessary with a washable marker or tailor's chalk for future reference.

Preparing Patterns for Cutting

Patterns from this book have to be transferred to either template material or to pattern-tracing paper or transfer cloth. Using the giraffe pattern on the template insert as an example, place a piece of pattern-tracing paper over the pattern and trace onto the paper using a pencil or marker. Transfer all instructions and markings to the paper.

Some patterns require you to lay a template on the fabric and trace around it. Wherever this is necessary, you will need to use template material. Using the Fun-to-Touch Play Mat as an example, the toy shapes need to be traced onto template material. The template is then traced onto the fleece, the fleece is folded with the marked side out, and you stitch on the marked line through both layers before cutting out, leaving at least ¼ inch beyond the marked/stitched line. In this book, templates are used for shapes that are stitched before being cut out.

The Wall Organizer project instructions recommend that you use transfer cloth and a marker. For this method, trace the pattern being used onto the transfer cloth, place the pattern on the fabric as directed with pattern and trace around the marked pattern using a black permanent fabric pen. The tracing will bleed through the transfer cloth onto the fabric. Follow the project instructions for further treatment of the traced shapes.

Assembly

Refer to the illustrations provided with each pattern for help in completing the steps.

Pressing

Pieces are most often joined with right sides together. After joining, the seams are pressed open or to one side unless otherwise specified. Laminated fabrics should be finger-pressed; no heat can be applied to the fabric surface. Refer to individual pattern instructions for specific pressing instructions as necessary.

Embellishments

Some projects have other shapes or notions added to their surfaces as a decoration. Follow the instructions carefully when adding embellishments to any project. ■

Fun-to-Touch Play Mat

Design by Chris Malone

Discover the wonderful world of soft, fuzzy and crinkly with this fun-to-touch play mat. Easy to make with small pieces of assorted fabrics, this gift is sure to stimulate the senses of a curious baby.

Project Note

There are many textured fabrics and trims that would be good to include in this play mat. Be sure that anything used is washable. Do not use any trims that are not securely attached and/or could become a choking hazard such as buttons and beads.

Adding fusible vinyl is a fun way to make a slick texture out of any fabric you choose for the play mat. Be aware that it cannot be ironed on directly and must always be protected from the heat of the iron.

Specifications

Mat Size: 39 inches square

Materials

- 6½ x19½-inch piece fusible vinyl
- 6½ x 19½-inch strip green Minky or similar substitute
- Assorted scraps fleece or velour in white, yellow, green, pink and black
- Assorted dot scraps or ⅔ yard total pink, blue, green and yellow
- ¼ yard or fat quarter purple dots
- ⅝ yard black with multicolored dots
- ⅔ yard white with multicolored dots
- Backing 39½ x 39½ inches
- Batting 39½ x 39½ inches
- Coordinating all-purpose thread
- Gold embroidery floss or pearl cotton
- ⅜-inch-wide grosgrain ribbon: 44 inches yellow, 32 inches each blue and pink, and 12 inches gold
- ⅝ yard 1¼-inch-wide white rickrack
- ⅝ yard ⅝-inch-wide yellow rickrack
- Small amount of polyester fiberfill
- Permanent fabric adhesive
- Template material
- Basic sewing supplies and equipment

Cutting

Prepare templates for toy shapes using patterns from insert and referring to the General Instructions on page 2. Transfer all pattern markings to fabric.

- Sun
- Flower
- Flower Center
- Butterfly Wings
- Butterfly Body

From green Minky:

- Cut three 6½-inch squares.

From fleece or velour scraps:

- Make templates using patterns given; cut as per instructions for toys.

From assorted dot scraps:

- Cut 6½-inch squares as follows: two green, four blue and six each yellow and pink.

From purple dots:

- Cut three 6½ x 12-inch rectangles.

From black with multicolored dots:

- Cut one 6½-inch by fabric width strip. Subcut strip into five 6½-inch squares.
- Cut two 2 x 36½-inch border strips.
- Cut two 2 x 39½-inch border strips.

From white with multicolored dots:

- Cut three 6½-inch by fabric width strips. Subcut strips into seven 6½-inch squares and six 6½ x 6¾-inch rectangles.

Assembly

Stitch right sides together using a ¼-inch seam allowance unless otherwise indicated.

Preparing the Blocks

1. To prepare the three gathered squares, machine-sew one line of long gathering stitches down the lengthwise center of a purple dots rectangle. Sew

an additional line ⅜ inch on each side of the centerline. Sew a line of gathering stitches a scant ¼ inch from each long edge and a second line ⅜ inch away (Figure 1). Anchor one end of each gathering line with a backstitch and leave remaining end loose with long strands to gather.

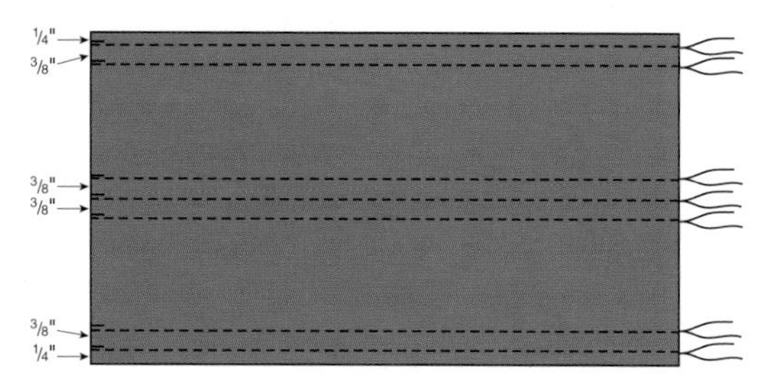

Figure 1

2. Pull bobbin thread on the center three lines to gather center of rectangle to a 6½-inch length. Pull the two bobbin threads at each stitching-line end to make a 6½-inch square. Adjust gathers evenly. Sew down the centerline and along each gathered outer edge with a regular stitch length to reinforce gathers. Repeat steps to make a total of three gathered squares.

3. To prepare rickrack squares, cut each size rickrack into three 6½-inch lengths. Pin the smaller yellow rickrack 1½ inches from an edge of a yellow dot square; stitch in place by sewing through the center of the rickrack. Pin the large white rickrack 1½ inches from an adjacent edge; stitch in place (Figure 2). Repeat to make a total of three rickrack squares.

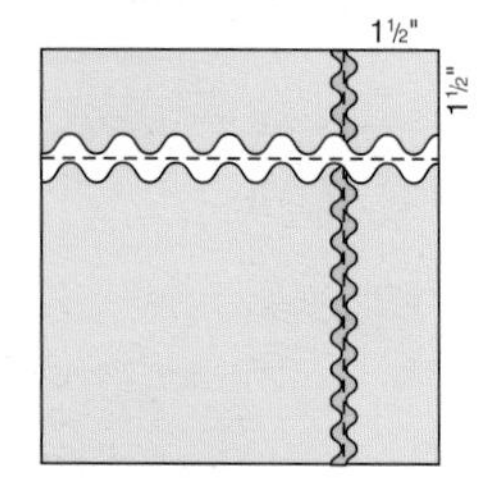

Figure 2

4. To prepare the vinyl coated "slick" squares, cut three 6½-inch squares from fusible vinyl. Follow manufacturer's directions carefully to fuse a vinyl square to the right side of three pink dot fabric squares.

5. To make the pocket covers for the toys, cut four 8-inch lengths from the pink, blue and yellow ribbons.

6. Pin two matching cut ribbons to the right side of a white dot 6½ x 6¾-inch rectangle, ⅜ inch down from a 6½-inch edge on each side with raw edges even. Baste to secure (Figure 3).

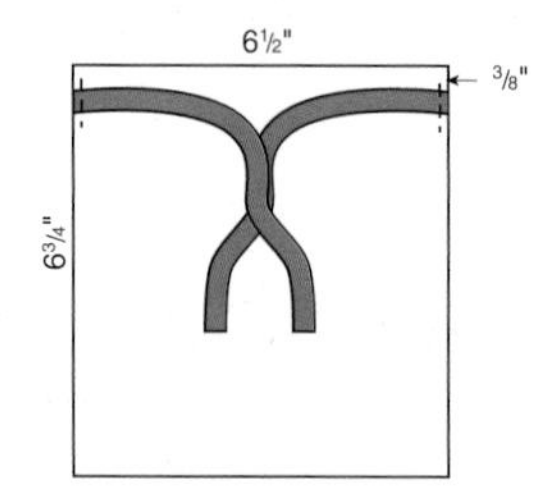

Figure 3

7. Pin a second white dot 6½ x 6¾-inch rectangle, right sides facing, to the rectangle with ribbons and sew both sides and across the top, taking care to not catch free ends of ribbons in stitching. Trim corners and turn right side out. Topstitch ⅛ inch from the seam (Figure 4).

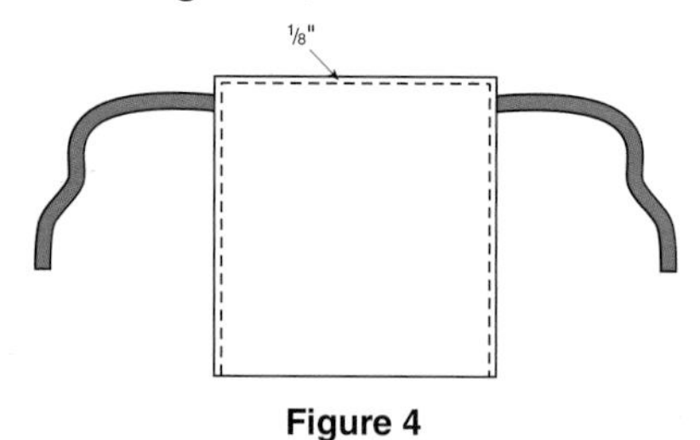

Figure 4

8. Repeat steps 6 and 7 to make a total of three pocket covers—one each with pink, blue and yellow ribbons.

9. To finish the pocket blocks, pin two matching ribbons to a white dot square ⅜ inch down from top edge on each side. Pin raw edge of pocket cover to bottom of the square. Baste to secure the ribbon ends and bottom edges (Figure 5).

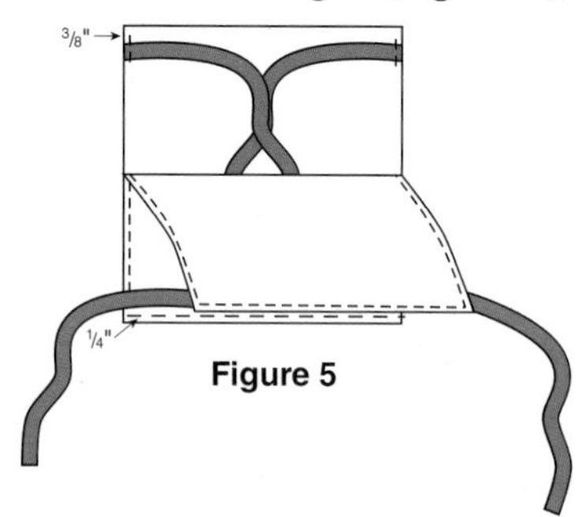

Figure 5

Completing the Play Mat

1. Referring to Placement Diagram, arrange and join prepared blocks (leaving the ribbons and tops of pocket covers free) in six rows of six blocks each, turning the textured blocks in varying directions for more interest. ***Note:*** *Insert pins into seam allowance only on the vinyl-coated squares as pin holes in the vinyl will be permanent.* Press seams in one direction, avoiding pressing vinyl areas.

2. Join the rows to make a 36½-inch square pieced center; press, avoiding vinyl areas.

3. Sew a 2 x 36½-inch border strip to top and bottom edges, and the 2 x 39½-inch border strips to opposite sides of play mat; press seams toward border strips as added.

4. Lay batting on flat surface; smooth with hands. Place backing, right side up, on batting and place pieced front, right side down, on top. With raw edges even, pin and sew all around, leaving a

6-inch opening on one side. Trim batting close to seam and trim corners. Turn play mat right side out. Press edges flat, avoiding the vinyl areas.

5. Fold in seam allowance on opening and whip-stitch opening closed.

6. To hold the layers in place, quilt the play mat by stitching near the seam lines between all the squares and between the pieced center and the borders. Sew two additional lines through the borders to finish.

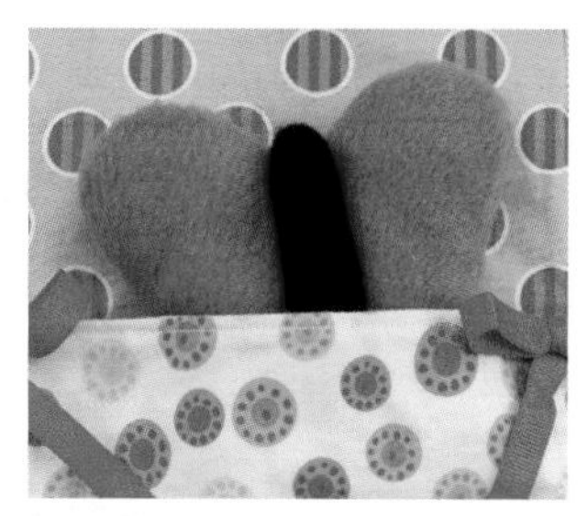

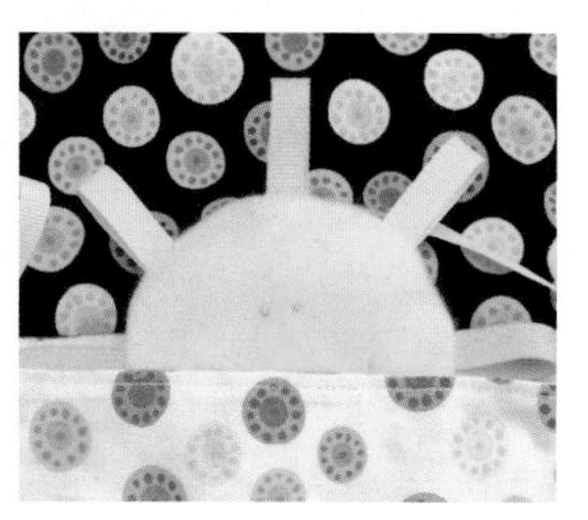

Completing the Toys

1. To make the flower toy, use prepared template to trace flower onto wrong side of fleece as directed on pattern. Fold fabric in half with complete outline on top and stitch all around on lines. Cut out ⅛ inch from seam and clip curves.

2. Make a slash through one side only where indicated on pattern. Turn flower right side out through this slash. Lightly stuff with fiberfill and whipstitch the slash closed.

3. Repeat steps 1 and 2 with flower center. Glue the flower center to the flower with the slashed sides facing. Stitch flower center to flower for additional security.

4. To make the butterfly toy, follow steps 1–3 for the flower toy, gluing the butterfly body to the butterfly wings. Stitch butterfly body to butterfly wings for additional security.

5. To make the sun toy, use the prepared template to cut out two circles as directed on pattern.

6. Transfer the face details to one of the circles and embroider the smile with gold pearl cotton or floss using a backstitch or outline stitch. Make a French knot for each eye.

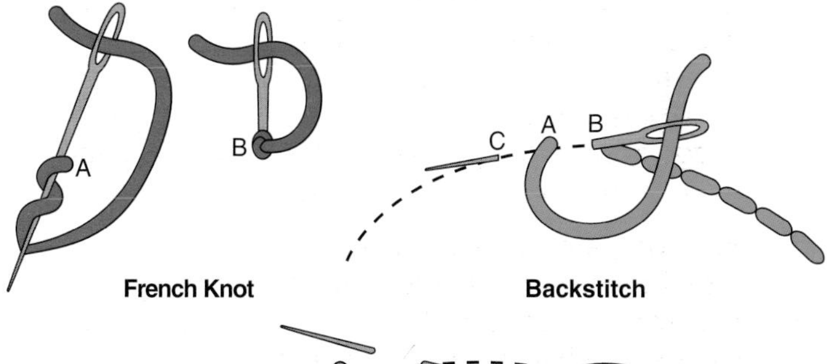

French Knot

Backstitch

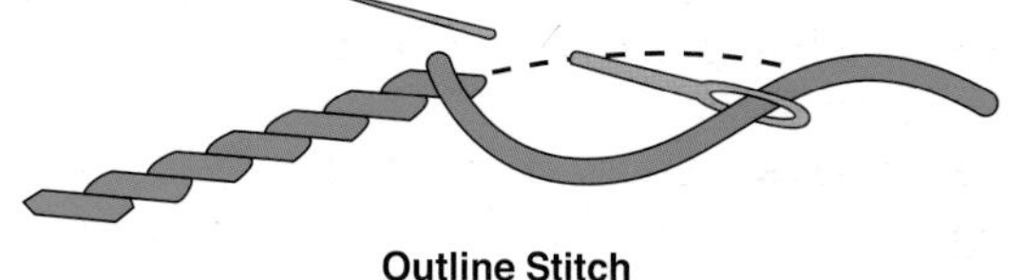

Outline Stitch

7. Cut the remaining yellow and gold ribbons into four 3-inch lengths. Fold each ribbon in half and pin evenly around the sun circle with raw edges even. Baste to hold (Figure 6).

Figure 6

8. Pin the two circles together, right sides facing, and sew all around, leaving a small opening. Clip curves and turn right side out. Lightly stuff sun shape with fiberfill. Fold in seam allowance on opening and whipstitch opening closed.

9. Place a toy on each pocket square; bring pocket cover up over toy and tie ribbons into bows at the sides to finish. ■

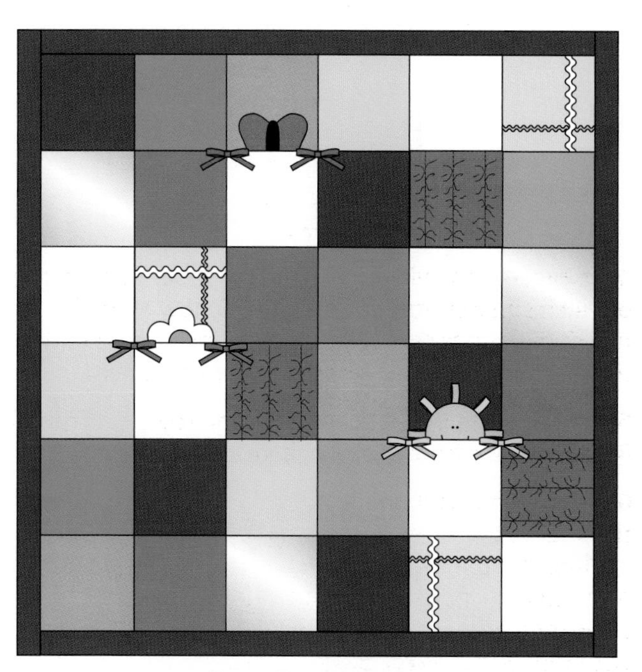

Fun-to-Touch Play Mat
Placement Diagram 39" x 39"

Sleepy-Time Giraffe

Design by Ahmelie Skistad

Make several of these sweet and easy soft giraffe rattles for baby shower gifts in under an hour. Small pieces of fabric and ribbon create this soft and huggable giraffe.

Specifications

Rattle Size: 7⅛ x 13½ inches

Materials

- ½ yard chenille, corduroy or faux fur (nap running selvage to selvage)
- Coordinating all-purpose thread
- Black embroidery floss or pearl cotton
- ¾ yard ¾–⅞-inch-wide coordinating ribbon
- Polyester fiberfill
- Jingle bell
- Pattern-tracing paper
- Basic sewing supplies and equipment

Cutting

Refer to the General Instructions on page 2 for preparing and using patterns from insert. Transfer all pattern markings to fabric.

- Sleepy-Time Giraffe

From chenille, corduroy or faux fur:

- Using the prepared pattern, cut one giraffe shape and one reversed giraffe shape, keeping the nap of the fabric running in the same direction on each piece.

From ribbon:

- Cut nine 2½-inch lengths.

Assembly

1. Transfer the closed-eye line to both giraffe shapes.

2. Using black embroidery floss or pearl cotton, hand-stitch along the marked lines using a blanket stitch (Figure 1). ***Note:*** *You may use black thread and a machine blanket or zigzag stitch.*

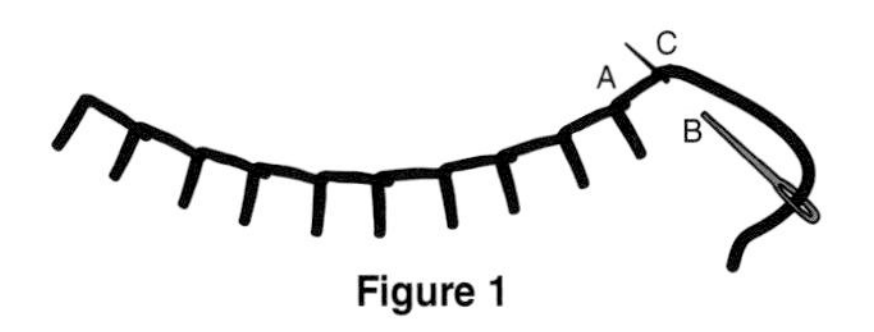

Figure 1

3. Fold each length of ribbon in half, wrong sides together, to make a loop; stitch across ends to secure (Figure 2).

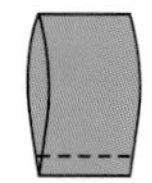

Figure 2

4. Evenly space, pin and machine-baste the ribbon loops between the double notches on the giraffe front (Figure 3).

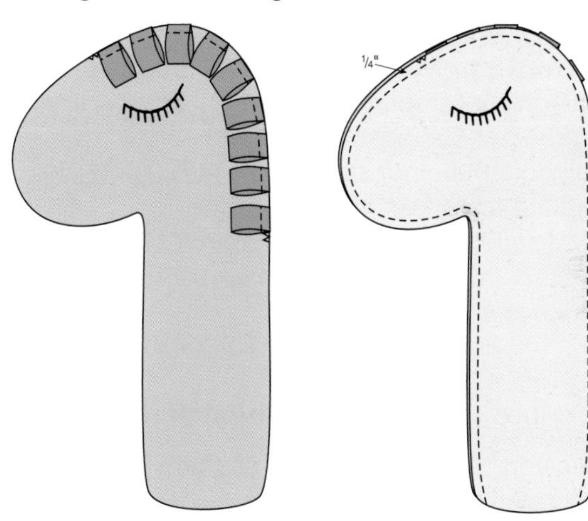

Figure 3 Figure 4

5. Place the two giraffe shapes right sides together, matching raw edges. Starting at one bottom edge and ending at the other, stitch around the shapes using a ¼-inch seam allowance, securing stitching at the beginning and end of seam (Figure 4).

6. Clip corners and curves, and turn right side out through the opening. Smooth seam edges with the eraser end of a pencil.

7. Stuff with fiberfill to desired fullness. Insert jingle bell into fiberfill, if desired.

8. Turn opening edges to the inside and hand-stitch opening closed to finish. ■

Peekaboo Block

Design by Jennifer Hagedorn

This colorful textured block will provide hours of fun for your baby. It's designed with textured fabrics and a secret door that reveals a fun surprise for Baby.

Specifications

Block Size: 3½-inch cube

Materials

- 8 (4-inch) fabric squares—textured fabrics, such as chenille and corduroy, and novelty prints* may be used
- Coordinating all-purpose thread
- 1-inch piece ½-inch or ¾-inch hook-and-loop tape
- 2-inch piece ½-inch-wide patterned ribbon
- Polyester fiberfill
- 3-inch square cellophane or clean, washed square of crinkly snack bag, such as a potato-chip bag (optional)
- Craft rattle, squeaker or jingle bell (optional)
- Cardstock or template material
- Air- or water-soluble marking pen
- Small hole punch or sharp tool
- Template material
- Basic sewing supplies and equipment

**Note: One square should be a fun peekaboo panel such as the lion's face used in the sample block.*

Completing the Block

Use a ¼-inch seam allowance throughout.

1. Use a very small hole punch or sharp tool to make a small hole in each corner of the template (Peekaboo Block Square) as indicated by the small dots on the pattern.

2. Place the punched template on the wrong side of each 4-inch fabric square and make a mark at each hole using the air- or water-soluble marker (Figure 1).

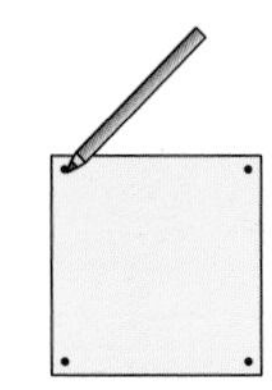

Figure 1

3. Choose two squares for the inner and outer faces of the flap.

4. Fold the ribbon in half with right side out and baste the raw edges to the center right edge of the inner flap square, raw edges aligned (Figure 2).

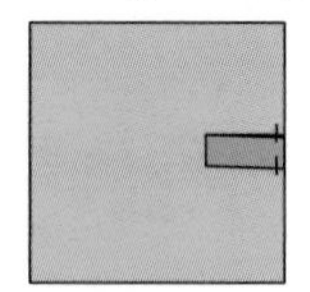

Figure 2

5. Lay the outer flap square right side down on top of the basted inner flap and sew around three edges leaving the edge opposite of the ribbon open (Figure 3).

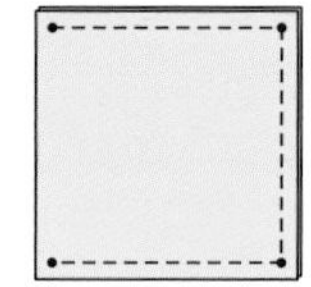

Figure 3

6. Turn the flap right side out; press and topstitch around the three sewn edges to add a decorative touch and further secure the ribbon (Figure 4).

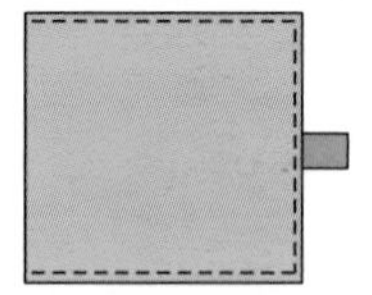

Figure 4

7. Insert the cellophane square into the flap for a soft noise element, if desired.

8. Sew the hook side of the hook-and-loop tape on the inner side of the flap, centered vertically and ¼ inch from the ribbon edge. Sew the remaining side of the hook-and-loop tape on the right side of

ROAR!
ROAR!

the peekaboo panel (the square that will be underneath the flap), centered vertically and ½ inch from one edge (Figure 5).

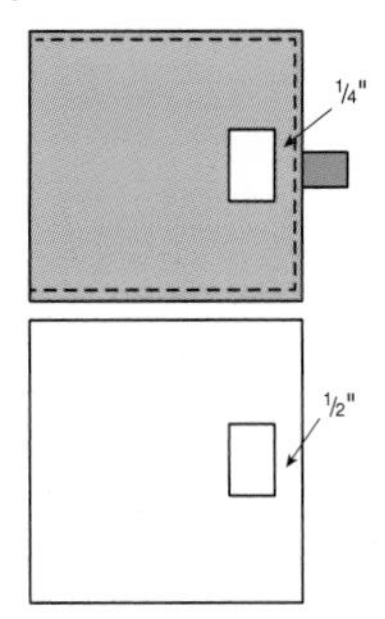

Figure 5

9. Lay out the remaining squares and assign each a letter from A to F as shown in Figure 6. Note that square B is the peekaboo panel. Lay squares A and B right sides together and sew one edge from dot to dot (Figure 7). Repeat until the A, B, C and D squares are attached in a row.

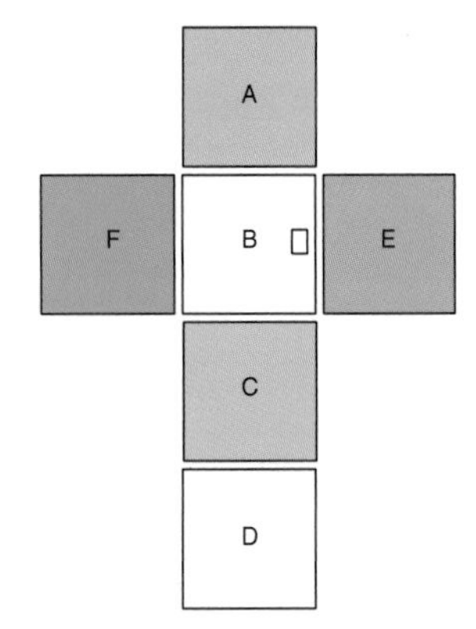

Figure 6

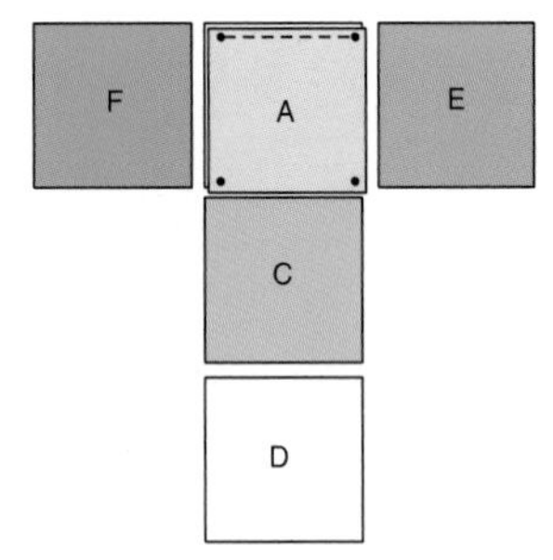

Figure 7

Tip

You can sew 2-inch folded ribbons in a variety of colors and textures into the seams for additional sensory stimulation.

10. Lay the E square right side down on the B square and sew together from dot to dot along the side edge (Figure 8).

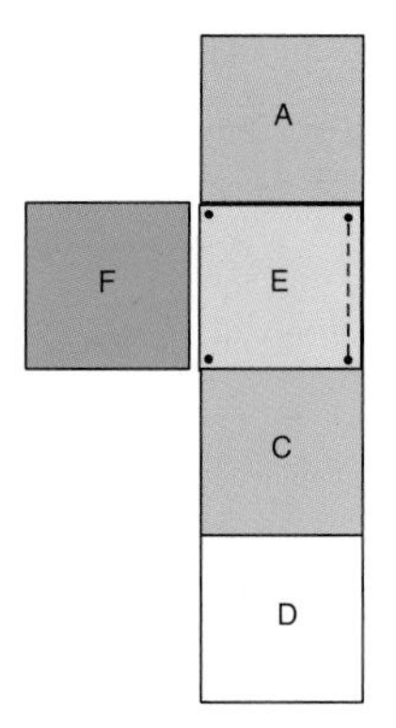

Figure 8

11. Open the E square so it is out of the way and lay the finished flap on the B square with the outer side facing up and the ribbon edge toward E. Lay the F square right side down on top and sew through all layers along the edge from dot to dot (Figure 9).

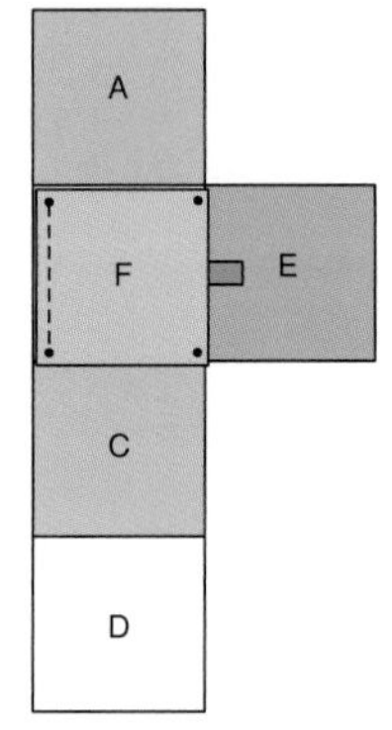

Figure 9

12. With right sides together, fold into a box shape and pin along adjacent edges. Sew along one edge from dot to dot (Figure 10). Repeat until all side edges are sewn.

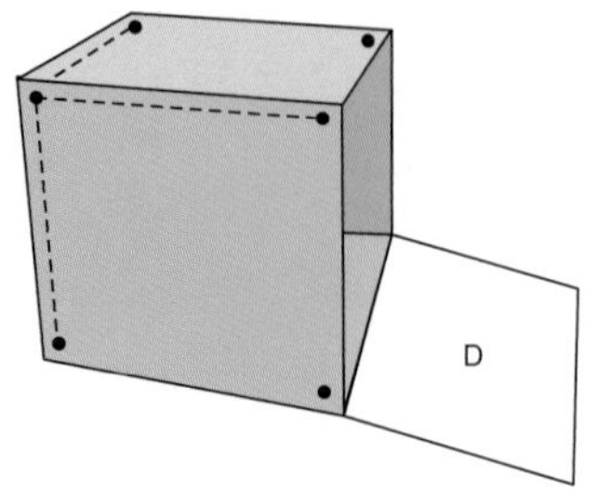

Figure 10

13. Fold the remaining square (D) into place and sew along three edges, leaving a 2-inch opening for turning (Figure 11).

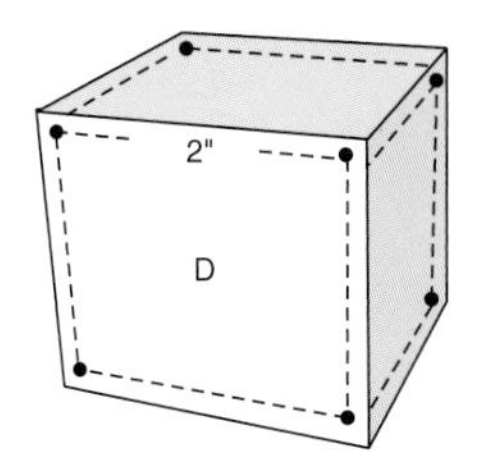

Figure 11

14. Turn right side out and stuff moderately with fiberfill, using a tool to press fill into the corners.

15. Insert optional noisemaker.

16. Securely hand-stitch the opening closed using an invisible ladder stitch (Figure 12). ■

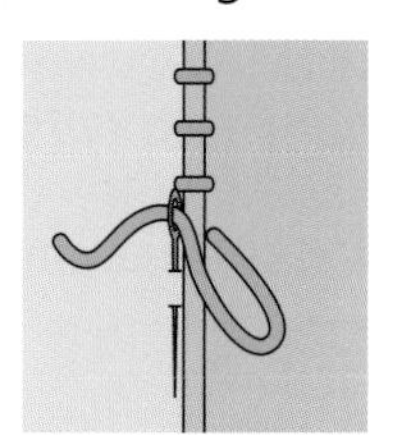

Figure 12

Organizers

Designs by Diane Bunker

Stash everything from baby toys to pacifiers in these two handy organizers. Make the one that best fits your needs, or make both as a gift set for double the organized storage.

Specifications

Vertical Organizer Size: 7 x 25 inches
Horizontal Organizer Size: 24½ x 7 inches

Materials

- 1 fat quarter green tonal for leaves and stems
- 1 fat quarter pink tonal for flowers
- 6 different fat quarters black-and-white print for binding
- 1¾ yards yellow tonal for background for both organizers
- 1 yard single-sided fusible ultra-firm stabilizer
- 15 x 50-inch rectangle thin cotton batting
- Coordinating all-purpose thread
- Black 40-wt. 100 percent rayon thread
- 2 (9 x 12-inch) sheets of double-stick fusible web
- ½ yard ⅛-inch-wide elastic
- 10 (18-inch long, 20-guage) cloth-covered floral wires
- Wire cutters
- Fast-grab tacky glue or fabric adhesive
- Pink seed bead mix
- Green seed bead mix
- Dual-tip black permanent fabric pen
- Transfer cloth or pattern-tracing paper
- Walking foot (optional)
- Darning foot
- ¼-inch foot or quilting foot (optional)
- Basic sewing supplies and equipment

Cutting for Vertical Organizer

Refer to the General Instructions on page 2 for preparing and using patterns from insert. Transfer all pattern markings to fabric. Refer to the Embellishments at the end of these instructions for preparing flowers and leaves with the transfer cloth or pattern-tracing paper.

- Organizers A (vertical and horizontal)
- Organizers B (vertical)
- Organizers Flower
- Organizers Leaf

From green tonal:

- Tear six ½ x 21-inch strips.
- Cut two 7½ x 21-inch rectangles (approximately).

From pink tonal:

- Cut two 8 x 21-inch rectangles.

From six black-and-white prints:

- Cut six A pieces from each print using pattern given for binding.
- Tear ½ x 21-inch strips from remaining prints.

From yellow tonal:

- Cut two 7 x 25-inch rectangles for back.
- Cut one 7 x 31½-inch rectangle for front lining.
- Cut three 7 x 11-inch rectangles for front.

From batting:

- Cut one 7 x 31½-inch rectangle.

From stabilizer:

- Cut one 7 x 25-inch rectangle.

Completing the Vertical Organizer

Use a ¼-inch seam allowance unless otherwise directed.

1. To make the binding, join the A pieces end to end to make a long strip (Figure 1). Press seams in one direction; trim excess seams at edges after pressing, if necessary.

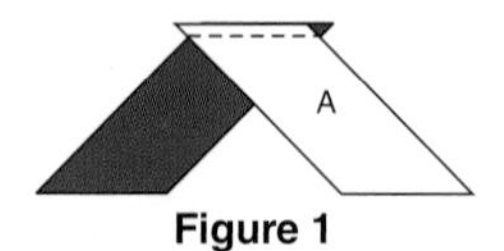

Figure 1

2. Fold the pieced strip in half wrong sides together along length and press to make the binding strip.

3. Iron the stabilizer to the wrong side of one 7 x 25-inch back rectangle referring to manufacturer's instructions.

4. Place the second 7 x 25-inch back rectangle right side up on the stabilizer side of the fused back

A
36

rectangle and baste the layers together around all edges using a ¼-inch seam allowance. Trim the edges as close to the stitching as you can (Figure 2).

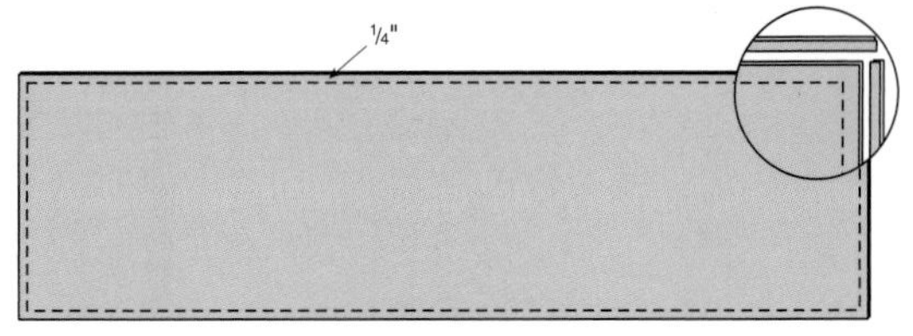

Figure 2

5. Pin the binding strip to one long side of the non-stabilizer side of the layered back rectangles and stitch. Wrap the binding strip to the back side and stitch in the ditch from the right side, catching the folded-over edge on the back side (Figure 3). Repeat on the opposite long side.

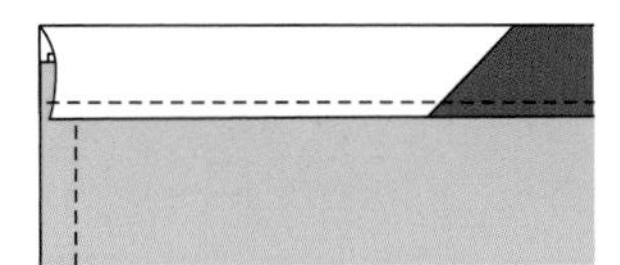

Figure 3

6. Join the three 7 x 11-inch front rectangles on the short ends to make a long strip; press seams open.

7. Sandwich the batting between the pieced strip and the 7 x 31½-inch front lining rectangle; machine-baste layers together ⅛ inch from outer edges all around (Figure 4). Trim ends of pieced strip even with lining/batting layers.

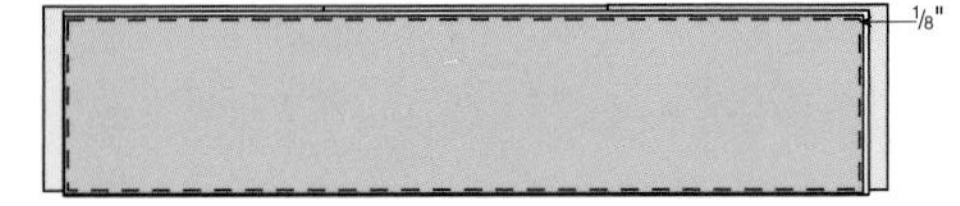

Figure 4

8. Bind both long edges as in step 5.

9. Measure 8¼ inches in from each end of the bound back piece and pin to mark (Figure 5).

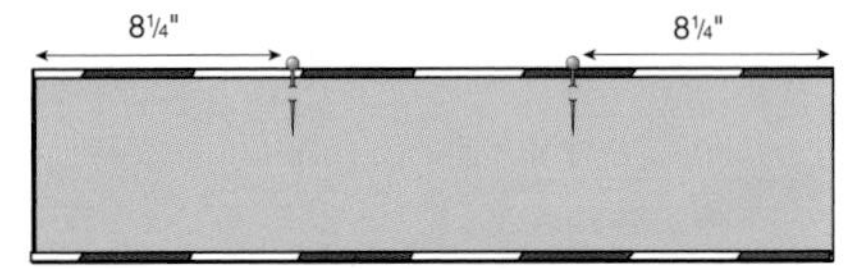

Figure 5

10. Referring to Figure 6, pin the bound front to the bound back at both ends and the sewn sections with seams at the pinned measurements and stitch the four pinned areas in place, securing stitching at the beginning and end of seams.

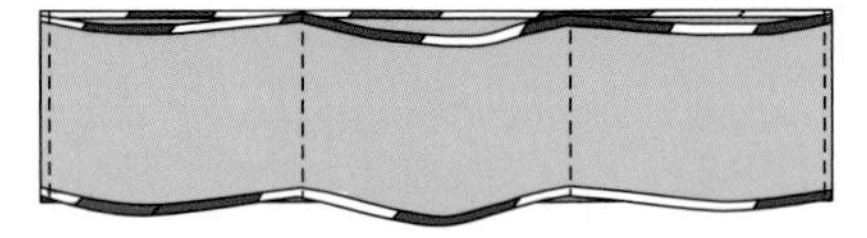

Figure 6

11. Cut a binding strip to fit each end allowing an extra ¼ inch at ends to turn in after stitching (Figure 7). Center, pin and stitch a binding strip to each end.

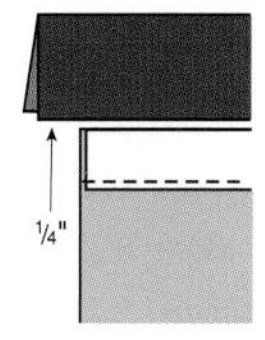

Figure 7

12. Fold over excess at each end and fold the strip to the back side to cover seam; hand-stitch in place.

13. To make a hanger from the remaining binding strip, press the strip open and then fold it right sides together along the length. Stitch along the length to make a tube (Figure 8). Trim edges close to seam and turn right side out. Trim to 10½ inches.

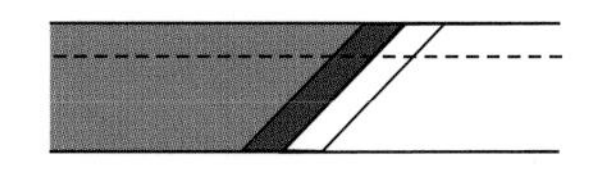

Figure 8

14. Twist two 10-inch lengths of floral wire together to make a stronger piece of wire. Snake the wire inside the tube, turn raw ends to the inside and hand-stitch closed. ***Note:*** *Wire should extend to each end of the tube.*

15. Hand-stitch the tube ends to the back corners of the top edge of the vertical organizer, making sure to catch the wire in the stitching. Form a nice curve in the wire for hanging as shown in the Placement Diagram.

Embellishments

1. Fuse a sheet of fusible web to the wrong side on one green and one pink rectangle. Peel off the paper backings and fuse same-fabric rectangles together to make double-layered pieces of fabric.

2. Trace the flower and the leaf shapes onto the transfer cloth using the thick end of the dual-tip permanent fabric pen.

3. Lay the traced leaf on top of the green fabric and go over the lines with the thin end of the pen. ***Note:*** *The ink will go right through.* Repeat to trace a total of 18 leaves. Repeat with the pink fabric to trace three flowers.

4. Thread your machine with black rayon thread and add a darning foot. Drop the feed dogs. Begin free-motion stitching with the leaves and outline the outer edge twice starting at the stem, then going up the center almost to the top, go back down and add the first side vein; go back to the center and add the vein on the other side. Stitch the next two veins and end at the stem to complete leaf stitching (Figure 9). Repeat for each traced leaf shape.

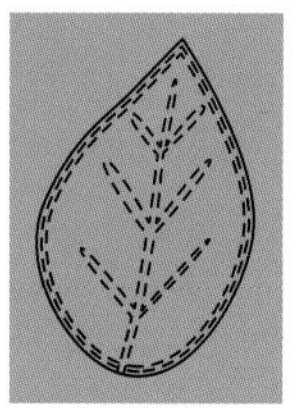

Figure 9

5. Repeat step 5 with the flowers starting at the flower center area and outlining the flowers twice. Add the three veins in each petal (Figure 10).

Figure 10

6. Cut the leaves and flowers out on the traced lines.

7. Change the presser foot back to the ¼-inch foot.

8. Cut each leaf from the center of the base to the second vein line (Figure 11).

Figure 11

9. Overlap the cut edges to make a pleat at the base of each leaf; tack down with a satin stitch with the feed dogs still down (Figure 12).

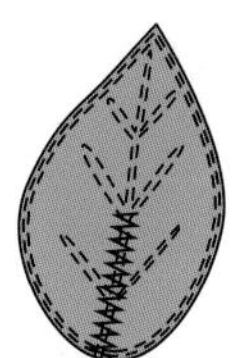

Figure 12

10. Fold each flower in half and in half again to resemble a fan. Satin-stitch at the flower center to hold the shape (Figure 13).

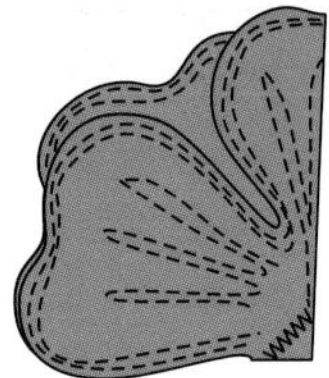

Figure 13

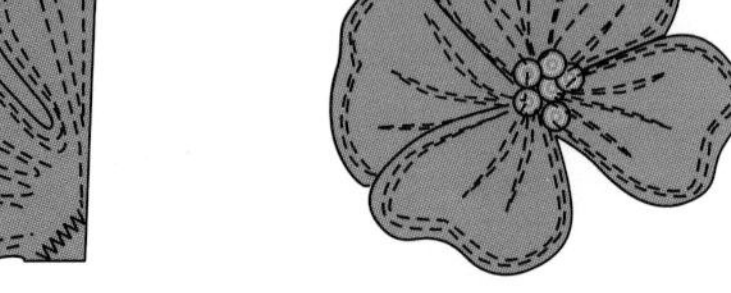

Figure 14

11. Open the flowers and hand-stitch pink seed beads to the center using black thread (Figure 14). Hand-stitch a flower to the top center of each pocket section of the organizer, referring to Placement Diagram.

12. Hand-stitch two leaves to one side and one to the opposite side of each flower just under the flower petals (Figure 15).

Figure 15

13. Cut three 10-inch lengths of floral wire. Begin wrapping a ½-inch black-and-white print fabric strip around one of the wires, adding a little fabric adhesive to the top of the wire to secure end. Wrap until you are to the end of the fabric strip, add a different strip and continue wrapping. Glue to secure the end and trim. Repeat to wrap two remaining lengths of wire.

14. Wrap each of these fabric-wrapped wires around something small such as a 2 oz. bottle to create a curved spiral—a double circle with one smaller than the other. Use the wrapped wire end to secure them together. Tack a bit off-center under each leaf-and-flower cluster (Figure 16).

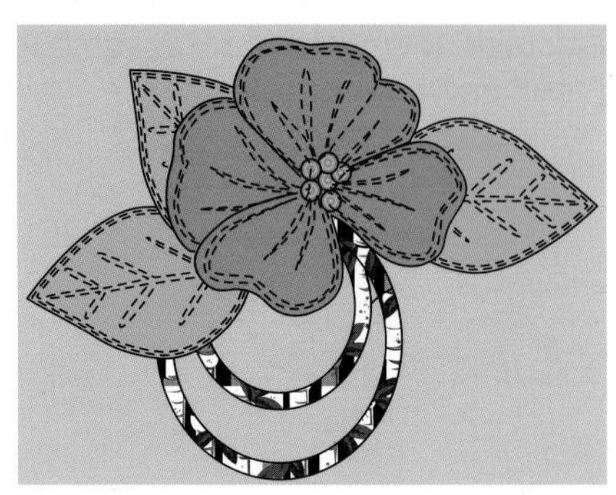

Figure 16

15. Cut six wires 6 inches long. Wrap wires with the previously torn ½ x 21-inch strips green tonal as in step 13.

16. Wrap a wrapped wire around a pencil, remove from the pencil and stretch a little; curl one of the ends a little tighter. Hand-stitch a few green seed beads to one end and along other areas as desired on the fabric-wrapped wire (Figure 17). Repeat with two more of the fabric-wrapped wires.

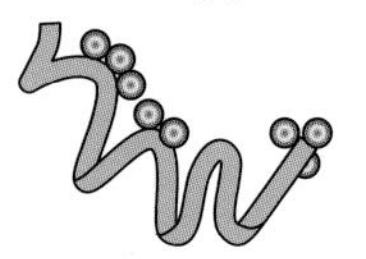

Figure 17

17. Hand-stitch a curled-and-beaded wire under each leaf-and-flower cluster next to the black-and-white wrapped wire.

18. Hand-stitch three leaves to each of the remaining fabric-wrapped wires. Bend the wire and stitch it under the black-wrapped wire to hang loose at the leaf end to finish each flower/leaf/stem cluster (Figure 18).

Figure 18

Vertical Organizer
Placement Diagram 7" x 25"

Cutting for Horizontal Organizer

From green tonal:

- Tear six ½ x 21-inch strips.
- Cut two 7½ x 21-inch rectangles (approximately).

From pink tonal:

- Cut two 8 x 21-inch rectangles.

From black-and-white prints:

- Cut 47 total A pieces using pattern given for binding.
- Tear ½ x 21-inch strips from remaining black-and-white prints.

From yellow tonal:

- Cut two 7 x 24½-inch rectangles for back.
- Cut one 7 x 38-inch rectangle for front lining.
- Cut three B pieces on fold of fabric using pattern given.

From batting:

- Cut one 7 x 38-inch rectangle.

From stabilizer:

- Cut one 7 x 24½-inch rectangle.

Completing the Horizontal Organizer

Use a ¼-inch seam allowance unless otherwise directed.

1. Make binding referring to steps 1 and 2 of Completing the Vertical Organizer.

2. Refer to steps 3–5 of Completing the Vertical Organizer to complete the back of the Horizontal Organizer using the 7 x 24½-inch fabric and stabilizer rectangles and the prepared binding, binding only one 24½-inch edge to finish as the top of the back of the organizer.

3. Join the three B rectangles on the short ends to make a long strip; press seams open.

4. Sandwich the batting between the joined B strip and the 7 x 38-inch front lining rectangle. Machine-baste layers together ⅛ inch from outer edges all around; trim batting and rectangle to match the curved top of the B strip (Figure 19).

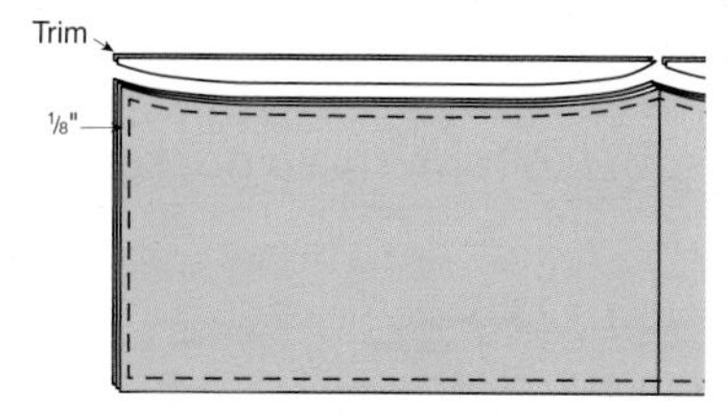

Figure 19

5. Pin and stitch the binding right sides together to the top curved edge of layered B strip using the ¼-inch foot.

6. Tack one end of the elastic on top of the binding on one end of the organizer matching elastic edge with stitched seam so the binding will enclose it (Figure 20). Wrap the binding to the lining side and hand-stitch one curved section at a time, being careful not to catch the elastic (Figure 21).

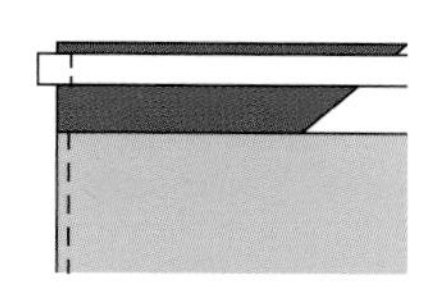

Figure 20

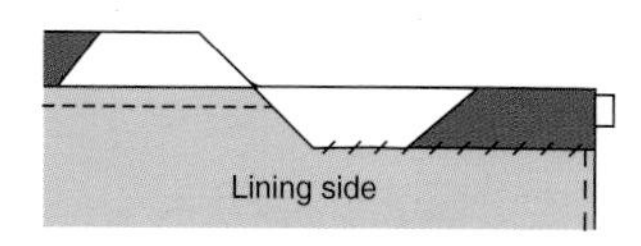

Figure 21

7. When you get to the end of a section, pull the elastic so the section measures 8 inches and machine-tack the elastic in place. Continue across the seam and tack the elastic again. Then begin hand-stitching to the next section. Repeat to make three sections. Trim excess elastic, if necessary.

8. Sew two lines of gathering stitches along the unbound edge of the front rectangle and pull to gather piece to measure 24½ inches long (Figure 22); adjust gathers evenly and machine-baste to hold shape.

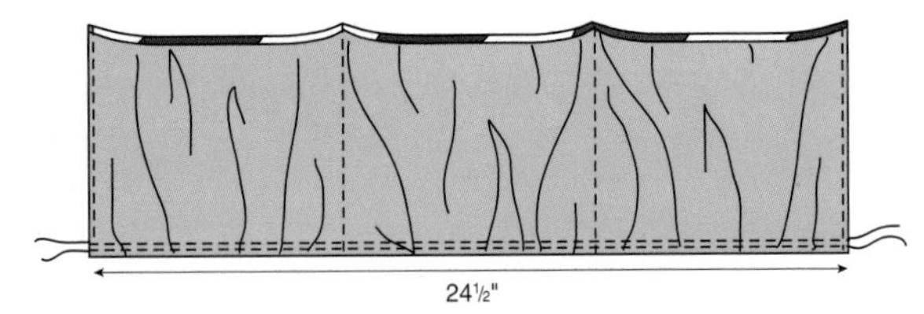

Figure 22

9. Measure and place a pin 8 inches in from each end on both the top and bottom edges of the back rectangle (Figure 23).

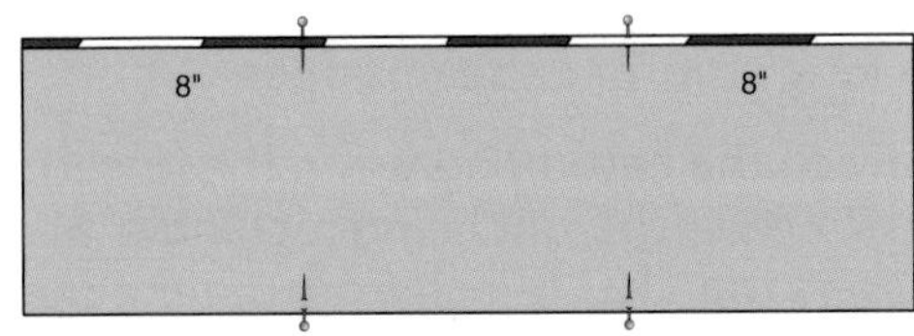

Figure 23

10. Pin the front of the organizer to the back at the sides and baste together. Topstitch the front sections seams down to the organizer back at the pin-marked spots to form three pocket sections (Figure 24).

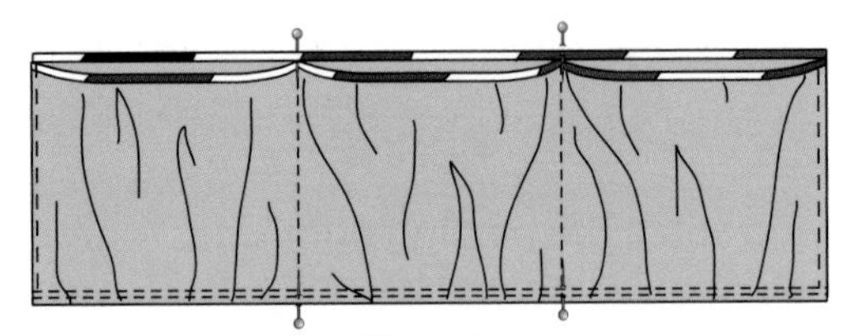

Figure 24

11. Machine-baste the front and back together along bottom edges.

12. Bind end and bottom edges referring to steps 11 and 12 for Completing the Vertical Organizer.

13. To make ties from the remaining binding strip, press the strip open and then fold it right sides together along the length. Stitch along the length, sewing the long edge to make a tube. Trim edges close to seam and turn right side out.

14. Cut four ties each 20 inches long. Turn in ends and hand-stitch closed. Find the center of each tie and fold it over the top of the organizer with one at each end and two on the middle sections. Sew in place (Figure 25).

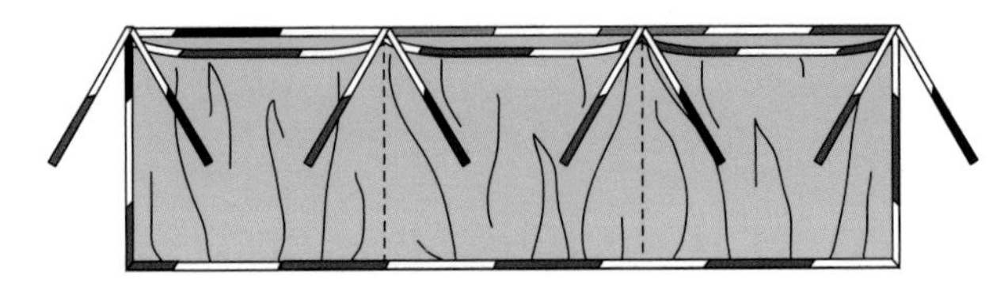

Figure 25

Embellishments

1. Referring to Embellishments for Vertical Organizer and the Placement Diagram, complete three flower-and-leaf clusters, without the long stem with attached leaves. Securely hand-stitch one cluster at the center top edge of each pocket to complete the Horizontal Organizer.

2. Tie to shelf pegs, dresser knobs or affix to wall and fill pockets with Baby's necessities. ■

Horizontal Organizer
Placement Diagram 24½" x 7"

Cuddle Me Blanket Set

Designs by Carol Zentgraf

Wrap your baby in these oh-so-soft and cuddly blankets.

Specifications

Blanket Size: 35 x 50 inches
Snuggle Square: 24 inches square

Materials

For one blanket:

- 1 yard Cuddle fleece print
- 3⅛ yards coordinating cotton print

For one snuggle square:

- 24-inch square each of two fleece prints
- ⅜ yard coordinating cotton print
- 6¾ yards ¼-inch-wide double-stick fusible web tape

For both:

- Coordinating all-purpose thread
- Press cloth
- Basic sewing supplies and equipment

Cutting

From Cuddle fleece print:

- Cut one 30 x 45-inch rectangle for blanket center.

From blanket cotton print:

- Cut two 4 x 51-inch side border strips along length of fabric.
- Cut two 4 x 36-inch top/bottom border strips along length of fabric.
- Cut one 36 x 51-inch backing rectangle along remaining length of fabric.

From the snuggle-square cotton print:

- Cut three 3-inch by fabric width strips for binding.

Blanket Assembly

Use a ½-inch seam allowance and sew seams with right sides together. Use a press cloth when ironing the fleece; do not touch the iron directly to the fleece.

1. Mark the center of each side of the blanket center.

2. Mark the center of each long side of each border strip.

3. Matching the center marks, pin the 51-inch border strips to opposite long sides and the 36-inch border strips to the top and bottom of the blanket center. ***Note:*** *Strips will extend beyond the quilt center at each end of each strip.* Sew the border strips in place, beginning and ending stitching ½ inch from the corners (Figure 1).

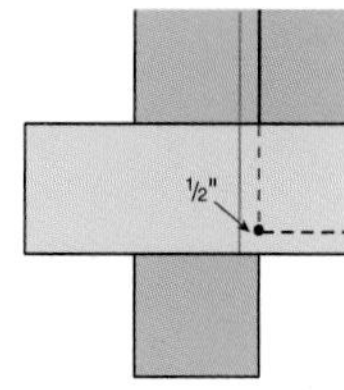

Figure 1

4. To miter the corners, fold each corner in half diagonally with right sides together and the border strips aligned (Figure 2).

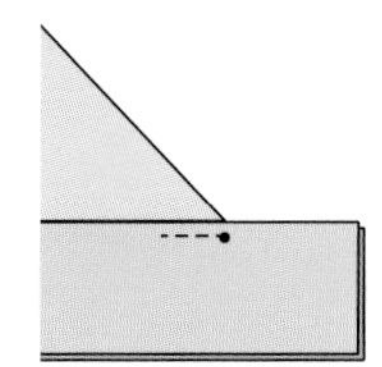

Figure 2

5. Using a clear ruler and fabric marker, draw a line from the corner of the stitching to the outer corner of the layered borders (Figure 3).

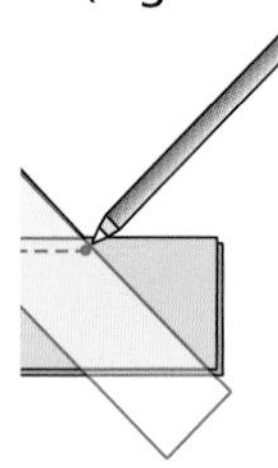

Figure 3

6. Sew along the marked line. Trim the excess fabric and press the seam open.

7. Sew the blanket front to the backing rectangle right sides together, leaving a 3–4-inch opening for turning. Turn right side out.

8. Turn opening edges to the inside along seam allowance; slipstitch the opening closed.

9. Topstitch ¼ inch around the edges of the blanket to finish.

Snuggle Square Assembly

1. To make the snuggle square, baste the fleece print squares together with wrong sides facing and edges even.

2. Join the binding strips on the short ends to make a long strip. Fold the strip in half along length with wrong sides together and press. Open the strip and press the long raw edges to the wrong side to meet in the center (Figure 4). Press the strip in half again.

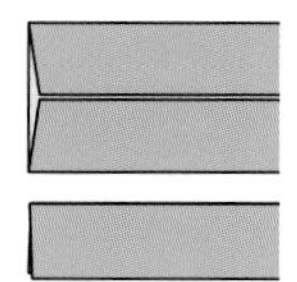

Figure 4

3. On the inside of the folded strip, apply fusible web tape along both long bottom edges (Figure 5). Remove the paper backing.

Figure 5

4. Insert the edge of the layered fleece square into the folded strip (Figure 6), making sure it is even on both sides. Press to fuse the binding in place, folding at corners to make miters and being careful not to touch the iron directly to the fleece.

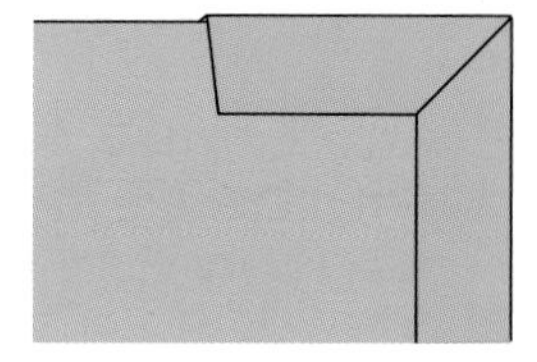

Figure 6

5. To end the binding, cut the strip 2 inches past the beginning end, turn the end under; overlap the beginning end into the folded end (Figure 7).

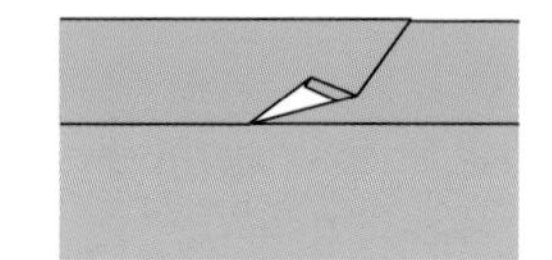

Figure 7

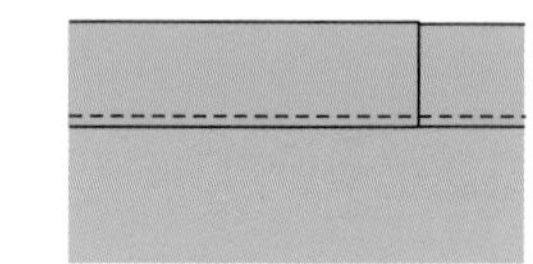

Figure 8

6. Edgestitch the binding in place to finish (Figure 8). ■

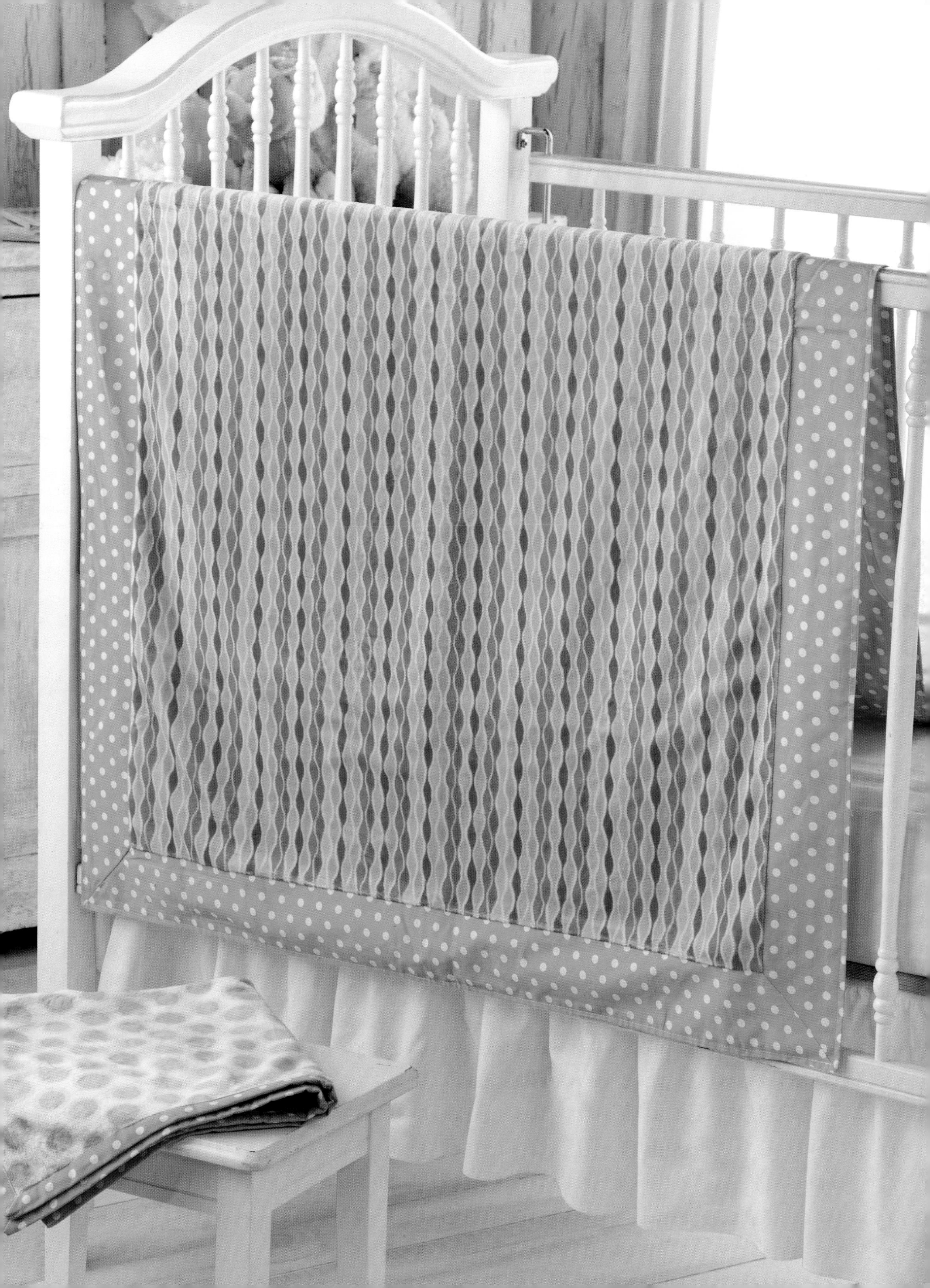

Tote-It-All Diaper Bag & Pad

Designs by Carol Zentgraf

Carry all of Baby's needs in this stylish bag. It's designed with both inside and outside pockets so everything is at your fingertips. A coordinating easy-to-clean changing pad folds and fits nicely into the interior pockets.

Specifications

Diaper Bag Size: 14 x 18 x 7 inches
Changing Pad Size: 14 x 22 inches

Materials

- ½ yard coordinating fabric for outside pockets and pad
- 1⅔ yards cotton print for outside of bag and pad binding
- 2 yards coordinating laminated fabric for bag lining and back side of pad
- ½ yard fusible fleece
- Coordinating all-purpose thread
- 10-inch strip and two 1-inch strips ½-inch-wide hook-and-loop tape
- 2 (½-inch) hook-and-loop dots
- 1 yard medium-weight fusible interfacing
- 2½ yards heavy-weight fusible interfacing
- ¼-inch-wide fusible web tape
- Teflon®-coated machine foot (optional)

Tip

***Stitching on Laminated Fabric:** If you do not have a Teflon-coated machine presser foot, you may cut a piece of masking tape or blue painter's tape to fit the bottom of your machine's regular presser foot. This will allow the laminated fabric to slide through the machine smoothly without sticking to the presser foot. It helps to use a little longer stitch length. A shorter stitch length makes too many holes in the fabric, which can weaken the fabric later in use.*

- Self-adhesive, double-sided basting tape
- Press cloth
- Basic sewing supplies and equipment

Cutting

From coordinating fabric:

- Cut two 9½-inch squares for outside pockets.
- Cut one 14 x 22-inch rectangle for changing pad.

From cotton print:

- Cut two 15 x 19-inch rectangles for bag front and back.
- Cut two 8 x 15-inch rectangles for bag sides.
- Cut one 8 x 19-inch rectangle for bag bottom.
- Cut two 6 x 22-inch strips for handles.
- Cut two 3-inch by fabric width strips for binding edges of the changing pad.

From coordinating laminated fabric:

- Cut two 15 x 19-inch rectangles for front and back bag lining.
- Cut two 8 x 15-inch rectangles for side lining.
- Cut one 8 x 19-inch rectangle for bottom lining.
- Cut two 9½-inch squares for outside pocket linings.
- Cut two 10 x 19-inch rectangles for inside pockets.
- Cut one 14 x 22-inch rectangle for changing pad.

From medium-weight fusible interfacing:

- Cut two 6 x 22-inch strips for handles.
- Cut two 9½-inch squares for outside pockets.

From heavy-weight fusible interfacing:

- Cut two 15 x 19-inch rectangles for bag front and back.
- Cut two 8 x 19-inch rectangles for bag sides.
- Cut one 8 x 19-inch rectangle for bag bottom.

From fusible fleece:

- Cut one 14 x 22-inch rectangle for changing pad.

Project Notes

Use a ½-inch seam allowance and sew seams with right sides together. Reverse stitching at the beginning and end of seams to secure.

Finger-press the seams on the laminated fabric or use a press cloth and a low-temperature setting on your iron; do not touch the iron directly to the laminated fabric. Use a Teflon foot when sewing on the right side of the laminated fabric.

Completing the Diaper Bag

1. Follow the manufacturer's instructions to apply the heavy-weight interfacing pieces to the wrong side of the outside bag front, back, side and bottom pieces. Repeat with the medium-weight interfacing pieces to the wrong sides of the handle strips and the outside pocket squares.

2. To make each handle, press an interfaced fabric strip in half with wrong sides together along length.

Open the strip and press the edges under to meet in the center (Figure 1).

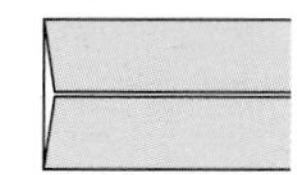
Figure 1

3. Press the strip in half again and bond the folded edges together with fusible web tape. Using coordinating thread, stitch the fused folded edges together 1/8 inch from the edge. Topstitch on the remaining long edge in the same manner. Repeat steps 2 and 3 with remaining handle strip to complete the handles.

4. To add the handles to the top edges of the bag front and back, use fusible web tape to adhere the ends of one handle to each bag rectangle, 4½ inches from the short side edges; machine-baste in place 1/8 inch from top edge (Figure 2).

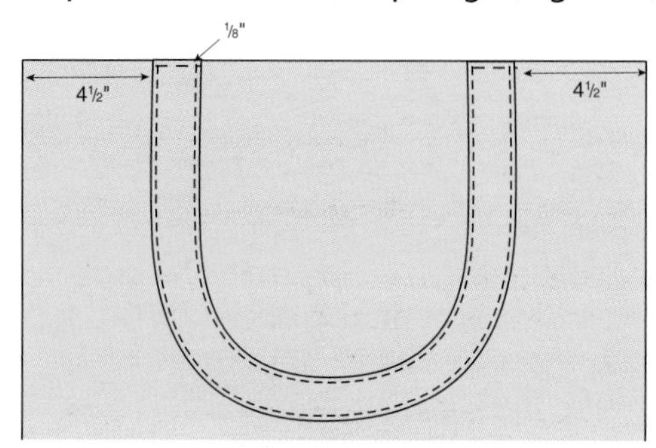

Figure 2

5. Sew the top edge of each outside pocket square to an outside pocket-lining square. Fold wrong sides together and press the seam edges. Topstitch along the top edges (Figure 3).

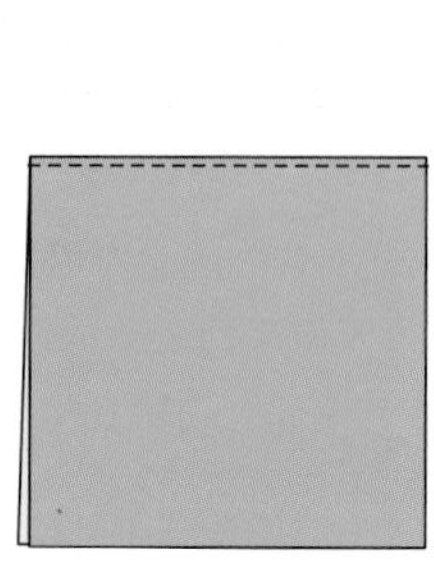
Figure 3

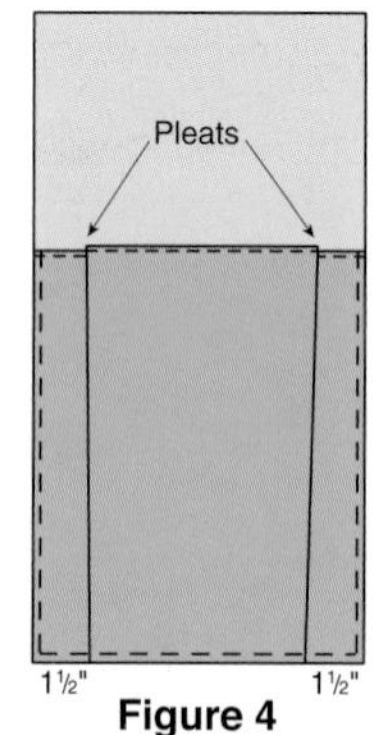

Figure 4

6. Pin each pocket to a side panel, laminated side facing the side panel, aligning the side and bottom edges. Make two small pleats in the bottom edge of the pocket 1½ inches from outer edge to fit the panel and baste to hold in place (Figure 4).

7. Sew the side panels to the bag front and back, ending the stitching ½ inch from the bottom edge (Figure 5).

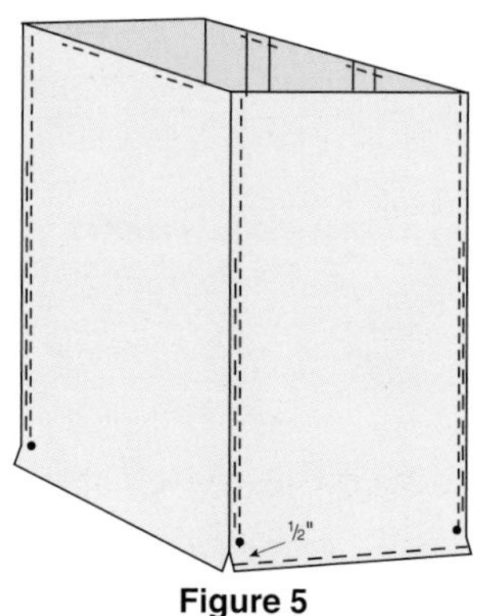

Figure 5

8. Sew the bottom panel to the bottom edges of bag, stitching to the stopped stitching between sides and front and back pieces (Figure 6). Trim the corners, turn right side out and press.

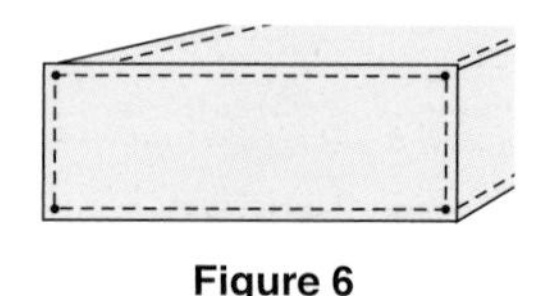
Figure 6

9. To make the lining pockets, turn under one long edge of each pocket piece 1 inch and topstitch in place. Topstitch ¼ inch from the top folded edges to finish pockets.

10. With the bottom and side edges even and the hemmed pocket edges at the top, use the double-stick basting tape to adhere a pocket to the right side of the lining front and back panels (Figure 7).

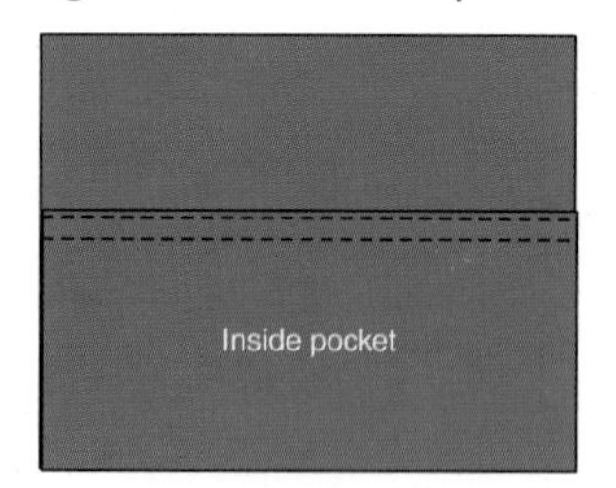

Figure 7

11. Follow steps 7 and 8 to assemble the lining, leaving an 8-inch opening in one bottom seam for turning; do not turn right side out.

12. Place the outer bag inside the lining with right sides together and the side seams and top edges even. Sew the top edges together. Turn right side out by pulling the outer bag through the opening in the lining. Turn the opening seam allowances to the inside and stitch the opening closed.

13. Insert the lining in the bag, press the top edges and topstitch all around.

14. Stitch the 10-inch hook-and-loop strips to the inside of the top edges, centering the strips between the handles (Figure 8).

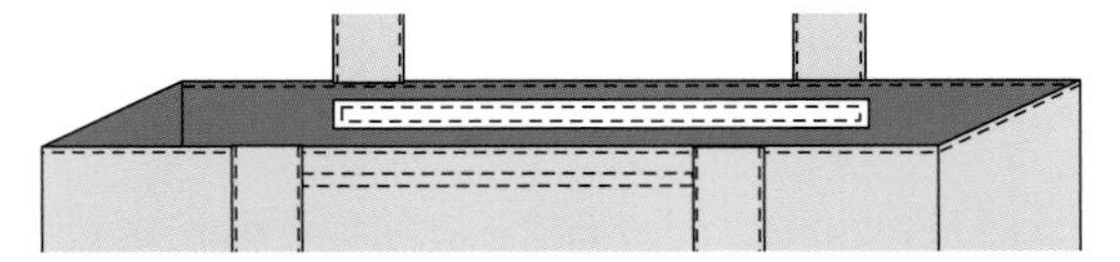

Figure 8

15. Sew a hook dot to the center of the inside top edge of each outside pocket and sew the loop dot to the bag, aligned with hook dot (Figure 9).

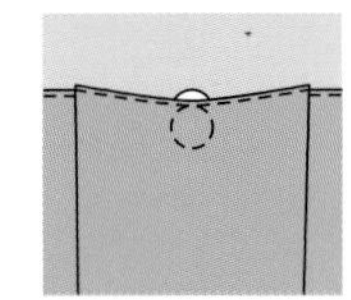

Figure 9

16. Sew a 1-inch hook strip on one outside side piece, ½ inch from top edge and ¼ inch from side seam (Figure 10). Repeat with loop strip on opposite edge of the side piece. Repeat on remaining side piece.

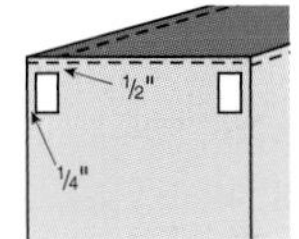

Figure 10

Completing the Changing Pad

1. Fuse the 14 x 22-inch fusible fleece rectangle to the wrong side of the same-size coodinating fabric rectangle.

2. With the fleece side facing the wrong side of the same-size laminated rectangle and raw edges even, baste the rectangles together.

3. Join the short ends of the binding strips with diagonal seams to make a long strip; trim seam allowance to ¼ inch (Figure 11). Press seams open.

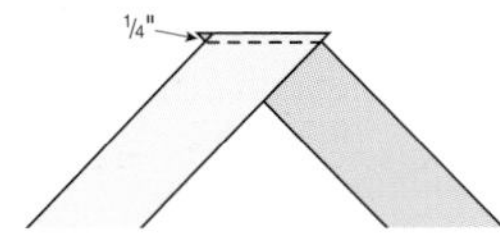

Figure 11

4. Cut the length to fit around the pad, allowing 6 inches extra for mitering corners and overlapping ends. Press the binding strip in half with wrong sides together along length.

5. Open the binding strip and press the long edges under to meet in the center. Apply a strip of fusible web tape along the inside of each folded edge (Figure 12).

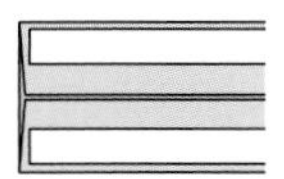

Figure 12

6. Remove the paper backing from the tape and wrap the binding around the edge of the pad, mitering the corners (Figure 13).

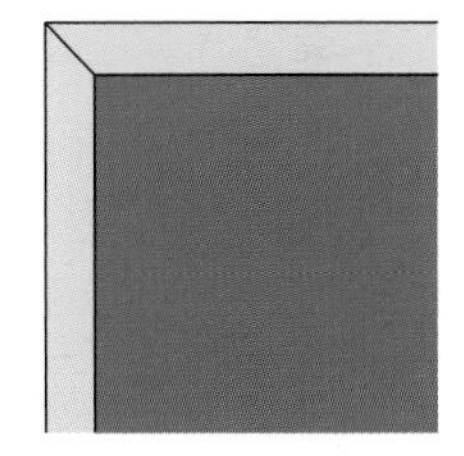

Figure 13

7. To end, trim the binding 2 inches past the beginning end and turn the short raw edge under. Wrap around the beginning end.

8. Fuse the binding in place on both sides using a press cloth on the laminated side.

9. Stitch close to the edge of the binding strip, being sure to catch the tape edge on the underside of the pad to finish (Figure 14). ■

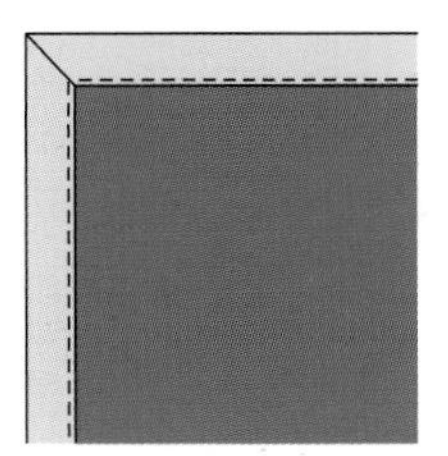

Figure 14

Dinnertime Bib, Place Mat & Wet Bag

Designs by April Forshee

This is a great set for the on-the-go mom! This laminated set can be wiped clean in an instant. The nonskid side on the place mat helps keep it in place and the laminate side makes it easy to clean.

Tip

Sewing With Laminates: *Laminated fabric cannot be handled like regular cotton fabric. However, using PUL (polyurethane laminated) fabric you may use the same sewing procedures you use on normal cotton fabrics, but there are some exceptions. The following is a list of special sewing tips to follow when sewing with laminated cotton fabrics.*

- *Do not use fusible interfacing. The heat and moisture from the iron will melt the laminate coating.*
- *Use a stitch length of 3 or larger. Shorter stitch lengths will create weaker seams.*
- *Use all-purpose thread and a size 14 needle.*
- *Use a Teflon®-coated presser foot. A roller presser foot is not recommended because it tends to scratch the laminate surface. You may also use masking tape cut to fit the underside of your regular presser foot to allow the laminate to slide through more easily.*
- *Bobby pins, paper clips or binder clips should be used instead of regular straight pins. Straight pins will leave permanent holes in the laminate.*

Bib

Specifications

Bib Size: 9 x 12½ inches

Materials

- ⅓ yard laminated cotton fabric (PUL)
- ⅓ yard flannel or other soft fabric
- Coordinating all-purpose thread
- 1 inch ¾-inch-wide hook-and-loop tape
- Bobby pins
- Chopstick or large knitting needle
- Tissue paper
- Teflon-coated presser foot
- Size 14 sewing machine needle
- Pattern-tracing paper
- Scrap of tissue paper
- Basic sewing supplies and equipment

Cutting

Refer to the General Instructions on page 2 for preparing and using patterns from insert. Transfer all pattern markings to fabric.

- Dinnertime Bib A
- Dinnertime Bib B
- Dinnertime Wet Bag C
- Dinnertime Wet Bag D

From laminated fabric:

- Cut one A piece on fold of fabric using pattern given.
- Cut one B piece using pattern given.

From flannel:

- Cut one A piece on fold of fabric using pattern given.

Completing the Bib

Use Teflon-coated presser foot when sewing with the presser foot touching the laminated fabric.

1. Mark the center front of the bottom edge of A and both long edges of B on the right side, inside the seam allowance (Figure 1).

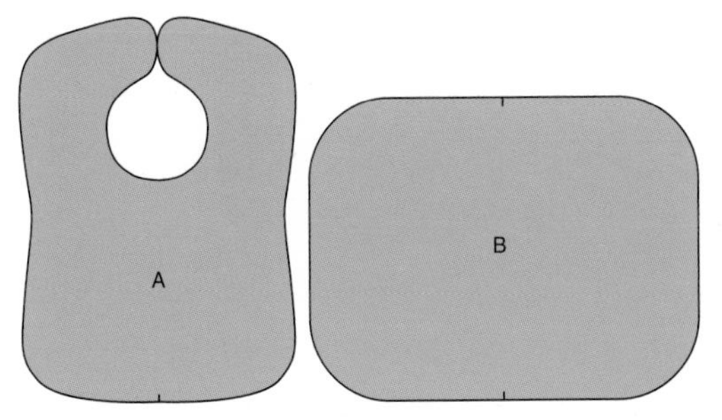

Figure 1

2. Mark the opening marks on the wrong side of the center front of the A piece.

3. Mark the corner darts on the wrong side of the B piece.

4. Fold and stitch darts on the marked dart lines on B; trim to 1/8 inch from sewn lines (Figure 2) and finger-press to open seams.

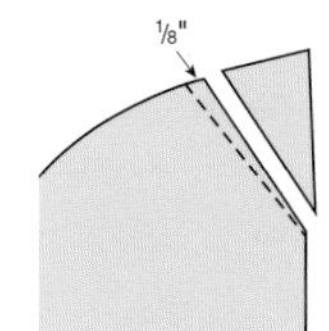

Figure 2

5. Fold B in half along length with wrong sides together, matching dart seams, and finger-press a crease to make a double-layered pocket (Figure 3). Secure with bobby pins.

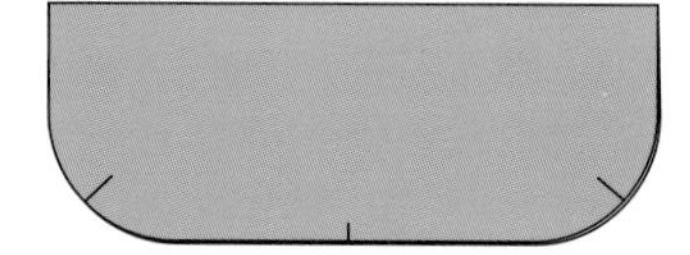

Figure 3

6. Topstitch the folded edge of the B pocket 1/4 inch and 1/2 inch from edge, and baste 1/8 inch from the raw curved edge (Figure 4).

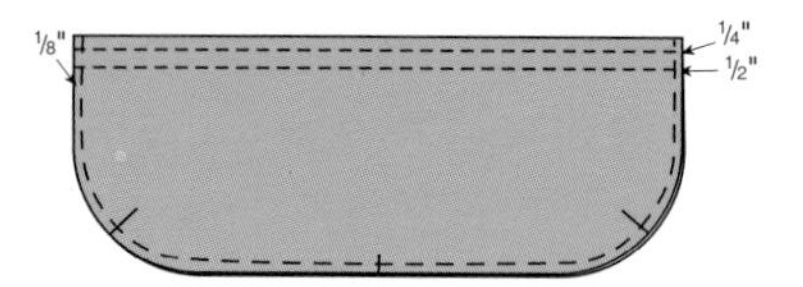

Figure 4

7. Matching the center marks, secure the B pocket on the bottom edge of A using bobby pins. Baste in place along the raw edges starting on one end of B and ending on the other side (Figure 5).

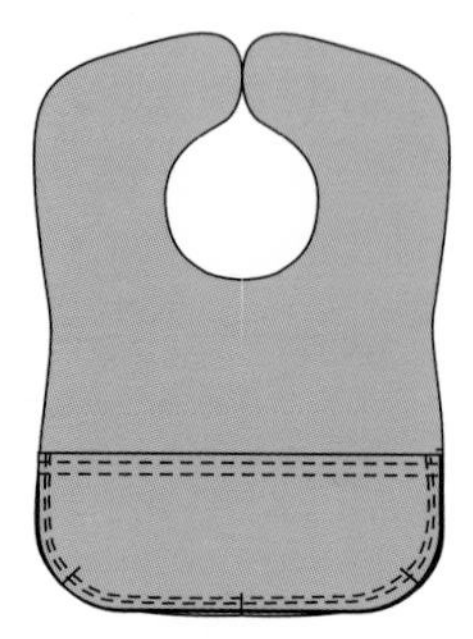

Figure 5

8. Place the basted A/B layers right sides together with the flannel A piece; secure with bobby pins. Stitch all around using a 3/8-inch seam allowance, leaving 5 inches open between marks (Figure 6). Clip and notch curves (Figure 7).

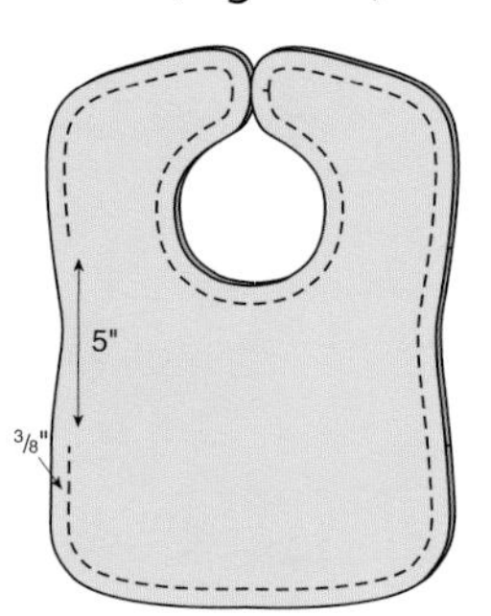

Figure 6

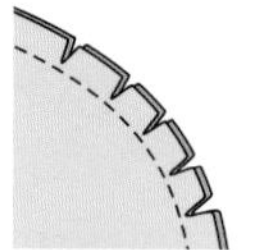

Figure 7

9. Turn right side out through the opening and use chopstick or large knitting needle to flatten seams from the inside; finger-press seams flat from the outside.

10. Finger-press opening edges to the inside along seam allowance; secure with bobby pins to hold.

11. Topstitch 1/4 inch from edge from the top of the pocket on one side to the top of the pocket on the opposite side (Figure 8), stitching opening closed at the same time.

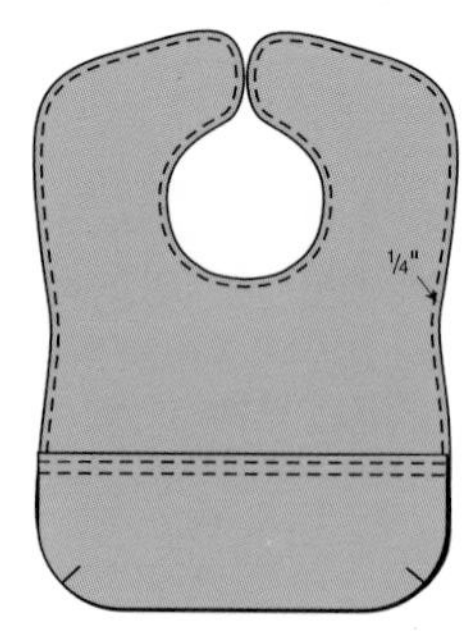

Figure 8

12. To finish, attach the hook side of the hook-and-loop tape to the laminate right side of the bib and the loop side on the flannel left side of the bib (Figure 9), placing a piece of tissue paper between the laminated side and the throat plate of the sewing machine for easier movement when stitching the hook-and-loop tape on the flannel side.

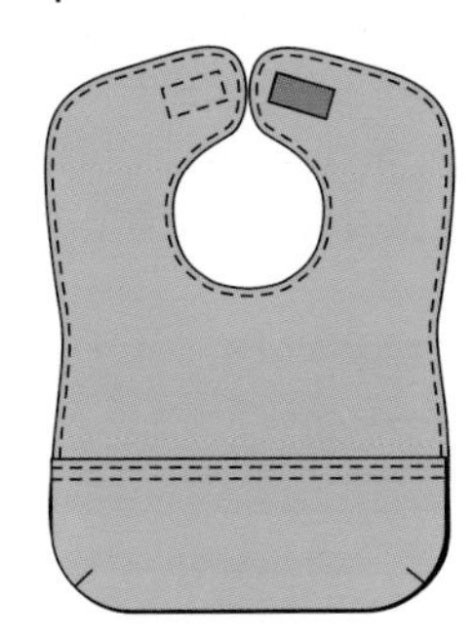

Figure 9

Place Mat

Specifications

Place Mat Size: 16¼ x 11¼ inches

Materials

- ⅜ yard laminated cotton fabric (PUL)
- ⅜ yard nonskid fabric
- Coordinating all-purpose thread
- Chalk or disappearing pen
- Bobby pins
- Teflon-coated presser foot
- Size 14 sewing machine needle
- Can, CD or other round object
- Basic sewing supplies and equipment

Cutting

From laminated fabric:

- Cut one 17 x 12-inch rectangle.

From nonskid fabric:

- Cut one 17 x 12-inch rectangle.

Completing the Place Mat

1. Mark rounded corners ⅜ inch from edge on the wrong side of the laminated fabric using a can, CD or other round object (Figure 10).

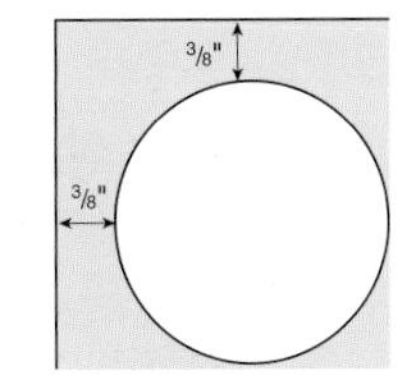

Figure 10

2. Place the marked laminated fabric rectangle right sides together with the nonskid fabric rectangle and secure edges with bobby pins.

3. Stitch all around from the marked side of the laminated fabric using a ⅜-inch seam allowance and stitching on the marked curved corners, leaving a 5-inch opening on one side. Trim corners and clip into curved seams (Figure 11).

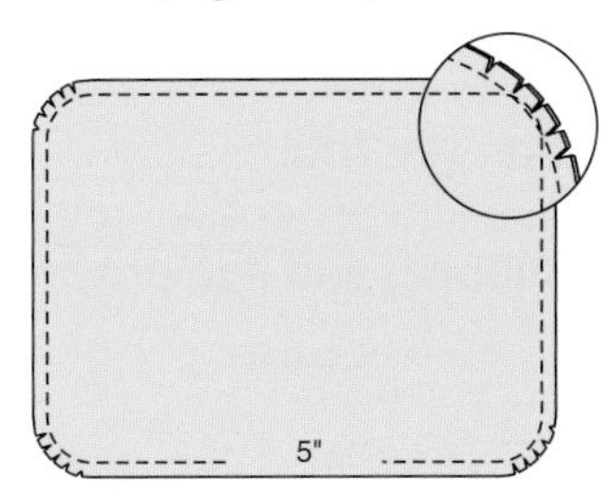

Figure 11

4. Turn right side out through the opening, finger-pressing seams open to help make edges flat. Fold opening edges to the inside along seam allowance and secure with bobby pins.

5. Attach the Teflon-coated presser foot to your machine; topstitch ¼ inch from edge using a 3.5 stitch length, stitching opening closed at the same time, to finish.

Wet Bag

Specifications

Wet Bag Size: 12 x 7¾ inches

Materials

- ⅞ yard laminated cotton fabric (PUL)
- Coordinating all-purpose thread
- 9 inches ¾-inch-wide hook-and-loop tape
- Chalk or disappearing pen
- Bobby pins
- Teflon-coated presser foot
- Size 14 sewing machine needle
- Basic sewing supplies and equipment

Cutting

From laminated fabric:

- Cut two C pieces on fold of fabric using pattern given (one for outer flap and one for flap lining).
- Cut four D pieces on fold of fabric using pattern given (two for outer bag and two for bag lining).

Completing the Flap

1. Transfer hook-and-loop placement lines to the right side of the C lining piece as marked on pattern (Figure 12).

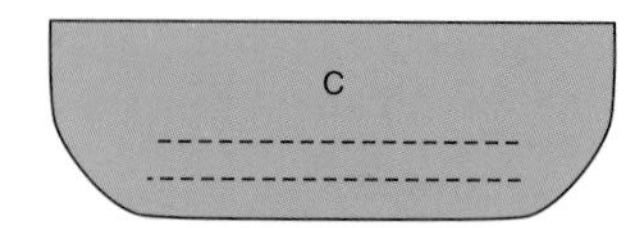

Figure 12

2. Place the hook part of the hook-and-loop tape on the marked line and secure with bobby pins; stitch in place along both long sides and each end to secure (Figure 13).

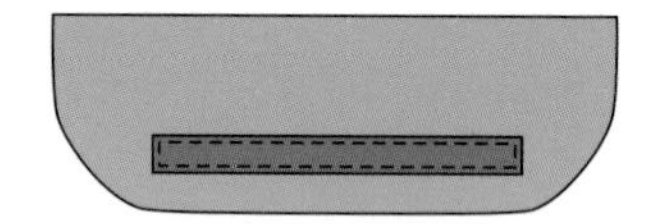

Figure 13

3. With right sides together, stitch the outer C piece to the C lining piece along the curved outer edges using a ⅜-inch seam allowance (Figure 14); clip curves.

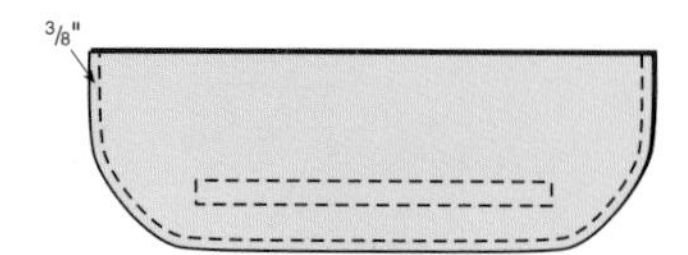

Figure 14

4. Turn right side out; finger-press seams open and flatten edges on the right side.

5. Baste the straight open edge closed ⅛ inch from edge.

6. Topstitch ¼ inch around curved edges to complete the flap (Figure 15); set aside.

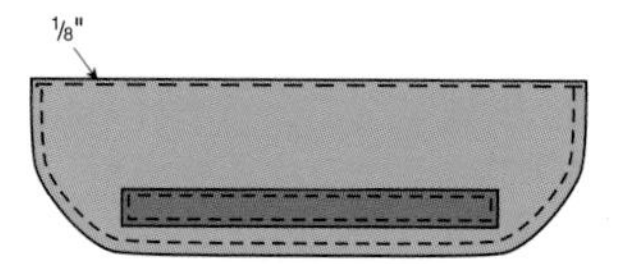

Figure 15

Completing the Bag

1. Mark hook-and-loop placement on the right side of one D outer bag piece.

2. Place the loop part of the hook-and-loop tape on the marked line and secure with bobby pins; stitch in place along both long sides and each end to secure.

3. With right sides together, stitch sides and bottom edges of the D outer bag pieces together using a ⅜-inch seam allowance. Finger-press seam open.

4. Pull the pieces apart and match cut raw corner edges and open seam allowances; secure with bobby pins. Stitch across corner edge using a ¼-inch seam allowance (Figure 16).

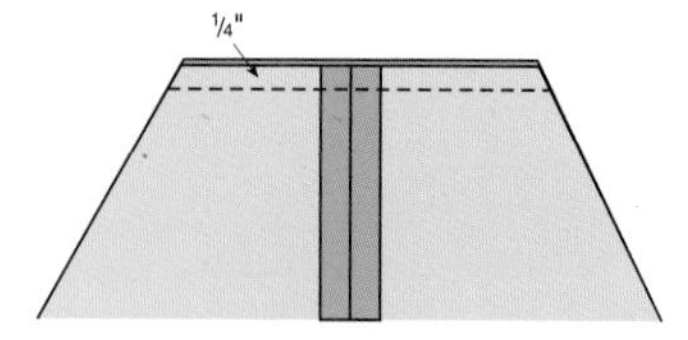

Figure 16

5. Repeat step 4 on the opposite corner of the outer bag.

6. Turn right side out; finger-press corner seams open and then flat.

7. Repeat steps 3–6 for bag lining except leave a 5-inch opening on the bottom seam for turning later; do not turn right side out.

8. Center the flap on the back of the outer bag (the one without the hook-and-loop tape) with right sides together; secure with bobby pins and then baste to hold (Figure 17).

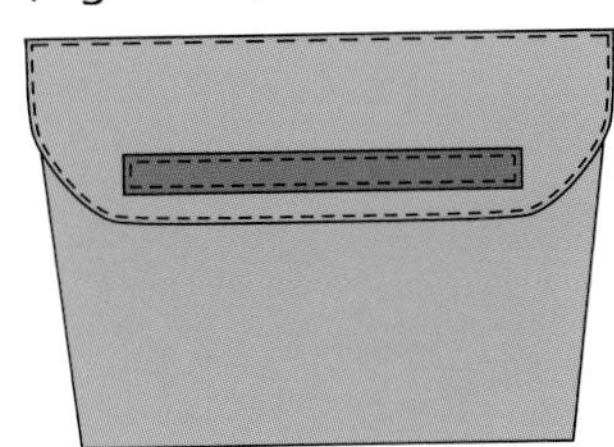

Figure 17

9. With right sides together, place the outer bag inside the bag lining, matching side seams. ***Note:*** *If the two bags don't match perfectly, adjust side seams as necessary to make them fit at this time.* Stitch along top raw edges to hold the layers together.

10. Reach through the opening in the bottom of the bag lining and pull the outer bag out through the opening.

11. Fold raw edges of the opening in the bag lining to the inside along seam line and stitch opening closed (Figure 18).

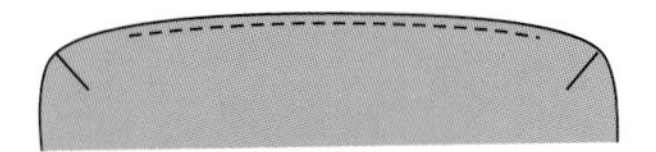

Figure 18

12. Tuck the bag lining inside the outer bag and finger-press top seam edges flat.

13. Topstitch ¼ inch around the top edge to finish (Figure 19). ■

Figure 19

On-the-Move Diaper Set

Designs by Holly Daniels

Make a handy diaper kit using pre-quilted fabric, fabric you quilt yourself, flannel or fleece. This kit holds travel-size wipes, diapers and a changing mat. Personalize it with a monogram to make the perfect gift.

Make Your Own Pre-Quilted Fabric

If you can't find the perfect pre-quilted fabric, make your own. Purchase ¾ yard each of two fabrics and cut one 27 x 42-inch rectangle from each fabric and one from thin batting.

Sandwich the batting rectangle between the two fabric rectangles and quilt as desired by hand or machine. Figure 1 shows some suggested simple quilting designs. Treat this quilted fabric just the same as the purchased pre-quilted fabric in the instructions.

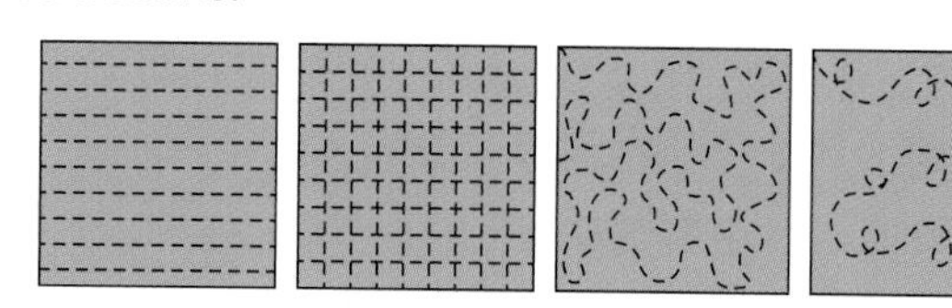

Figure 1

Specifications

Diaper/Wipe Holder Size: 11 x 16 inches
Changing Mat Size: 15 x 23 inches

Materials

- 3-inch scrap square each of 2 contrasting fabrics (optional monogram)
- ½ yard contrasting binding fabric
- ¾ yard pre-quilted fabric (or ¾ yard each 2 fabrics and a 27 x 42-inch rectangle of thin batting)
- Coordinating all-purpose thread
- 1 large snap
- 6-inch square fusible web (optional monogram)
- ⅛ yard lightweight fusible interfacing
- Pattern-tracing paper
- Saucer
- Paper and pencil
- Computer with printer (optional)
- Basic sewing supplies and equipment

Cutting

Refer to the General Instructions on page 2 for preparing and using patterns from insert. Transfer all pattern markings to fabric.

- On-the-Move Diaper Set A (Alternate Pocket Pattern)
- On-the-Move Diaper Set B (Alternate Pocket Pattern)
- On-the-Move Diaper Set C Tab Pattern
- On-the-Move Diaper Set 2½-inch Circle
- On-the-Move Diaper Set 2-inch Circle

From pre-quilted fabric:

- Cut one 11 x 16-inch rectangle for Diaper/Wipe Holder.
- Cut two 6½ x 11-inch rectangles for inside pockets (or cut A and B pieces using pattern given for alternate inside pockets).
- Cut one 15 x 23-inch rectangle for Changing Mat.

From binding fabric:

- Cut two C tab pieces using pattern given.
- Cut 2½-inch bias strips to total 170 inches after joining on ends with diagonal seams.

From lightweight fusible interfacing:

- Cut one C tab piece using pattern given.

Making Bias Binding

1. Join the 2½-inch bias strips on the short ends with diagonal seams (Figure 2) to make a 170-inch long strip; press seams open.

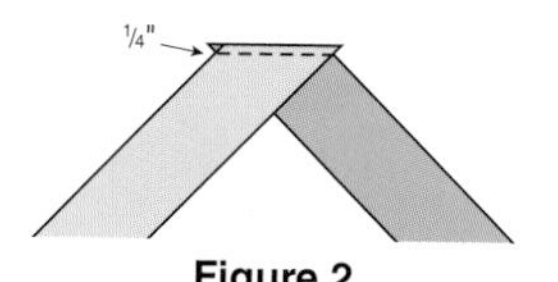

Figure 2

2. Fold the bias strip with wrong sides together along the length and press to make a double-layered binding strip. Set aside for use on the Diaper/Wipe Holder and the Changing Mat. ***Note:*** *Straight-grain binding doesn't fold around curved edges easily; bias binding has some stretch that will allow it to be easily wrapped around curves.*

Completing the Diaper/Wipe Holder

1. Pin and stitch raw edges of folded bias binding to one long straight edge of the right side of each 6½ x 11-inch pocket rectangle, trimming excess at the end of each after stitching (Figure 3).

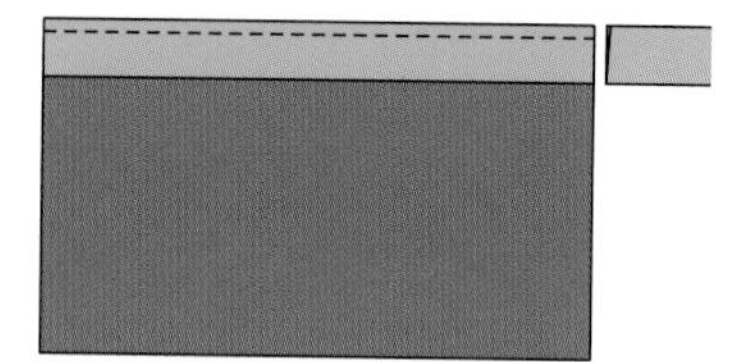

Figure 3

2. Press the binding up over seam and turn to the back side; hand-stitch in place to finish the top edge of the pockets (Figure 4).

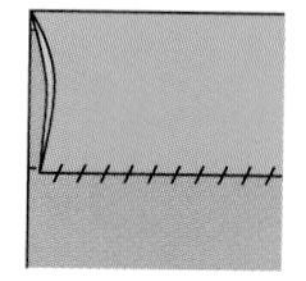

Figure 4

3. Apply monogram, if desired. To make a letter, print the chosen letter 1½ inches tall using word-processing software and a font of your choice. ***Note:*** *For best results, choose a simple sans-serif font with rounded edges and print in reverse or a mirror image—Arial Rounded MT Bold sized at 130 points was* *used in the sample. You may substitute a heart motif or other shape as desired.*

4. Trace the letter and both the 2-inch and 2½-inch circles, using patterns given, on the paper side of the square of fusible web leaving ¼ inch between pieces when tracing.

5. Fuse the letter and the 2-inch circle to the wrong side of the scrap squares and the 2½-inch circle to the wrong side of the leftover binding fabric. Cut out shapes on traced lines and remove paper backing from each piece.

6. With long edges of rectangle vertical, fuse the larger circle to the right side of the 11 x 16-inch holder rectangle 1 inch from the right-hand–side edge and 3½ inches down from the top edge (Figure 5).

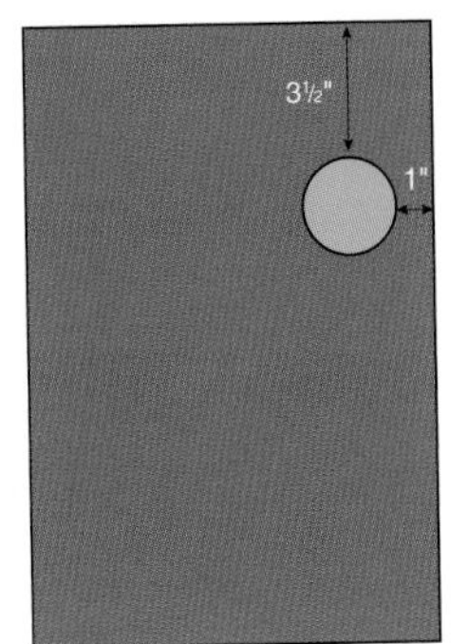

Figure 5

7. Center and fuse the 2-inch circle on the fused 2½-inch circle and then fuse the letter on the 2-inch circle (Figure 6).

Figure 6

8. Using a straight stitch and thread to match the fabric, sew around the edge of the smaller circle to secure. Repeat using a small zigzag stitch around the edges of the letter (Figure 7).

Figure 7

9. To make closing tab, bond the lightweight fusible interfacing C piece to the wrong side of one fabric C piece. Layer and pin the fused C piece right sides together with the remaining fabric C piece and stitch around curved edges using a ¼-inch seam allowance, leaving the straight end open (Figure 8). Clip curves and turn right side out; press edges flat. Topstitch close to edges, if desired.

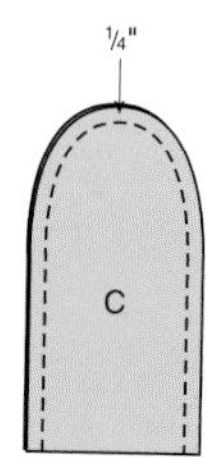

Figure 8

10. Center the raw edge of the tab 1½ inches from the bottom edge on the right side of the holder rectangle and stitch to secure (Figure 9).

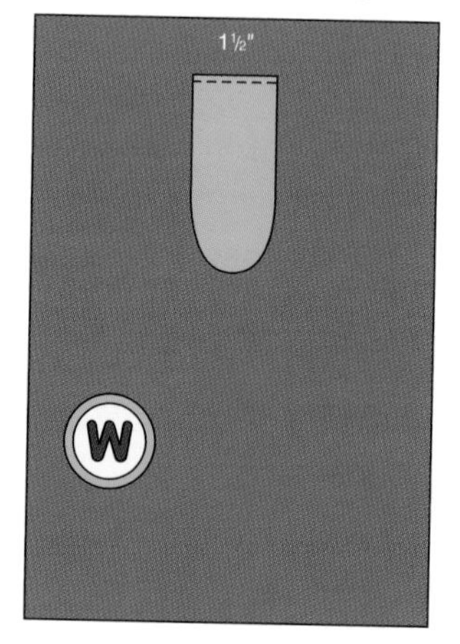

Figure 9

11. Fold the tab down and over the raw edge, covering stitches; stitch ½-inch rectangle shape to secure (Figure 10).

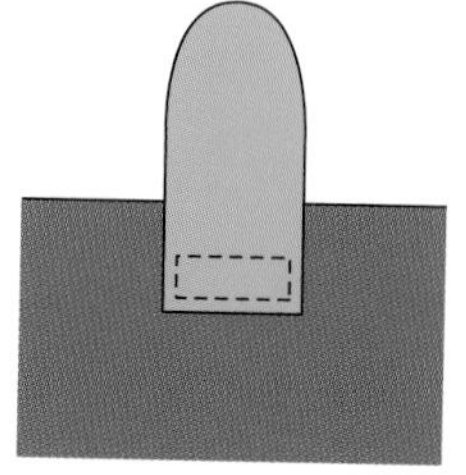

Figure 10

12. Place a bound pocket rectangle right side up on each end of the wrong side of the holder rectangle; baste edges in place keeping tab out of stitching (Figure 11).

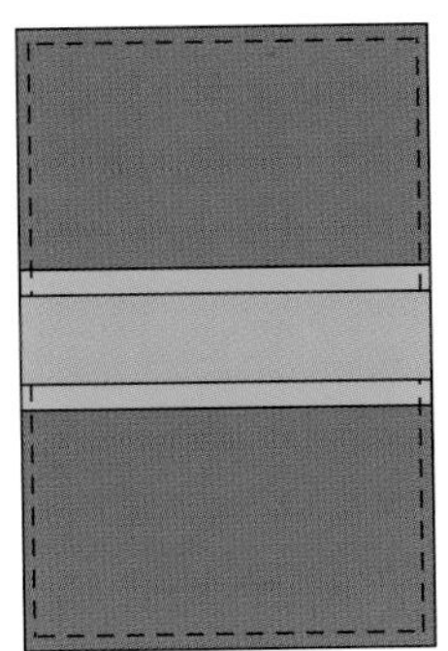

Figure 11

13. Use a saucer to round the outer corners of the layered unit (Figure 12).

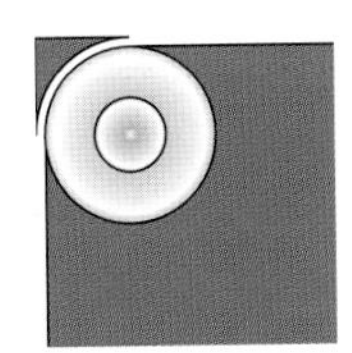

Figure 12

14. Bind edges of the holder rectangle as in steps 1 and 2, again keeping tab out of stitching.

15. Apply the male part of the snap to the end of the inside center edge of the tab and female part of the snap 1 inch from the edge in the center of the opposite end to finish.

Completing the Changing Mat

1. Use a saucer to draw a curved edge on each corner of the 15 x 23-inch pre-quilted rectangle; cut away excess to the marked lines.

2. Bind edges with bias binding referring to steps 1 and 2 of Completing the Diaper/Wipe Holder to finish.

Alternate Pockets for Diaper/Wipe Holder

1. Use A and B pieces for inside pockets.

2. Bind the curved edge of each A piece and outward (convex) curved edge of each B piece as in steps 1 and 2 of Completing the Diaper/Wipe Holder.

3. Place the bound A and B pieces on the ends on the wrong side of the 11 x 16-inch pre-quilted rectangle, overlapping A over B (Figure 13).

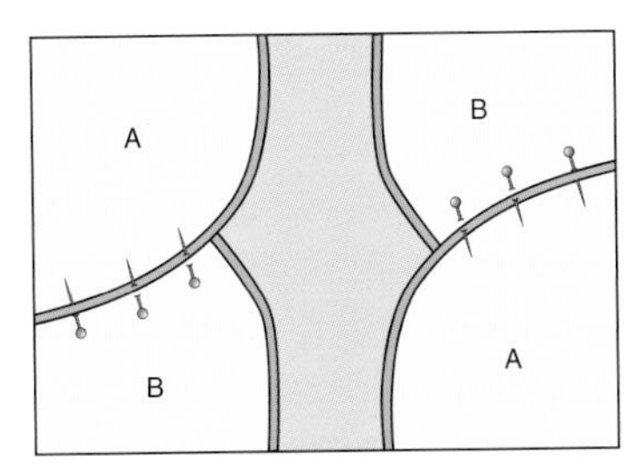

Figure 13

4. Pin pieces together at the overlapped edges. Remove pinned A/B units and machine-stitch together in the ditch of the binding on the A piece from the outside to make a one-piece pocket (Figure 14).

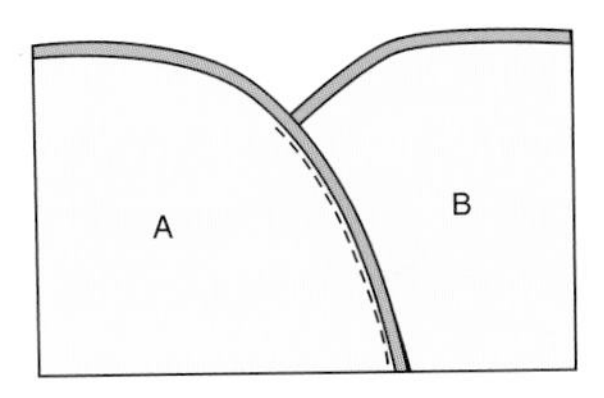

Figure 14

5. Complete the holder as for Completing the Diaper/Wipe Holder steps 3–15 to finish. ■

Appliquéd Diaper Covers

Designs by Chris Malone

These pull-on diaper covers are cute coming and going. Stitch them in various colorful fabric patterns and adorn them with fun appliqués.

Specifications

Diaper Cover Size: Size varies

Materials

- Gray, white, pink, purple, green and yellow fabric scraps for appliqués
- ⅜ yard cotton fabric for each diaper cover
- Coordinating all-purpose thread
- 1 yard single-fold bias tape to match cotton fabric
- Scraps lightweight fusible web
- Pearl cotton or embroidery floss: purple, black and blue
- Embroidery needle
- ⅝ yard ½-inch-wide elastic
- ¾ yard ¼-inch-wide elastic
- Pattern-tracing paper
- Template material
- Basic sewing supplies and equipment

Cutting

Refer to the General Instructions on page 2 for preparing and using patterns from insert. Transfer all pattern markings to fabric.

- Appliquéd Diaper Covers Back
- Appliquéd Diaper Covers Front

From fabric scraps:

- Cut appliqué pieces as per instructions and patterns.

From cotton fabric:

- Cut front and back diaper cover pieces as per patterns. Small and large-size patterns are given. To make a cover that is larger or smaller than those provided, alter the cutting lines on the side, bottom and legs as necessary.

From ½-inch-wide elastic:

- For best results, measure waist of baby and add 1 inch for length of elastic needed. If making the cover for a gift, cut as follows: 17 inches for small size (3–6 months) and 20 inches for large size (12–24 months).

From ¼-inch-wide elastic:

- Measure around the baby's leg and add 1 inch for length and cut two pieces of elastic for legs. If making the cover for a gift, cut for each leg as follows: 11 inches for small size (3–6 months) and 13 inches for large size (12–24 months).

Completing the Appliqué

1. Use templates to trace selected appliqué motifs onto paper side of fusible web. Cut shapes apart and follow manufacturer's instructions to apply fusible web to wrong side of scrap fabrics as directed on patterns. Cut out each shape on drawn lines and remove paper backing.

2. Arrange appliqué shapes according to pattern layering numbers on diaper cover back, centered about 2¾–3¾ inches down from top edge of cover. When satisfied with arrangement, fuse in place.

3. Machine-stitch appliqué edges with matching threads. ***Note:*** *Models are finished with a short, narrow blanket stitch; a zigzag or satin stitch would also be appropriate. Follow instructions for Individual Diaper Covers for embroidery, if used.*

Completing the Diaper Cover

Note: *French seams, which appear as a regular seam on the outside, but encase all the raw edges on the inside, were used on the models. This type of seam is durable and will withstand lots of wash and wear. If preferred, sew a standard ½-inch seam and serge or zigzag the edges to finish.*

1. Place the diaper front and back pieces wrong sides together, matching side seams.

2. To make a French seam, sew a scant ¼-inch seam along side and bottom edges. Trim the seams to ⅛ inch and turn wrong side out.

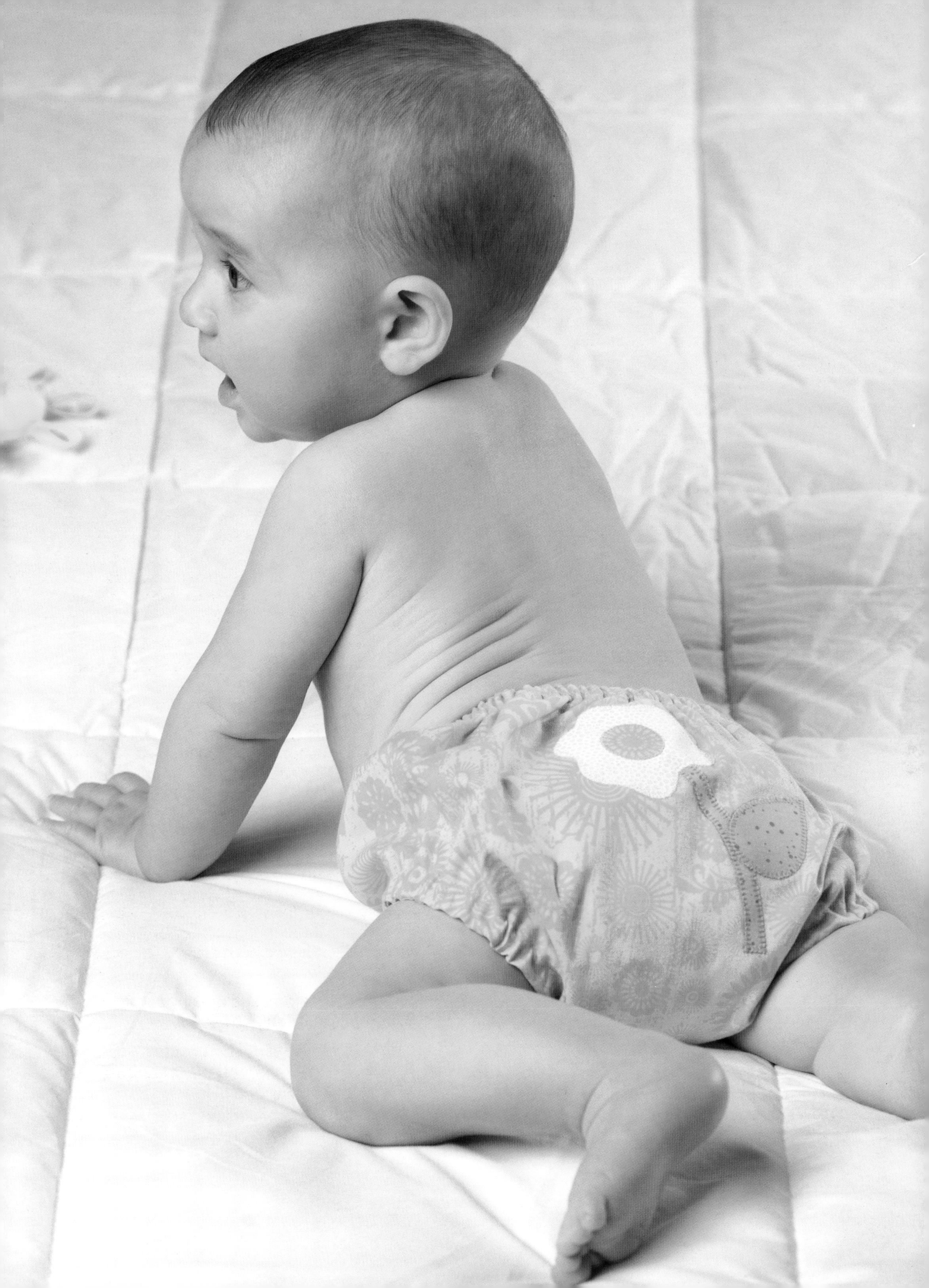

3. Crease along the stitched seam and sew another seam ¼ inch from the folded edge to enclose the first seam (Figure 1). Repeat to stitch both side seams and the bottom seam in this manner.

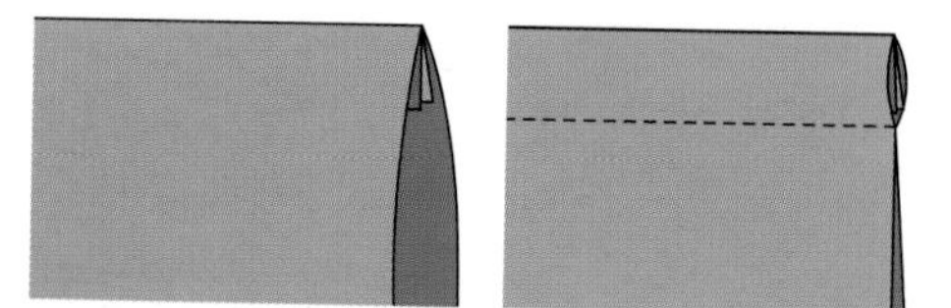

Figure 1

4. For elastic casing at the waist, press a ¼-inch hem to the wrong side at the top edge. Fold over an additional ¾ inch and press. Stitch close to the upper and lower folded edges of the casing, leaving a 1½-inch opening for the elastic (Figure 2).

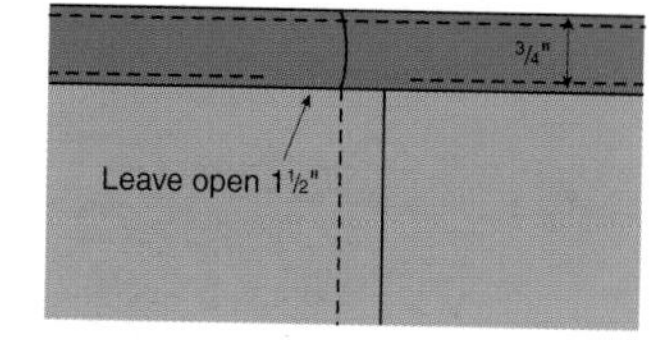

Figure 2

5. Insert the ½-inch-wide elastic into the casing opening. Overlap the ends ½ inch and stitch together securely by machine or hand (Figure 3).

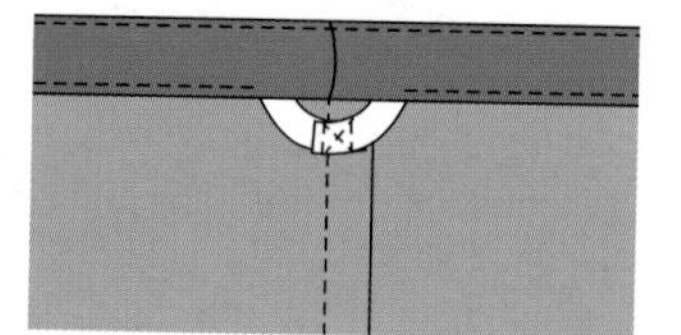

Figure 3

6. Push the elastic back in place and finish the stitching on the casing, stretching the elastic as necessary to make area flat while stitching, taking care not to catch elastic in stitching.

7. To make the casing for the leg opening, open one end of a piece of bias tape and fold in a ¼-inch hem on the short end. Pin this end of the bias tape right sides together along the leg opening starting with the folded end at the bottom seam line of the leg opening. With raw edges even, sew a ¼-inch seam all around (Figure 4).

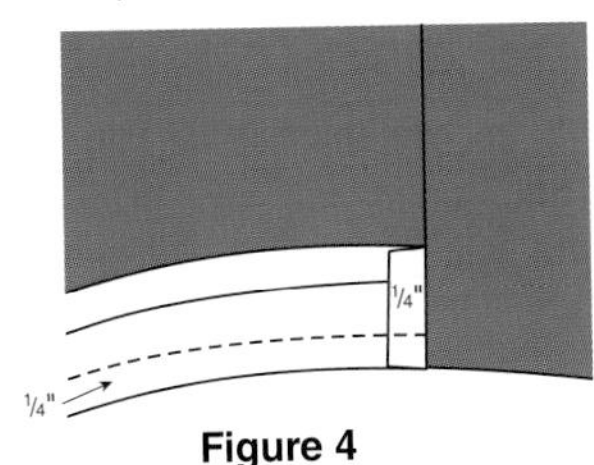

Figure 4

8. Trim bias tape ¼ inch past the starting point; turn under ¼ inch and finish stitching (Figure 5). ***Note:*** *Folded ends will just meet.*

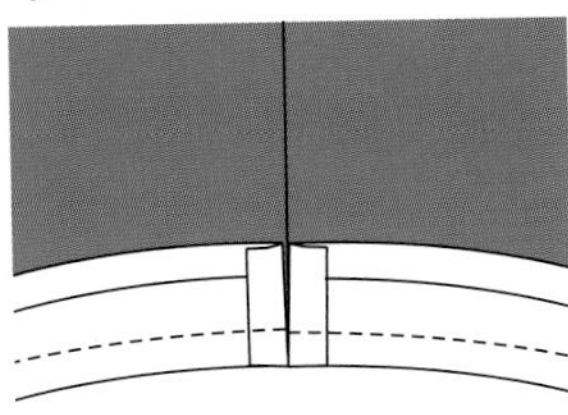
Figure 5

9. Trim seam to ⅛ inch. Fold bias tape all the way to the inside, forming casing. Stitch close to edge of the bias tape (Figure 6).

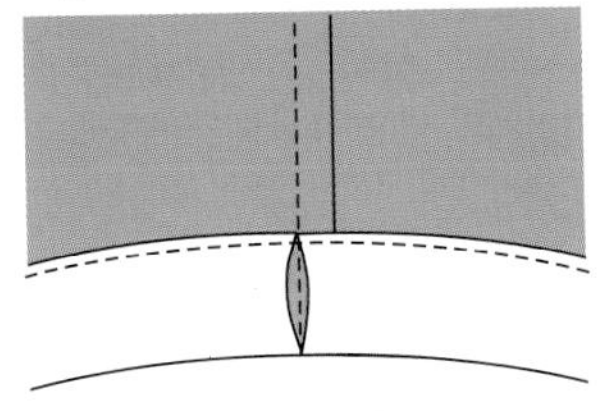
Figure 6

10. Insert one of the ¼-inch-wide elastic pieces into the casing through the opening in the bias tape. Pull through the casing and out the other end. Overlap the ends ½ inch and stitch together securely by machine or hand. Pull elastic to pull stitched ends inside casing. Whipstitch the folded edges of the bias opening closed.

11. Repeat steps 7–10 for second leg.

Individual Diaper Covers

Flower Motif Diaper Cover: Sample diaper cover was made with yellow print cotton fabric.

Butterfly: Sample diaper cover was made with white with multicolored dots cotton fabric. Use purple pearl cotton or floss to stem-stitch antennae with a French knot at each end. Sew "flight path" with a running stitch.

Car: Sample diaper cover was made with purple with green dots cotton fabric. Use purple pearl cotton or floss to make a running stitch for the road.

Hippo: Sample diaper cover was made with blue print cotton fabric. Use black pearl cotton or floss to stem-stitch smile and eyebrows. Make French knots for eyes. Use blue pearl cotton or floss to stem-stitch water. ■

Coming Up Flowers Jacket & Booties

Designs by Carol Zentgraf

This soft fleece jacket and booties set is simple to make and is the perfect gift for the new baby.

Specifications

Jacket and Booties Size: 18 months

Materials

- Scraps of coordinating cotton prints for flowers
- ½ yard 60-inch-wide fleece
- Coordinating all-purpose thread
- Assorted size coordinating felt buttons for flower centers
- 1¼ yards ⅜-inch-wide double-sided satin ribbon
- Contrasting 12-wt. and 30-wt. cotton threads
- Water-soluble stabilizer
- Pattern-tracing paper
- Small flower-making tool and templates
- Seam sealant
- Basic sewing supplies and equipment

Cutting

Refer to the General Instructions on page 2 for preparing and using patterns from insert. Transfer all pattern markings to fabric.

- Coming Up Flowers Jacket Front
- Coming Up Flowers Jacket Back
- Coming Up Flowers Jacket Sleeve
- Coming Up Flowers Bootie Top
- Coming Up Flowers Bootie Sole

From cotton print scraps:

- Cut as directed on the purchased flower template tool and templates.

From fleece:

- For jacket, cut one each left and right front; on the fold of fabric cut two sleeves and one back.
- For booties, cut two each tops and soles.

From ribbon:

- Cut four 11-inch lengths for jacket and bootie ties.

Completing the Jacket & Booties

Use a ¼-inch seam allowance and sew seams with right sides together. Finger-press seams open to avoid flattening the nap of the fleece.

1. Using all-purpose matching thread, sew the jacket fronts to the jacket back at the shoulder seams.

2. Set up your sewing machine with 12-wt. cotton thread in the needle and 30-wt. matching thread in the bobbin. Select a blanket stitch on your machine.

3. Cut 2-inch-wide strips of water-soluble stabilizer. Place a strip on top of and under each edge as you blanket-stitch the edges. ***Note:*** *The stabilizer ensures smooth, even stitches and prevents them from sinking into the nap of the fleece.* Stitch along outer edges of the jacket front/back and sleeves; **do not stitch** along edges that will be sewn together. Position the blanket stitches so the straight portion of the stitch runs along the fabric edge (Figure 1).

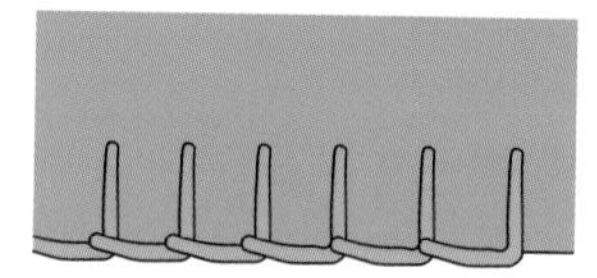

Figure 1

4. Repeat step 3 to stitch around bootie top edge (Figure 2).

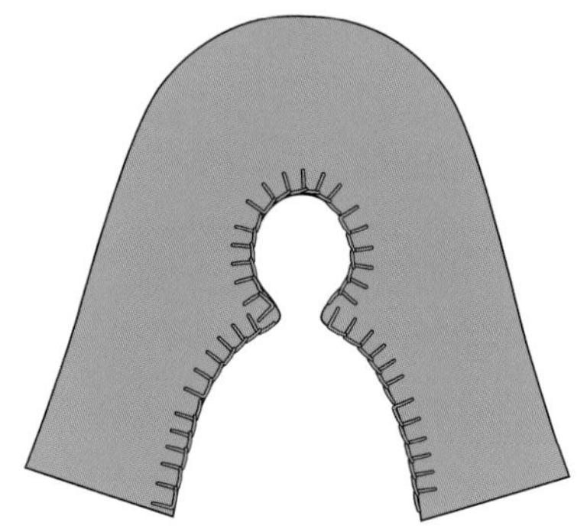

Figure 2

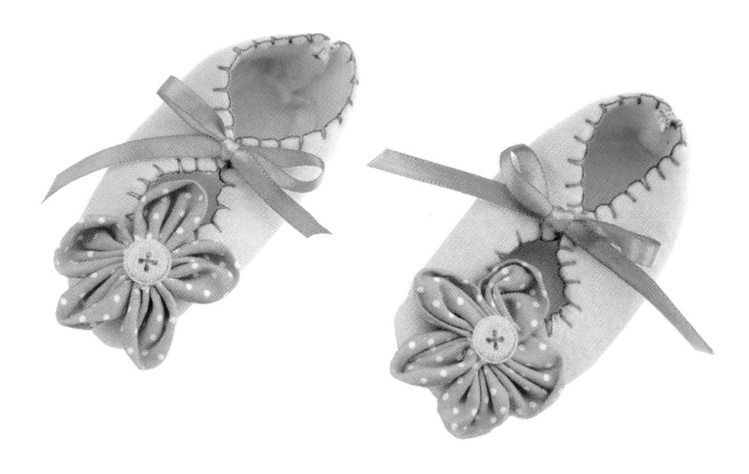

5. Cut away the excess stabilizer. Use warm water to gently dissolve the remaining stabilizer. Let the pieces dry flat on a terry-cloth towel or machine-dry them on an extra-low gentle setting.

6. Sew a sleeve to each armhole edge of the jacket, matching the center top of the sleeve to the shoulder seam. With edges and the underarm seams aligned, sew the side seams from the end of the sleeves to the bottom of the jacket (Figure 3). Turn right side out and finger-press the seams open to finish the jacket stitching.

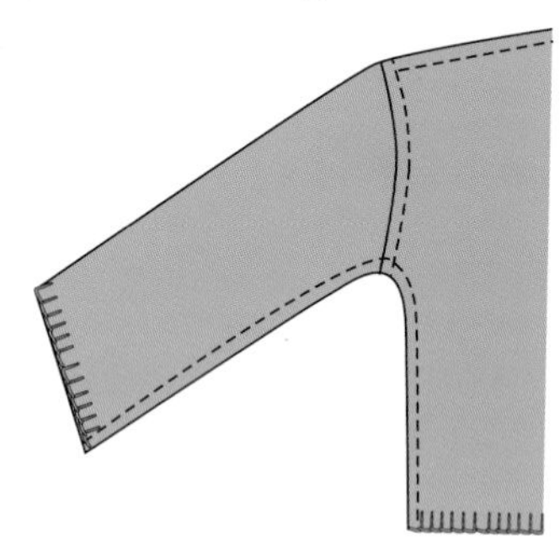

Figure 3

7. To make each bootie, sew the back seam of the bootie top with right sides together (Figure 4). Sew the bootie top to sole (Figure 5) with right sides together and trim the seam allowance close to the stitching. Turn right side out to finish.

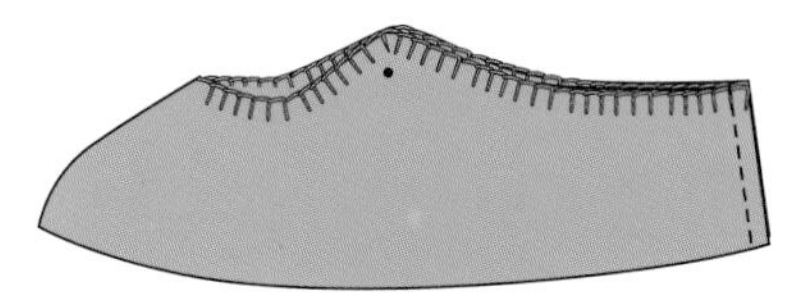

Figure 4

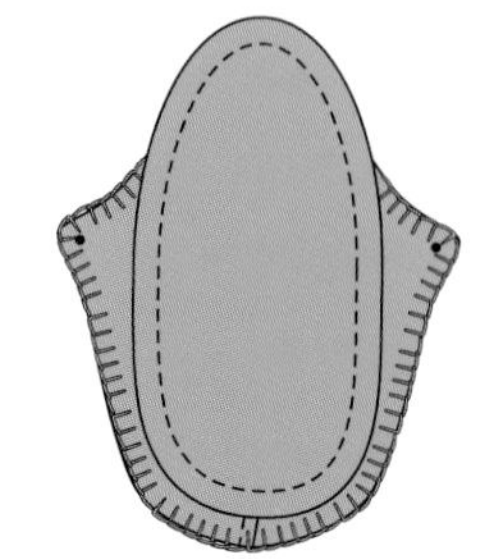

Figure 5

Embellishment & Finishing

1. Follow the manufacturer's instructions and use the flower templates to make flowers with the cotton prints. Make two complete flowers and four three-petal flowers for the jacket. Make one complete flower for each bootie.

2. Position the flowers on the jacket fronts and the bootie tops referring to the photo of the projects for positioning.

3. Securely hand-stitch the flowers to the fleece.

4. Sew felt buttons to the centers of the complete flowers and to the bottom of each three-petal flower. ***Note:*** *For added safety, stitch around the edges of all felt buttons to secure. Secure knots with seam sealant.*

5. Securely sew one 11-inch length of ribbon to each side of the jacket front neckline for ties.

6. Make a small hole in each side of the bootie top as marked by dots on pattern and slide one 11-inch length of ribbon through the slits on each bootie (Figure 6) to finish. ■

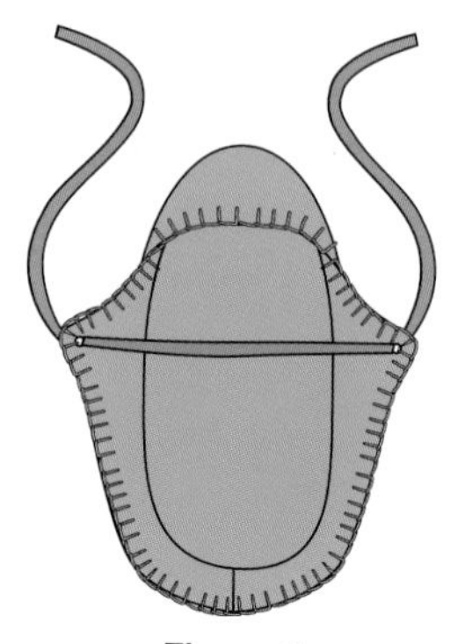

Figure 6

Tidy Tot Bib

Design by Chris Malone

This colorful bib with crumb pocket is a great gift for new parents. A quick hook-and-loop closure makes it easy to fasten on a wiggly baby.

Specifications

Bib Size: 9 x 12½ inches

Materials

- Assorted scraps 8 colorful prints
- Fat quarter or ⅜ yard green dot
- Batting 10 x 14 inches
- Coordinating all-purpose thread
- 1-inch square hook-and-loop tape
- Pattern-tracing paper
- Basic sewing supplies and equipment

Cutting

Refer to the General Instructions on page 2 for preparing and using patterns from insert. Transfer all pattern markings to fabric.

- Tidy Tot Bib

From scraps:

- Cut the following:
  - A—2½ x 4½-inch rectangle.
  - B—3½ x 4½-inch rectangle.
  - C—5½ x 4½-inch rectangle.
  - D—3½ x 4½-inch rectangle.
  - E—3½ x 2½-inch rectangle.
  - F—3½-inch square.
  - G—3½-inch square.
  - H—4½ x 6½-inch rectangle.

From green dot:

- Cut one 10½ x 3½-inch I rectangle.
- Cut two 10½ x 4-inch pocket strips.
- Cut one bib shape for backing using pattern given.

From batting:

- Cut 1 bib shape using pattern given.

Assembly

Stitch right sides together using a ¼-inch seam allowance unless otherwise indicated. Patchwork seams are pressed open.

1. Referring to Figure 1 for patchwork piecing, sew D to E and F to G and add to H to make the center row; press.

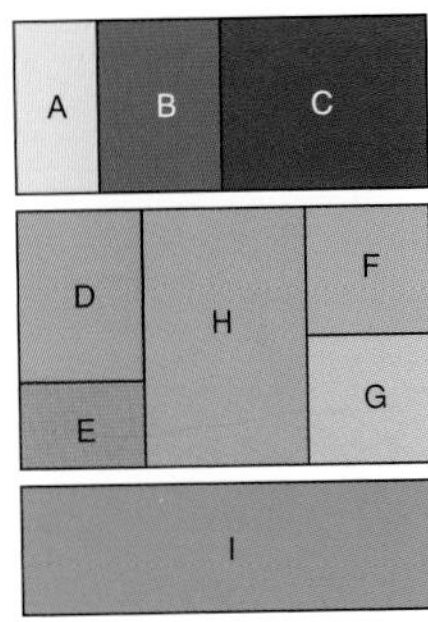

Figure 1

2. Sew A to B to C to make the top row; press. Sew this row to the top of the center row; press.

3. Add the I rectangle to the bottom to complete a patchwork rectangle; press.

4. To make the pocket, sew the two 10½ x 4-inch rectangles together on one long edge. Flip one piece over along seam edge so wrong sides are facing; press. Topstitch ⅛–¼ inch from seam (Figure 2).

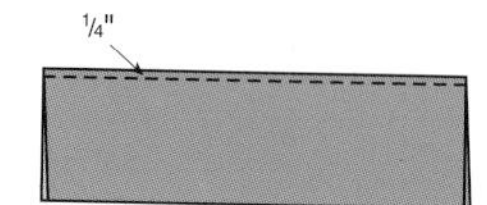

Figure 2

5. Fold patchwork piece in half along length, making sure seams between rows are aligned. Use the bib pattern to cut one bib front from the patchwork piece, aligning the bottom seam line (top of I rectangle) with the mark on the pattern (Figure 3).

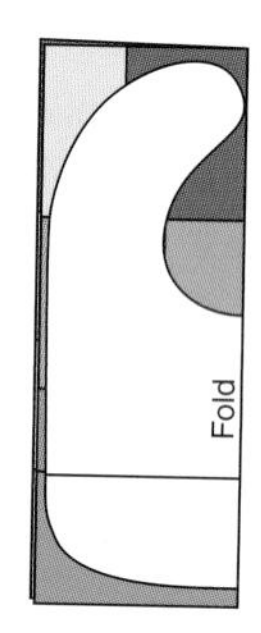

Figure 3

6. Unfold and pin the pocket to bottom of bib front, aligning top finished edge of pocket with the top edge of the I rectangle. Trim bottom corners of pocket to match bib and baste pocket in place (Figure 4).

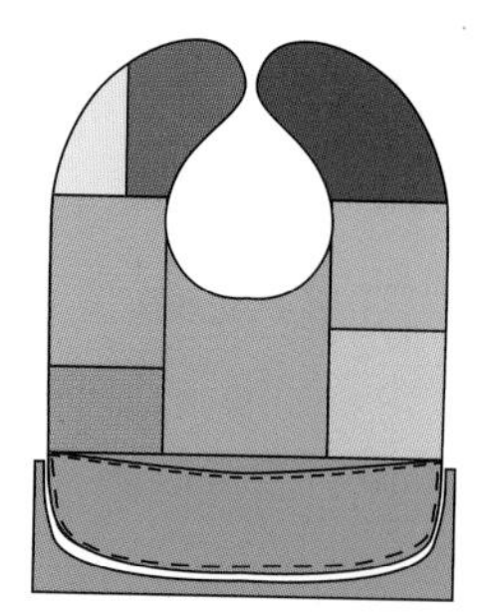

Figure 4

7. Place bib front and bib backing right sides together and pin to batting. Sew all around, leaving a 3-inch opening as indicated on pattern.

8. Trim batting close to seam; clip curves and turn bib right side out through opening; press edges flat.

9. Fold opening seam allowance to the inside and whipstitch opening closed.

10. Topstitch ⅛ inch from edge all around bib.

11. To finish, sew the hook square to the right side of a bib neck strap; sew the loop square to the wrong side of the remaining strap so they overlap to fasten (Figure 5). ■

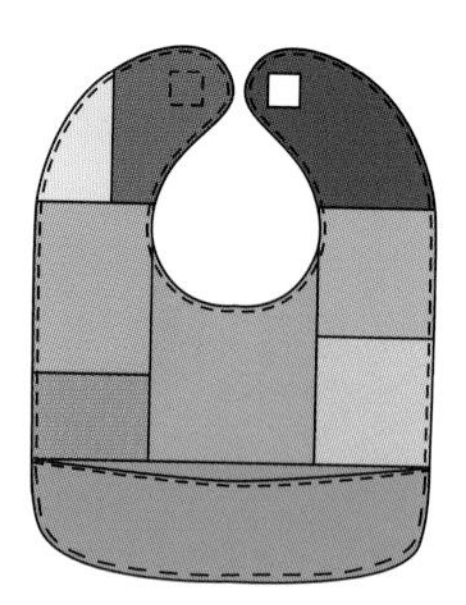

Figure 5

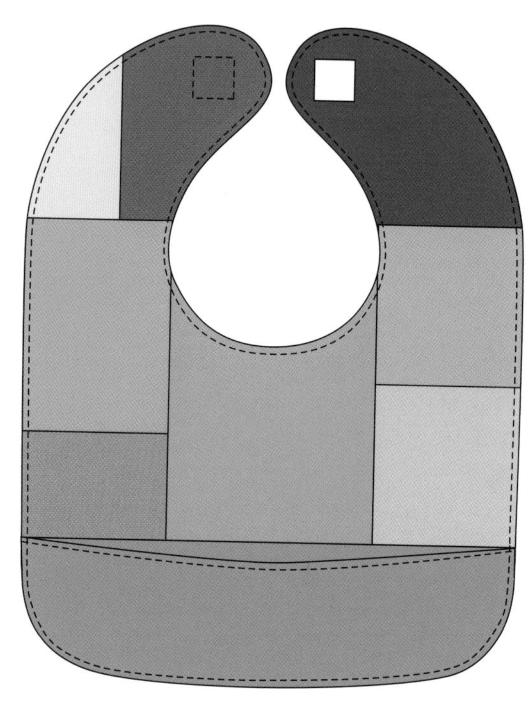

Tidy Tot Bib
Placement Diagram 9" x 12½"

Ruffles & Roses Hat

Design by Linda Turner Griepentrog

Protect your little cutie from the sun and wind with this ruffled floral hat. The ties keep it in place in even the strongest breezes.

Specifications

Hat Size: 22½-inch circumference x 5 inches tall

Materials

- ¼ yard coordinating lining print
- ½ yard floral print
- Coordinating all-purpose thread
- Rayon machine-embroidery thread to match ribbon
- ¾ yard jumbo rickrack
- 1⅜ yards ⅞-inch-wide striped grosgrain ribbon
- ¾ yard ⅝-inch-wide grosgrain ribbon
- ½-inch-wide fusible web tape
- 1½-inch felt flower button
- Pattern-tracing paper
- Basic sewing supplies and equipment

Cutting

Refer to the General Instructions on page 2 for preparing and using patterns from insert. Transfer all pattern markings to fabric.

- Ruffles & Roses Hat Section

From coordinating lining print:

- Cut six hat sections using pattern given.

From the floral print:

- Cut six hat sections using pattern given.
- Cut one 5½ x 42-inch ruffle strip.
- Cut one 1¼ by fabric width strip.
  Subcut into two 1¼ x 13-inch tie strips.

Ruffle Preparation

All seam allowances are ¼ inch.

1. Press a crease line down the center length of the ruffle strip. Unfold the ruffle strip, and using the fusible web tape, fuse the striped ribbon in place ¾ inch from the pressed crease line along the ruffle length (Figure 1).

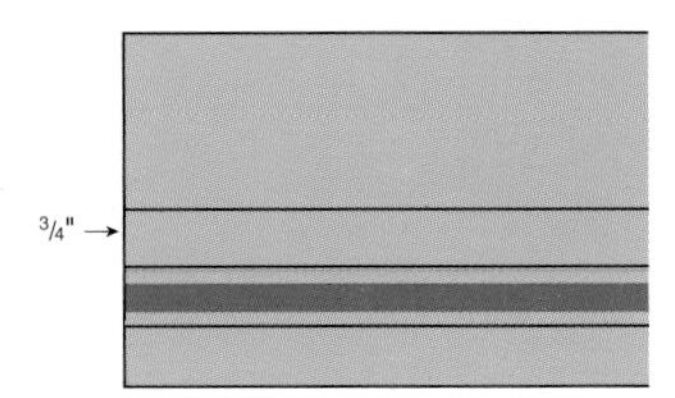

Figure 1

2. Using machine-embroidery thread, sew an appliqué stitch along the ribbon edges and a decorative flower stitch down the center of ribbon. ***Note:*** *See photo for stitching detail. If you don't have these exact stitches, choose something similar, or a simple straight stitch and zigzag.*

3. With right sides together, join the ruffle strip on the short ends, matching the ribbon ends. Press the seam open and refold the ruffle along the pressed centerline.

4. Matching the long raw edges of the ruffle strip, sew a line of basting stitches ⅛ inch from the edge, leaving thread tails long enough to pull.

5. Quarter-mark the ruffle length, starting at the center back seam.

Hat Assembly

1. Join three floral print hat sections from point to lower edge; repeat for the second set of three sections (Figure 2).

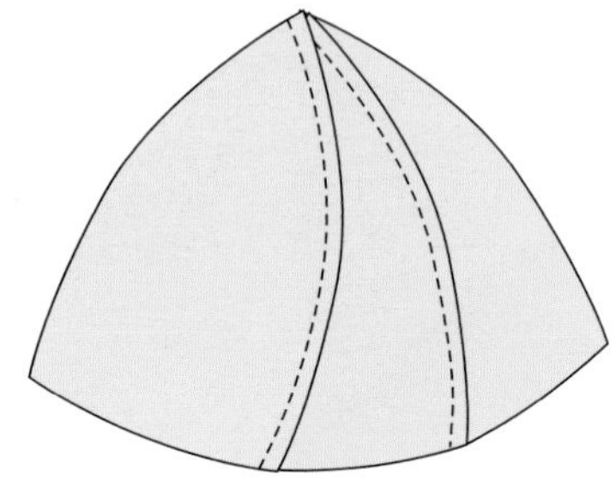
Figure 2

2. Matching the hat section edges, join the two hat halves; press seams open (Figure 3). Turn right side out.

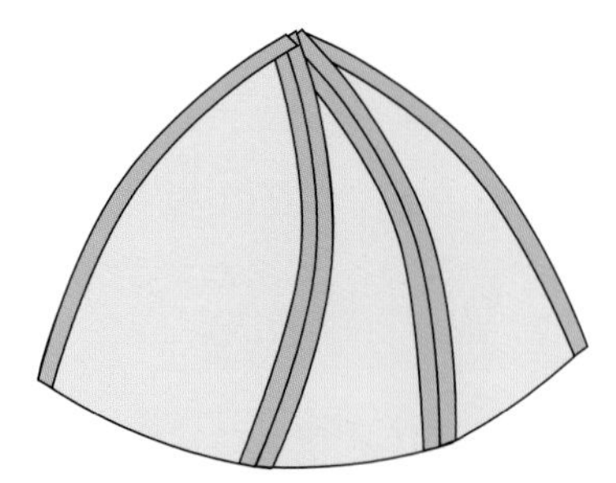

Figure 3

3. Repeat steps 1 and 2 for the hat lining but do not turn right side out.

4. With wrong sides together, slip the floral print hat into the completed lining, matching seam lines; baste around the lower edge (Figure 4).

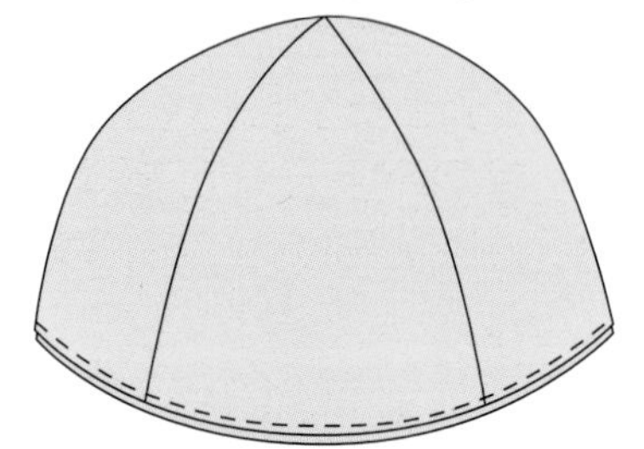

Figure 4

5. Turn right side out and pin the rickrack around the lower hat edge with the points against the cut edge. Turn under the beginning and ending rickrack ends. Baste a scant ¼ inch from the edge, down the rickrack center (Figure 5).

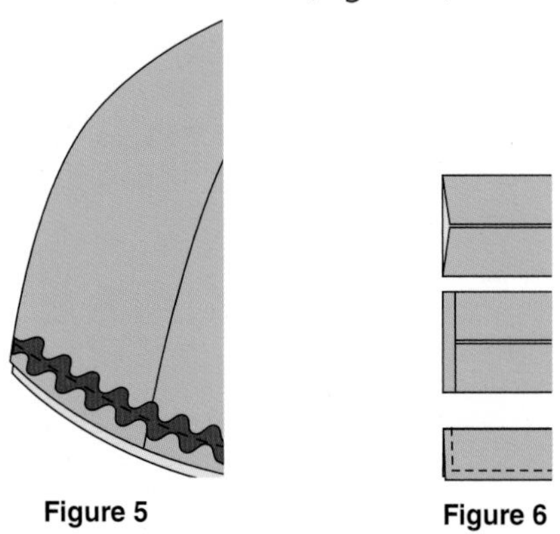

Figure 5

Figure 6

6. To make the ties, fold the long edges of each strip to the center and press. Press one end to the inside, then fold the strip in half again; press and stitch the long edge and the pressed-under short end to finish (Figure 6).

7. Quarter-mark the hat lower edge, beginning at center back where the rickrack joining is placed.

8. With right sides together, match the ruffle and hat quarter markings and pin. Pull up the gathering threads to fit the ruffle to the hat size. Adjust the gathers evenly. Pin in place.

9. Pin a tie in place at each side marking, matching the unfinished end to the hat/ruffle raw edge. Sew ¼ inch from the cut edges to join the ruffle and ties to the hat (Figure 7).

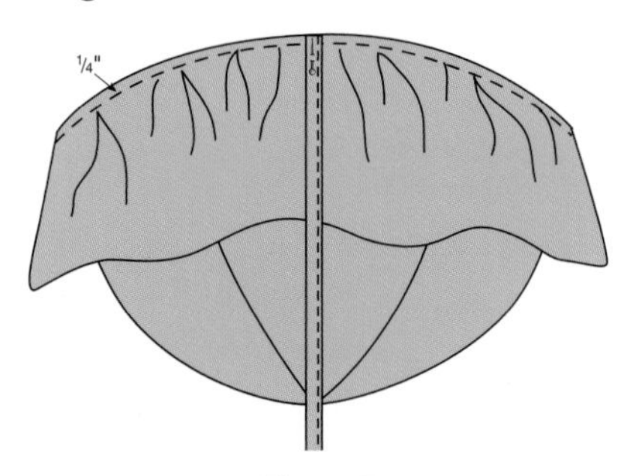

Figure 7

10. To cover the inside raw edges, lap the ⅝-inch-wide ribbon over the stitched seam allowances and use a narrow zigzag to stitch it in place (Figure 8). Turn under the end at the starting point.

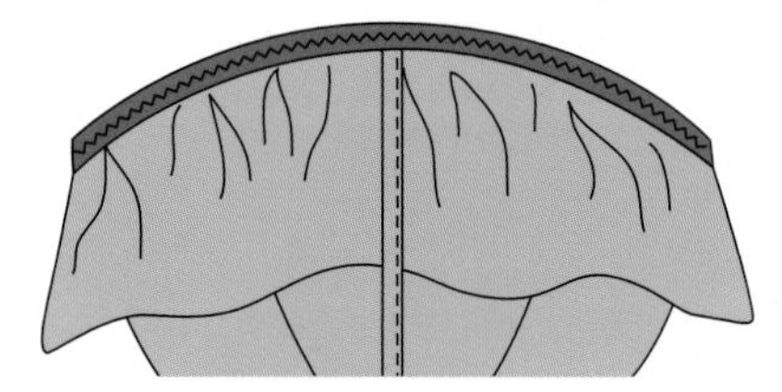

Figure 8

11. Hand-stitch the upper ribbon edge to the hat lining.

12. Using doubled thread, stitch the felt flower button to the hat top covering the intersection of the hat seams. Stitch down the edges of the felt flower for added security.

13. Lightly press the hat along the rickrack seam to finish. ■

Hatful of Posies

Design by Lynn Weglarz

Easy to make and fun to wear, this soft and warm fleece hat with a bouquet of posies on top is the perfect way to keep your baby warm on those cold winter days.

Specifications

Hat Size: 16-inch circumference x 6 inches tall (9½ inches tall, including flowers)

Materials

- ¼ yard outerwear fleece B (stems)
- ¼ yard outerwear fleece C (flowers)
- ⅜ yard outerwear fleece A (hat)
- Coordinating all-purpose thread
- Pattern-tracing paper
- Basic sewing supplies and equipment

Cutting

Refer to the General Instructions on page 2 for preparing and using patterns from insert. Transfer all pattern markings to fabric.

- Hatful of Posies Flower

Note that the longest measurement for each piece should be cut in the direction with the greatest stretch.

From outerwear fleece B and C:

- Cut flower pieces from C as directed on pattern.
- Cut one 6 x 8-inch strip from B for stem.

From outerwear fleece A:

- Cut one 11 x 17-inch piece for hat.
- Cut one ½ x 9-inch strip to tie fringe.

Completing the Hat

1. Cut 1-inch-wide by 4½-inch-deep fringes along one long edge of the 6 x 8-inch stem strip to make eight fringe pieces (Figure 1).

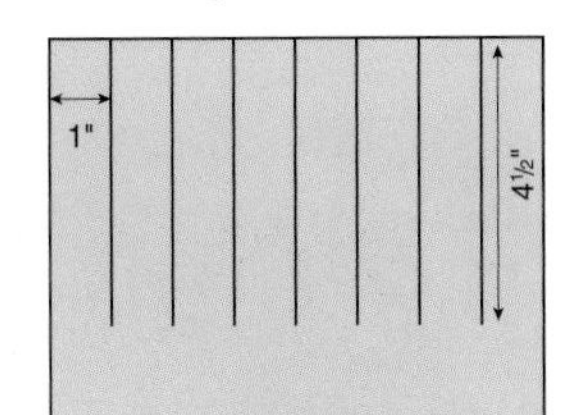

Figure 1

2. Fold the fringe strip in half with wrong sides together along the length. Stitch close to the bottom, unclipped edge (Figure 2).

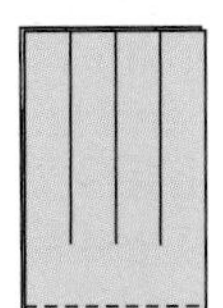

Figure 2

3. Trim the end of all fringe pieces at a 45-degree angle (Figure 3). Set aside.

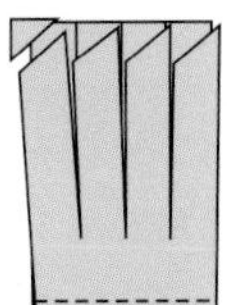

Figure 3

4. With right sides together, fold the 11 x 17-inch hat rectangle in half matching short ends. Using a ½-inch seam allowance, stitch (or serge) the seam to form a tube (Figure 4).

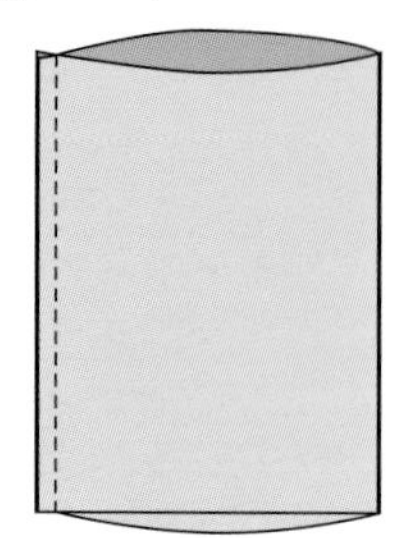

Figure 4

5. Press side seam open and then fold under one end of tube 2½ inches and stitch to hem (Figure 5). ***Note:*** *A three-step zigzag is recommended. If the seam is serged, press seam to one side.*

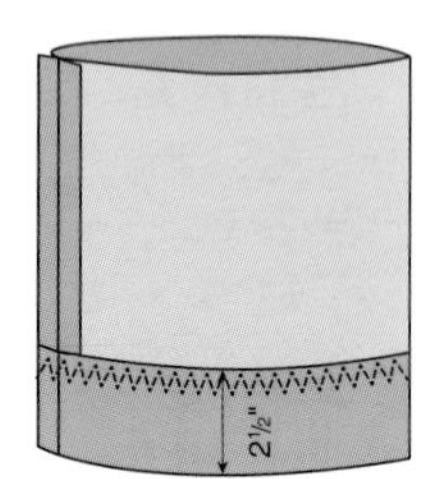

Figure 5

6. With right sides together, lay hat flat with seam centered (Figure 6).

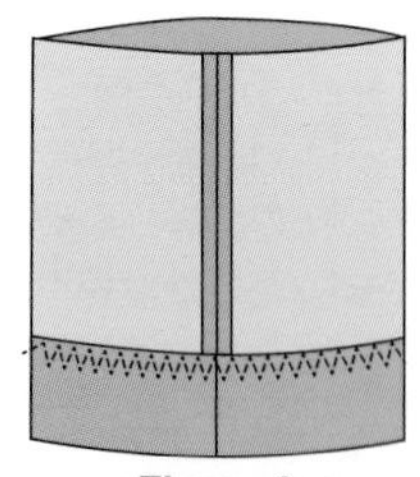

Figure 6

7. Insert fringe piece into hat with stitched straight edge matching and centered behind hat seam (Figure 7). Stitch ½ inch from edges (Figure 8).

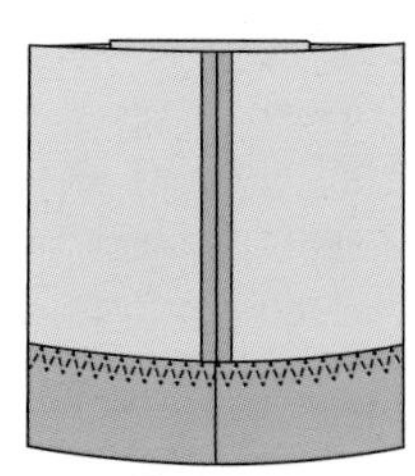

Figure 7

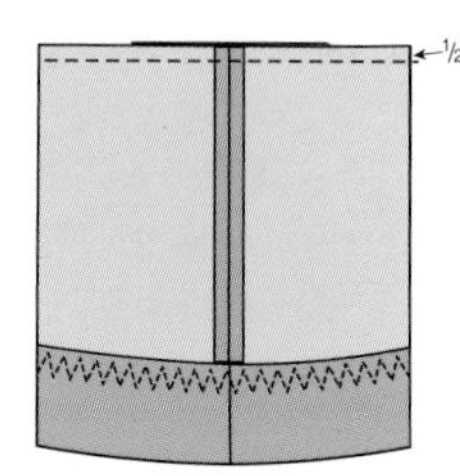

Figure 8

8. To create the corners, mark a 45-degree angle line from the stitched edge to the sides on each end and stitch (Figure 9). Turn hat right side out (Figure 10).

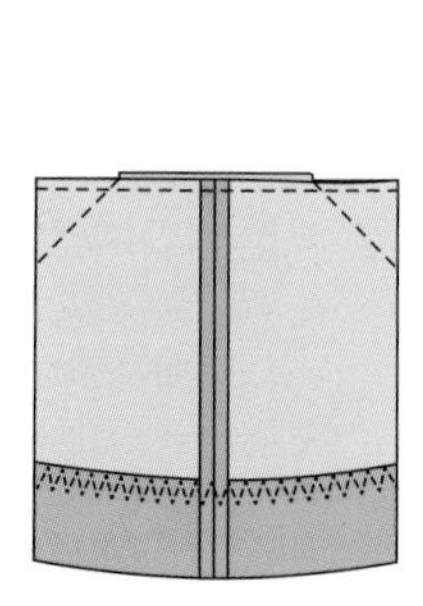

Figure 9

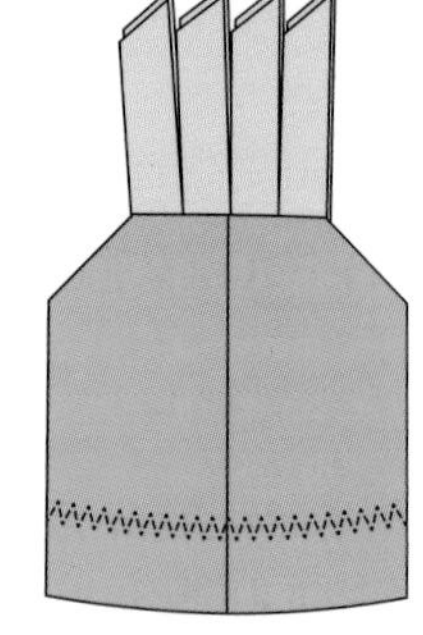

Figure 10

9. Securely tie fringe with the 9-inch strip about ¾ inch from bottom edge; trim ends of tie strip if needed (Figure 11).

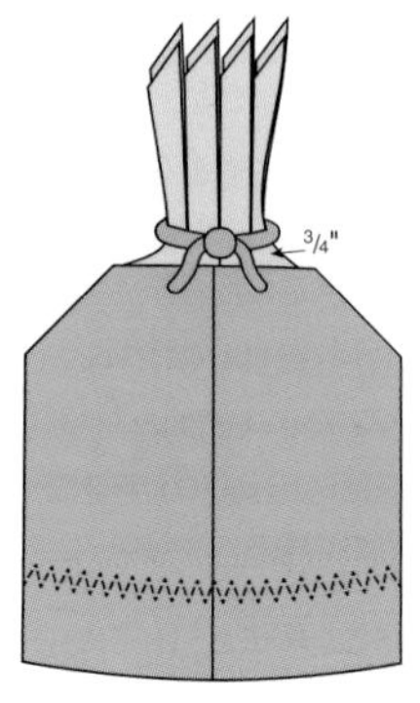

Figure 11

10. Make a very small snip in the center of each flower. Push the pointed end of one fringe/stem through a flower and tie a knot (Figure 12). Repeat with all fringe/stems and flowers to finish the hat.

Figure 12

11. Turn up hemmed edges of hat to create a cuff, if desired. ■

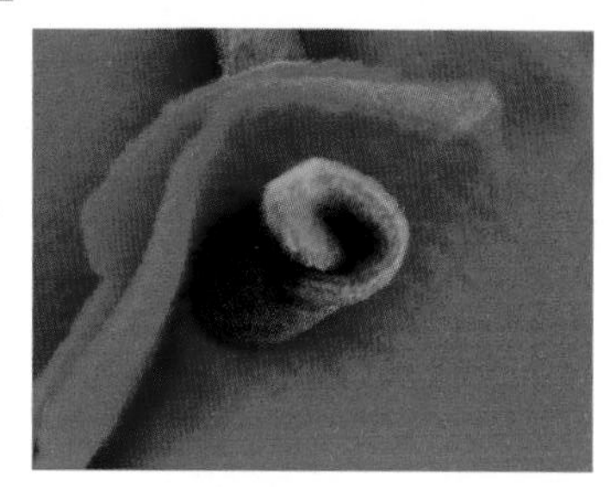

Chic Beret

Design by Sue Marsh

This adorable beret is sure to add flair to your baby's wardrobe.

Specifications
Hat Size: Size varies

Materials
- Assorted scraps 4-inch squares cotton or felted wool for pins
- ⅛ yard hatband fabric
- ¼ yard or 10-inch square bow fabric (optional)
- ⅜ yard main hat fabric
- ⅜ yard coordinating lining fabric
- Coordinating all-purpose thread
- Size 5 pearl cotton
- Assorted colored felt buttons
- 1-inch pin back for each pin
- Large colored felt button
- ¾ yard ¾-inch-wide elastic
- ⅛ yard lightweight fusible interfacing
- Pattern-tracing paper
- Basic sewing supplies and equipment

Cutting
Refer to the General Instructions on page 2 for preparing and using patterns from insert. Transfer all pattern markings to fabric.
- Chic Beret A & B or C & D (depending on size needed)
- Small Circle
- Pin Background
- Heart
- Medium Circle

From scrap cotton or felted wool squares:
- Cut small and medium circles, pin background, flower and heart pieces as directed in instructions and patterns.

From hatband fabric:
- Cut one 3 x 19½-inch strip (toddler) or 3 x 16½-inch strip (infant) for hatband.

From bow fabric:
- Cut one 6½ x 8½-inch rectangle for optional bow.
- Cut one 2½ x 3½-inch rectangle for optional bow knot.

From main hat fabric:
- Cut two A1 or B1 circles (depending on size needed) using pattern given; cut out the center in one piece as marked on the pattern so you have one large whole circle and one large circle with a hole in the center (Figure 1).

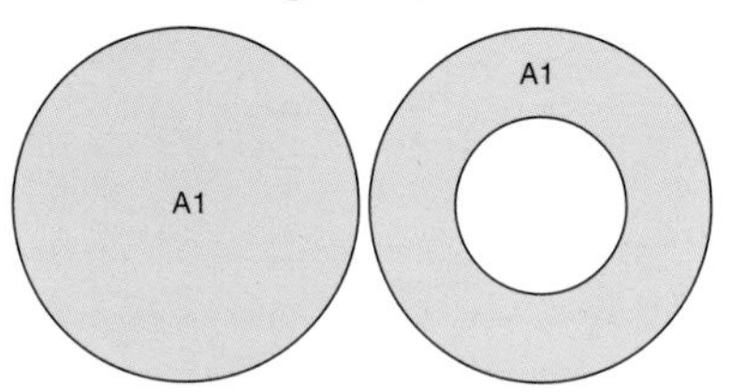

Figure 1

From coordinating lining:
- Cut two A2 or B2 pieces (depending on size needed) using pattern given; cut out center in one piece as marked on the pattern so you have one large whole circle and one large circle with a hole in the center, again referring to Figure 1.

From lightweight fusible interfacing:
- Cut one 3 x 19½-inch strip (toddler) or 3 x 16½-inch strip (infant).

Completing the Beret
Use a ¼-inch seam allowance for all machine stitching.

1. Place the A1 (B1) circles right sides together and sew around the outer edges (Figure 2).

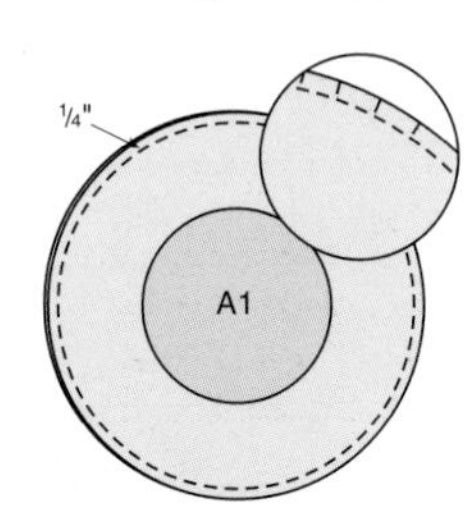

Figure 2

2. Clip into curved edge of the stitched seam and turn right side out. Smooth seam and press edges flat.

3. Repeat step 1 with A2 (B2) lining.

4. Place the stitched A2 (B2) lining inside the stitched-and-turned A1 (B1) beret circles (wrong sides together); baste ¼ inch around inner edge (Figure 3).

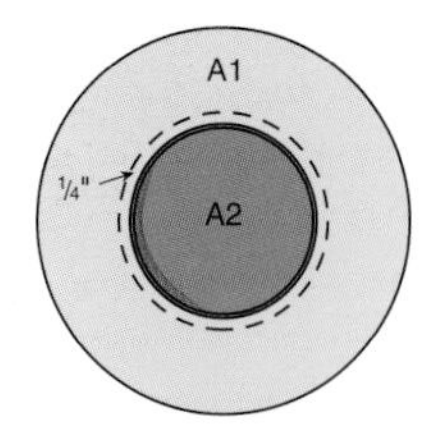

Figure 3

5. Fuse the interfacing strip to the wrong side of the hatband strip.

6. Press one long edge of the fused hatband strip ¼ inch to the wrong side; unfold.

7. Join the hatband strip on the short ends; press seam open and fold pressed edge to the wrong side again (Figure 4).

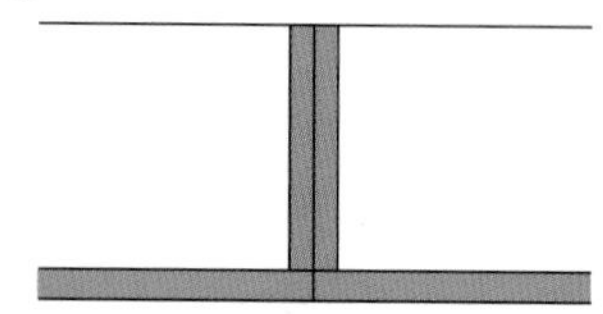

Figure 4

8. Pin the hatband to the center opening of the beret/lining unit, matching raw edges. Sew all around (Figure 5).

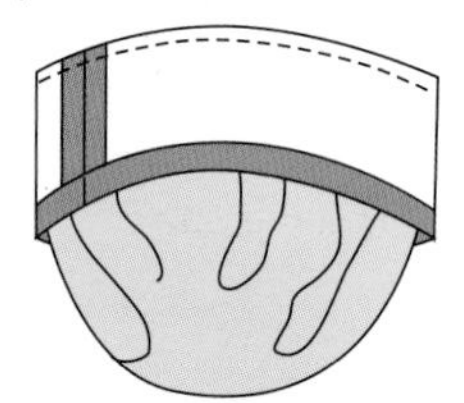

Figure 5

9. Fold the hatband to the inside, enclosing the previously stitched seam (Figure 6); hand-stitch hatband edge to the lining, leaving a 2-inch opening to insert the elastic.

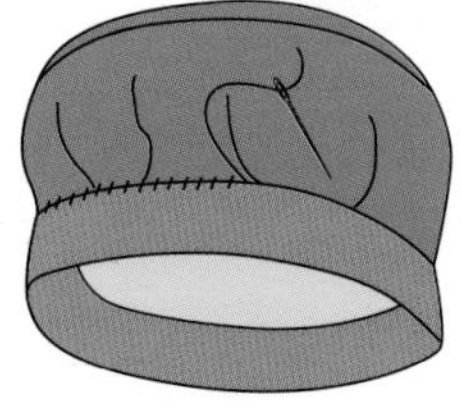

Figure 6

10. Measure child's head and cut a piece of ¾-inch-wide elastic to this size.

11. Thread the elastic through the opening in the hatband (Figure 7); overlap elastic ½ inch and secure layers together. Stretch elastic to pull into band; hand-stitch the opening closed.

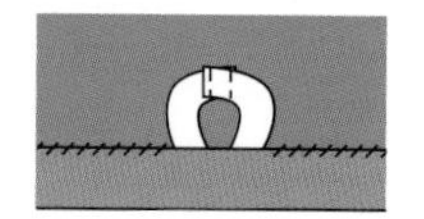

Figure 7

12. To finish beret, topstitch close to both edges of the hatband, being careful not to catch elastic in stitching (Figure 8).

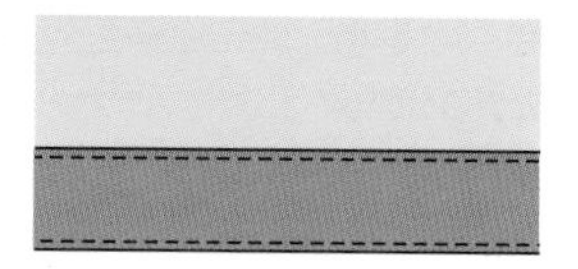

Figure 8

Completing the Pins

1. Select desired pin style.

2. Cut two background circles and desired pieces for chosen pin style. For example, for Circle Pin, you will need two background circles and one each small and medium circles.

3. Center and hand-stitch your chosen design to one background circle using pearl cotton and a buttonhole stitch.

4. Securely hand-stitch a felt button or buttons to the stitched top layer, adding additional security by stitching around the edges of all felt buttons.

5. Layer the stitched top layer with the remaining background circle wrong sides together and sew edges with pearl cotton and a buttonhole stitch.

6. Sew a pin back to the back side of the pin to finish. ***Note:*** *You may use hook-and-loop tape on the pins and hat instead of a pin back for additional safety measures.*

7. Attach the pin to the hatband as desired.

Completing the Bow

1. Fold the 6½ x 8½-inch bow rectangle with right sides together to make a 6½ x 4¼-inch rectangle. Sew along the 6½-inch side, leaving 2½ inches in the center unstitched (Figure 9). Press seam open.

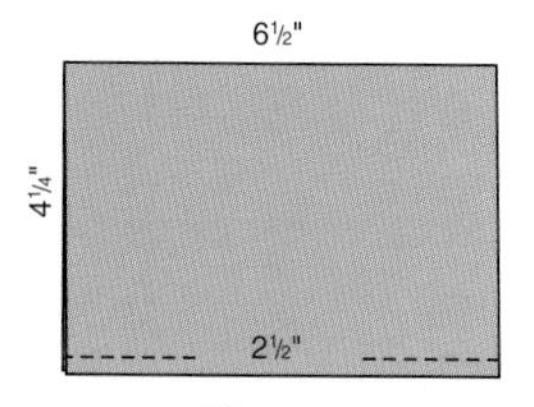

Figure 9

2. Rotate stitched rectangle so seam is centered; stitch across each end (Figure 10).

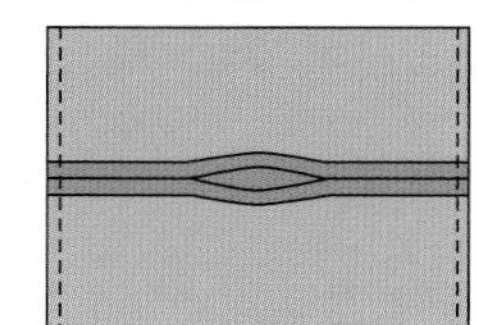

Figure 10

3. Turn right side out through the opening; press edges flat. Turn opening edges to the inside and hand-stitch opening closed to finish the bow.

4. Fold the 2½ x 3½-inch knot rectangle with right sides together to make a 1¼ x 3½-inch rectangle; join edges on the 3½-inch side. Press seam open and turn right side out.

5. Rotate seam so it is in the center. Turn raw edges to the inside and press. Join the short ends together to form the knot.

6. Insert bow through the knot and center the knot on the bow (Figure 11).

Figure 11

7. Sew a large felt button to the center of the bow knot, securing the outside edge of the button with additional stitches.

8. Position bow on hatband as desired; hand-stitch in place at knot edges to finish. ■

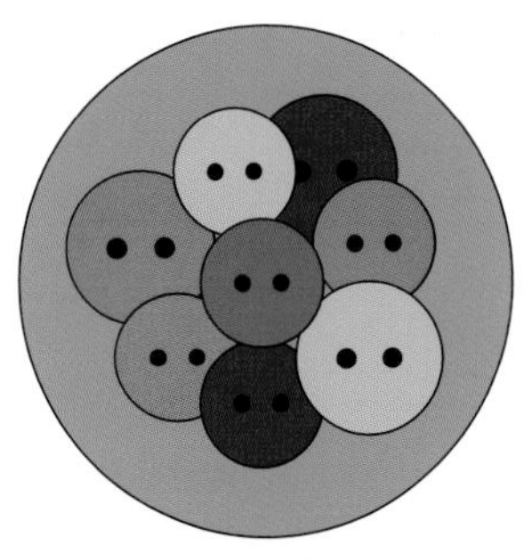

Button Pin
Placement Diagram
2½-inch Diameter

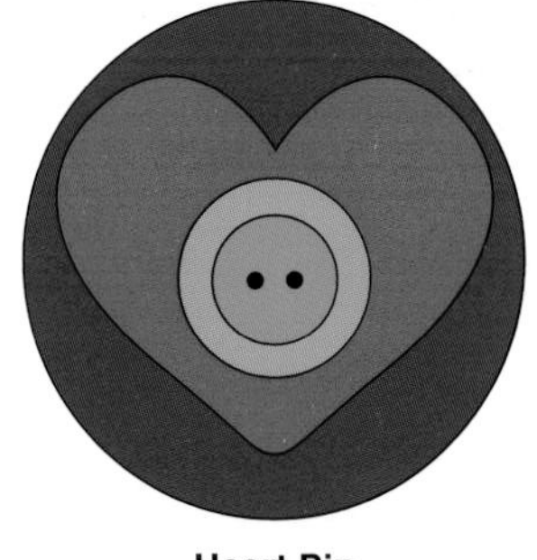

Heart Pin
Placement Diagram
2½-inch Diameter

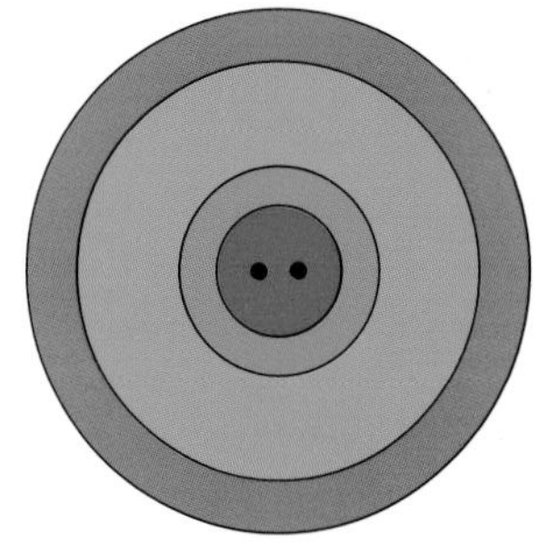

Circle Pin
Placement Diagram
2½-inch Diameter

Flower Pin
Placement Diagram
2½-inch Diameter

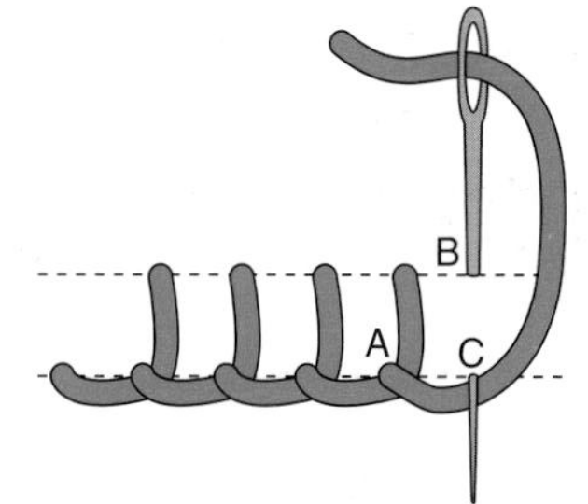

Buttonhole Stitch

As an alternative option to the bow, create these cute pins to embellish your beret. Use felt buttons and stitch down securely.

Gone Fishin' Hat

Design by Carol Zentgraf

Protect your baby's head with this adorable fishing-style hat. Hook-and-loop chin straps help keep the hat in place.

Specifications

Hat Size: 19½-inch circumference x 2½ inches tall

Materials

- ½ yard cotton print for hat
- ½ yard coordinating print for lining
- Coordinating all-purpose thread
- ½ yard medium-weight fusible interfacing
- 2-inch-long strip soft hook-and-loop tape
- Tube-turning tool (optional)
- Pattern-tracing paper
- Basic sewing supplies and equipment

Cutting

Refer to the General Instructions on page 2 for preparing and using patterns from insert. Transfer all pattern markings to fabric.

- Gone Fishin' Hat Top
- Gone Fishin' Hat Crown
- Gone Fishin' Hat Brim

From cotton print:

- Cut one each hat top, brim and crown as directed on patterns.

From coordinating print for lining:

- Cut one each hat top, brim and crown as directed on patterns.
- Cut two 2 x 8-inch strips for straps.

From medium-weight fusible interfacing:

- Cut one each hat top, brim and crown as directed on patterns.

Assembly

Use a ½-inch seam allowance and sew seams with right sides together.

1. Apply fusible interfacing pieces to the wrong side of each corresponding cotton print hat piece.

2. To make the hat, join the short ends of the crown piece. Press the seam open.

3. Pin and stitch the crown to the hat top, clipping the curve as needed to fit smoothly (Figure 1).

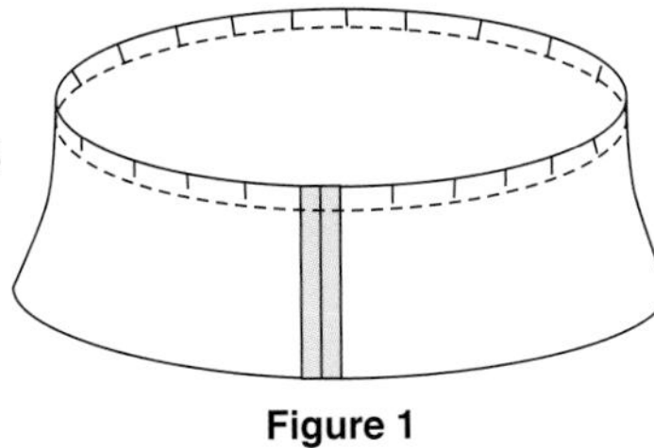

Figure 1

4. Press seam toward crown. Turn right side out and edgestitch seam in place (Figure 2).

Figure 2

5. Join the short ends of the brim. Pin and then stitch the brim to the bottom edge of the crown, clipping the curve as necessary. Press seam allowance toward the crown and edgestitch in place to complete the outer hat.

6. Repeat steps 2–5 with the lining pieces, leaving a 3-inch opening in the crown/brim seam for turning.

7. Place the lining and outer hat right sides together and stitch all around brim edges.

8. Turn right side out through opening in lining. Press opening seam allowance edges to the inside and stitch opening closed.

9. Press brim edges flat and topstitch ¼ inch from the edge all around.

10. To make the straps, fold each 2 x 8-inch strip in half along the length with right sides together. Sew the edges together along the long edge and one short edge. Trim seam allowances. Turn right side out, using a tube-turning tool if available. Press the straps flat. Turn the raw end edges of each strap ½ inch to the inside; press.

11. Pin the open end of each strap on opposite sides of the inside of the hat (crown and brim seams are center back of hat), extending the end ½ inch onto the crown (Figure 3). From the outside of the hat, stitch in the ditch of the brim/crown seam to secure each strap end.

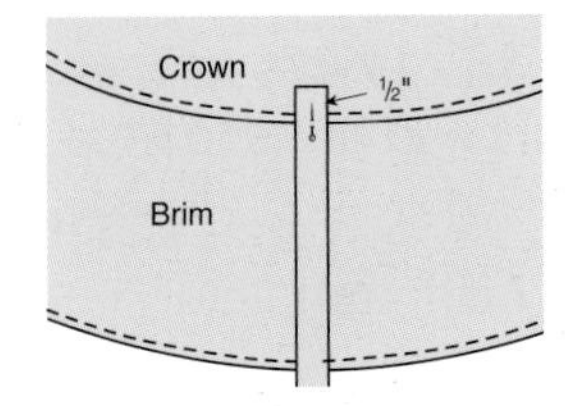

Figure 3

12. Trim the hook-and-loop tape strip to ⅜ x 2 inches. Separate and sew the hook piece to the inside of one finished end of one strap and the loop piece to the outside of the finished end of the remaining strap to finish (Figure 4). ■

Figure 4

Paisley Nursing Cover

Design by Little Lizard King

This stylish nursing cover is lightweight and easy to tuck into a small pocket in any tote. The cover is designed with a slight bow in the top to allow Mom to see Baby during nursing while still providing adequate modesty.

Specifications

Cover Size: Approximately 31½ x 23¼ inches

Materials

- 1⅛ yards blue paisley print
- 15 inches ½-inch flexible boning
- 2 (1-inch) D rings
- All-purpose thread to match fabrics
- Basic sewing supplies and equipment

Cutting

From blue paisley print:

- Cut one 33 x 25-inch rectangle for cover.
- Cut two 2 x 25-inch strips for long neck straps.
- Cut two 2 x 10-inch strips for short neck straps.

Completing the Cover

Use a ½-inch seam allowance throughout.

1. Fold edges of the 33 x 25-inch rectangle ¼ inch to the wrong side and press to hold.

2. Fold over two 25-inch sides and the bottom 33-inch edge ½ inch, completely enclosing the raw edges; press to hold.

3. Sew around the three double-folded edges to make finished edges.

4. Fold over the remaining 33-inch (top) edge ¾ inch and press to hold; do not sew. Set aside.

5. Place the two 2 x 25-inch long neck strap pieces right sides together. Sew around three sides, leaving one short end open for turning. Clip corners (Figure 1).

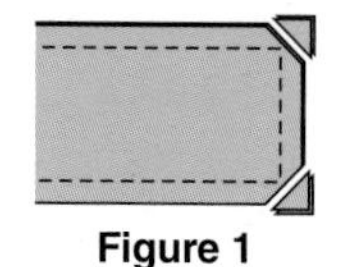

Figure 1

6. Turn the strap right side out; press edges flat. Topstitch close to stitched edges (Figure 2).

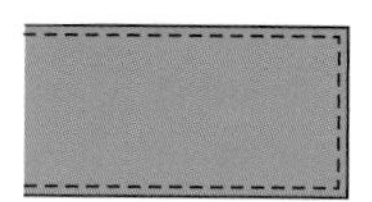

Figure 2

7. Repeat steps 5 and 6 with the short strap pieces.

8. Thread the short strap through the two D rings. Fold the strap in half, and keeping the D rings to the right of the presser foot, sew strap together 1 inch to the left of the D rings/folded edge to keep D rings at the center of the strap (Figure 3).

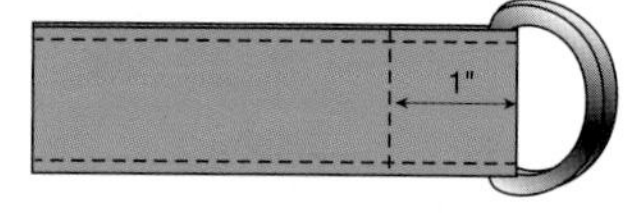

Figure 3

9. Make a mark at the top center point of the nursing cover. Measure and mark a line 7½ inches to the left of the center point (Figure 4).

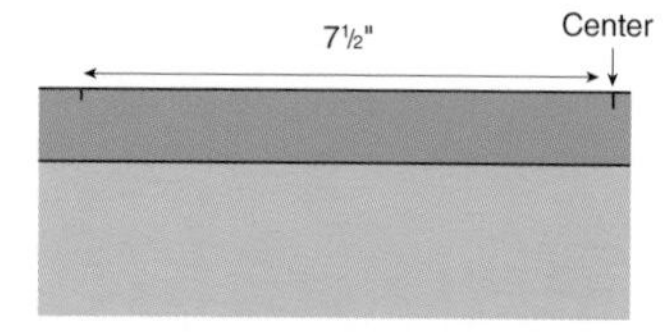

Figure 4

10. Tuck the raw end of the long neck strap under the folded edge at the mark (Figure 5). Pin to secure.

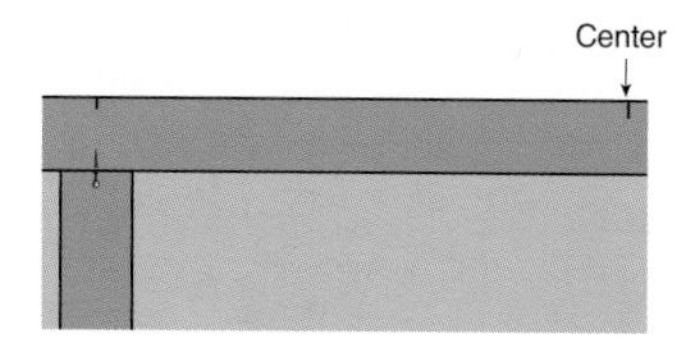

Figure 5

11. Measure and mark 7½ inches to the right of the center point. Tuck the raw end of the short strap under the folded edge as in step 10. Pin to secure.

12. Insert the boning between the straps under the top folded edge. ***Note:*** *The boning will overlap the neck straps. You can either sew over the boning or trim it slightly to fit between straps.* Pin the folded top edge to secure hem/casing. The boning will form a half circle "raised hoop" for the mother to see the baby while nursing.

13. Flip up both neck straps, over the hem/casing fold. Pin to secure.

14. Stitch close to the inside edge of the folded hem/casing along the entire width of the top edge to hem and enclose the boning.

15. For added security, stitch a square shape over the strap areas of the top edge (Figure 6). ■

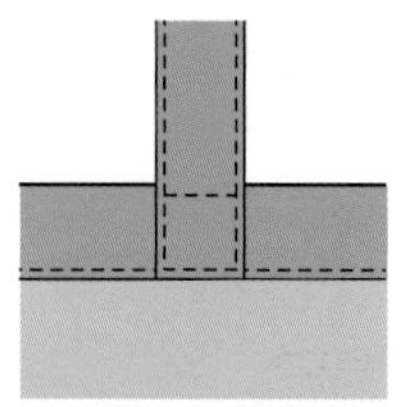

Figure 6

ISBN: 978-1-59635-633-7

1 2 3 4 5 6 7 8 9

For my amazing wife, April; my children, Gabrielle, Addison, and Asher; and my mother.

—Jay Dawes

CONTENTS

PART III Suspension Training Programs

EXERCISE FINDER

Exercise name	Page #	Exercise level
Reverse biceps curl	75	Intermediate
Dual-arm internal rotation	76	Intermediate
Single-arm inverted row	77	Advanced
Split fly	78	Advanced
Single-arm biceps curl	79	Advanced
Single-arm reverse biceps curl	80	Advanced
Upper-Body Flexibility and Mobility Exercises		
Pec stretch	81	Beginner
Single-arm pec stretch	82	Beginner
Single-arm kneeling pec stretch	83	Beginner
Overhead lat stretch	84	Beginner
Rear deltoid stretch	85	Beginner
Bent-over rear deltoid stretch	86	Beginner
Chapter 6 Lower-Body Exercises		
Excursions	88	Beginner
Single-leg reaching Romanian deadlift	89	Beginner
Reverse lunge with knee drive	90	Beginner
Deep squat	91	Beginner
Iso squat	92	Beginner
Split squat	93	Beginner
Overhead squat	94	Beginner
Lateral squat	95	Beginner
Iso lateral squat	96	Beginner
Lateral lunge	97	Beginner
Sprinter lunge	98	Beginner
Leg sweep	99	Beginner
Calf raise	100	Beginner
Suspended reverse lunge	101	Beginner
Lying leg curl	102	Beginner
Triangle squat	103	Beginner
Pigeon stretch	104	Beginner
Figure-four stretch	105	Beginner
Reaching hip flexor stretch	106	Beginner
Reverse lunge	107	Intermediate
Single-leg calf raise	108	Intermediate
Reverse lunge with chop and lift	109	Intermediate
Reverse lunge with horizontal push	110	Intermediate
Suspended single-leg deadlift	111	Intermediate
Suspended knee extension	112	Intermediate
Drop squat	113	Intermediate
Drop split squat	114	Intermediate

(continued)

ACKNOWLEDGMENTS

I would like to thank my family, friends, and colleagues for their continuous support and encouragement—especially Mark Stephenson, who introduced me to this training modality. I would also like to thank the team at Human Kinetics, especially Justin Klug, Roger Earle, Laura Pulliam, Ann Gindes, and Neil Bernstein, for helping this project become a reality. Finally, thank you to TRX® for their support and for endorsing this work—especially Chris Frankel, Marisa Christie, Miguel Vargas, Steve Katai, Rachel Mandeville, Tenae Roth, and Nick Vay.

INTRODUCTION

Over the years, Suspension Training® has continued to grow in popularity. Spawned from traditional gymnastics training, suspension training takes advantage of the physical laws of nature to improve physical fitness. Using the basic principles of physics, Suspension Training allows the user to manipulate the resistance created by one's own bodyweight to provide the necessary physical stressors for developing and maintaining health and fitness.

Suspension Training as we know it today became popular as a way to develop and maintain fitness among certain populations when traditional fitness equipment was not available. For example, U.S. Navy SEALs used Suspension Training when deployed in austere environments to maintain their fitness and occupational readiness. However, to create such devices, they typically used GI belts and nylon webbing designed to secure equipment to pallets. This concept was eventually commercialized and is now used in a wide variety of health clubs, by sports teams at every level, and in rehabilitation settings.

Working with older first responders (i.e., police, firefighters), masters athletes, and collegiate athletes, many of whom with multiple chronic injuries, required our training staffs to create modifications that could help them maintain and improve performance without aggravating any preexisting conditions. Introducing Suspension Training into their regular training programs provided a safe, versatile, and effective way for them to attain their goals. We found that individuals who started with a regular routine of suspension training experienced increased functional strength, decreased chronic pain, lower injury rates, and better results when performing traditional weightlifting and resistance training routines.

Suspension Training has a place in practically every type of training program. It can be used to develop core strength, mobility, joint strength and integrity, and basic and foundational strength, as well as to target specific strength goals. It can serve as a stand-alone training program or be used with another training program. Whatever the goals, suspension training can help an individual achieve success and improve training outcomes.

Science of Suspension Training

At this time, research on Suspension Training is minimal. However, several basic scientific principles support its use as a training modality. Part I presents some of the science behind Suspension Training and explains how to use these principles to guide training and maximize results.

CHAPTER 1

Foundation of Suspension Training

It is generally well accepted that performing resistance training on a regular basis can help maintain and improve health, fitness, and quality of life. However, people often encounter obstacles to resistance training, such as time, space, equipment, and cost. Suspension Training® offers a unique approach to resistance training that requires only one portable piece of equipment, and it can be done almost anywhere. In addition, Suspension Training exercises can be used to address a wide range of fitness needs such as enhancing and maintaining general fitness, improving sport performance, and as a rehabilitation or injury prevention tool. This mode of training can be used as a stand-alone exercise regime or be integrated it into a more traditional training program to add variety and prevent staleness and boredom. Additionally, Suspension Training is popular among those who are traveling or who do not have access to a training facility because of its versatility and portability. Based on this, it is no wonder this form of training has become so popular.

Although Suspension Training seems to be a very straightforward concept, a good deal of science is involved in setting up a workout. Suspension Training is based on principles of anatomy, exercise physiology, physics, and biomechanics. The better these principles are understood, the more Suspension Training will make sense as a training option. However, one of the primary goals of this book is to keep it simple. This chapter presents some basic principles to help the reader manipulate training programs and learn how to progress or regress exercises to change the intensity of a training program. It also presents foundational program design concepts to help in the development of fun, challenging, and productive training sessions.

By using a single-point anchor, Suspension Training allows users to take advantage of some basic principles of physics, including Newton's law of gravitation using force vectors, center of gravity, and pendulum. Creating resistance or force requires changing the direction of the force. The Suspension Trainer™ has a single-point anchor with straps, handles, and foot cradles that are perpendicular to the floor when it is allowed to hang, as a result of the object's center of gravity. When a person grabs the handles, mass increases (due to the person's body mass), resulting in a change in the object's center of gravity. Changing the angle of the straps on the Suspension Trainer changes the application, or direction of the force on the musculoskeletal system, thereby increasing the force of pull, or resistance placed on the body. The result of these forces, or force vectors, and the center of gravity being pulled away creates gravitational potential energy. A single-point anchor system creates a pendulum, converting gravitational potential energy and kinetic energy into work, or resistance.

A variety of ways are available to manipulate the intensity or difficulty of a Suspension Training program based on these principles. For the purposes of this text, *intensity* will be defined as increasing the load on the musculoskeletal system, or increasing the absolute load (i.e., amount of weight which must be moved) such as when changing the vector resistance, angle, or pendulum. *Difficulty* will be defined as any variations that may increase the complexity, or stability demands of a movement or action (e.g., single-arm, single-leg, balance, coordination). Stepping toward or away from the single-point anchor (depending on the exercise), and thus increasing the angle of pull, increases the intensity of an exercise. Ground contact is necessary to resist the forces that are trying to bring the mass back to perpendicular. The wider the floor contact base in the direction of the force vector is, the easier it is to resist the force vector. On the contrary, the narrower the ground contact base in the direction of the force vector is, the more difficult it is to resist the force vector. Consider the game tug of war. As one opponent pulls, creating a force vector, the other opponent must split the feet from front to back to keep from being pulled forward. This increases the base of support along the direction of pull created from the resultant vector, increasing stability along this vector.

There are three methods for varying the intensity or difficulty, or both, of a single-point anchor Suspension Trainer. These methods include:

- changing the stability demands of the exercise (e.g., from dual handles to a single handle, or by altering stance),
- manipulating the angle of pull, and
- changing the position of the center of gravity.

Base of Support

The body's base of support and center of gravity affect exercise intensity. Increasing the base of support makes a person more stable, which makes the exercise easier. Narrowing the base of support increases the difficulty by reducing stability. The most difficult base of support is a single limb (one foot, one arm). See figure 1.1 for examples of base of support levels.

FIGURE 1.1 Bases of support: *(a)* easy, *(b)* moderate, *(c)* harder, *(d)* hardest.

Angle of Pull

Changing the angle of pull increases exercise intensity. It also changes the angle of the body in relation to the ground. Also, increasing the lever arm, or movement arm, of gravitational pull increases the exercise intensity. In other words, the farther the person is from vertical, the greater the resistance will be. See figure 1.2 for examples of angles.

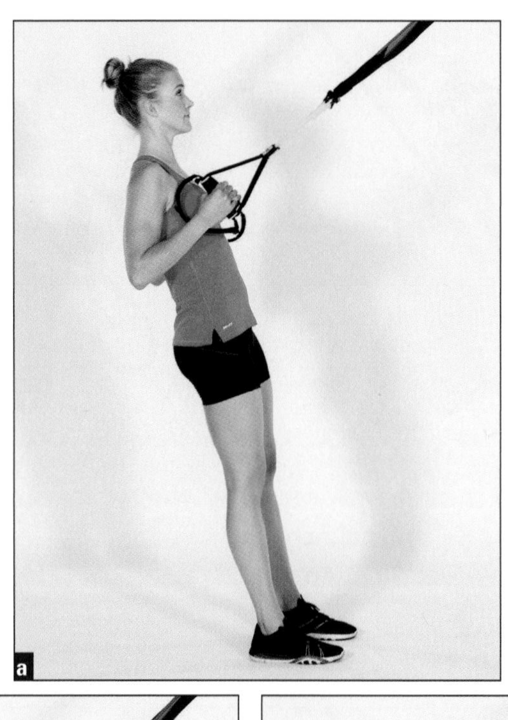

FIGURE 1.2 Angles of pull: *(a)* easy, *(b)* moderate, *(c)* harder.

Pendulum

The pendulum is used in ground exercises in which the feet are placed in the Suspension Trainer and the hands are off the ground. The center of gravity in relation to the perpendicular gravitational pull determines exercise intensity. Exercises in which the head and feet are on the same side in relation to the anchor point are more difficult than those in which the head and feet are on opposite sides of the anchor point—with some exceptions. See figure 1.3 for pendulums.

FIGURE 1.3 Pendulums: *(a)* easy, *(b)* moderate, *(c)* harder.

Handles

Using a single handle can increase the difficulty and intensity of some exercises by increasing the amount of neuromuscular control and stability needed to maintain the position. The single-handle grip also creates a significantly greater training demand on the core. When performing exercises unilaterally, on the side of the body with the free arm or leg, gravity tends to pull the body into rotation. Resisting the rotation is an excellent way to build trunk stability and reduce injury potential. Furthermore, unilateral type exercises (i.e., one hand or one foot in the straps) create off-center loading and require greater joint stabilization than traditional bilateral exercises, in which the loads moved are more evenly distributed. Used appropriately, this can provide a great alternative method of developing joint strength and stability.

For single-handle exercises to be safe, the handles must remain together during the exercise. This can be accomplished by grasping one handle in each hand (see figure 1.4*a*). Next, pass the handle in the right hand through the left-handle triangle (see figure 1.4*b*). Now take the handle in the right hand and pass it through the left-handle triangle (see figure 1.4*c*). Firmly pull down, cinching the handles together (see figure 1.4*d*). Test the security prior to performing the exercise.

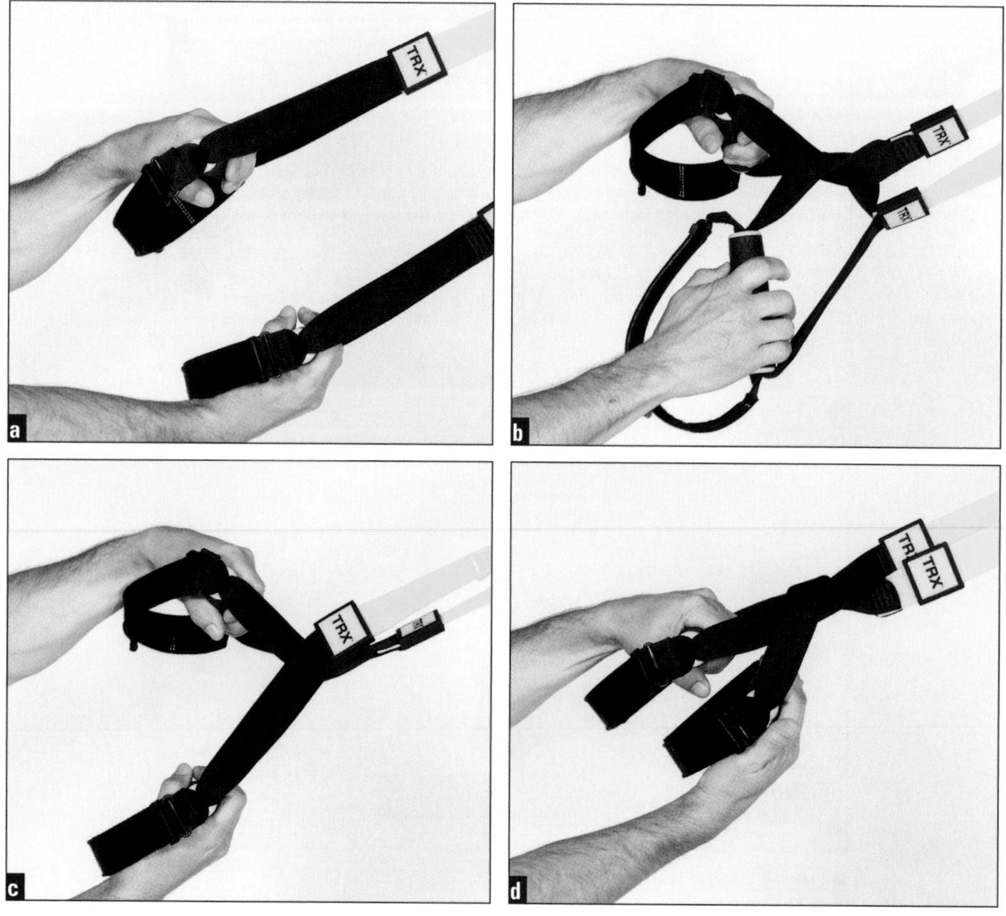

FIGURE 1.4 Single-handle setup.

Exercises using one limb, either an arm or a leg, require the double-handle setup for most individuals (see figure 1.5). The use of a single handle when a single arm or leg is in contact with the ground requires high levels of coordination, balance, and strength. Only experienced individuals with high levels of strength should attempt such progressions.

FIGURE 1.5 Double-handle setup.

Stance

Foot position is important for modifying the intensity of exercises performed while standing. The wider the base of support is, the lower the intensity and difficulty of the exercise will be. The narrower the base of support is, the more intense and difficult the exercise will be. Any base of support can be adjusted during the exercise to increase or decrease difficulty. The following are the seven basic positions:

- *Shoulder-width*—Stand so that the instep of the foot is in line with the armpits (see figure 1.6*a*).
- *Hip-width*—Stand so that the feet and ankles are directly under the hips (see figure 1.6*b*).
- *Feet together*—Stand so that the feet are touching (see figure 1.6*c*).
- *Staggered*—Stand so that the feet are hip-width apart and the toes of one foot are in line with the instep of the other foot (see figure 1.6*d*).
- *Single-leg*—Stand on one foot (see figure 1.6*e*).
- *Lunge*—Stand so that the feet are hip-width apart. Move one leg backward and the other forward. Bend the forward knee until the shin is perpendicular to the foot. Bend the knee of the back leg until it forms a 90-degree angle. The foot of the front leg should be flat on the ground. The heel of the back foot should be raised, and the weight should be supported on the ball of the foot (see figure 1.6*f*).
- *Plank*—Stand so that the upper body, hips, and legs are in line with one another forming a long ridged lever (see figure 1.6*g*).

FIGURE 1.6 Suspension Training stances: (*a*) shoulder-width, (*b*) hip-width, (*c*) feet together, and (*d*) staggered.

FIGURE 1.6 Suspension Training stances: *(e)* single-leg *(f)* lunge, and *(g)* plank.

Suspension Training can be a very effective way to improve health, fitness, and performance. An understanding of the basic scientific principles behind Suspension Training will help in the creation, progression, and regression of a variety of exercises regardless of training level. The chapters that follow describe how to use these principles to develop comprehensive training programs.

CHAPTER 2

Benefits of Suspension Training

As mentioned in chapter 1, Suspension Training is very popular because of its versatility, portability, and cost effectiveness. This chapter outlines the many benefits of this unique form of body weight training.

Functional Training

Functional training is a popular buzzword in the fitness community. Over the years, the term has been used to describe exercises performed with a variety of novel types of training equipment (e.g., balance discs, kettlebells, resistance tubing, Indian clubs). However, it is important to stress that a device does not make an activity functional. Furthermore, performing exercises that look similar to those in which one would like to improve, but whose underlying physical characteristics are different, may hinder performance. For example, running while towing a weighted sled can be functional; however, if the sled is weighted too heavily, the runner will have to counteract the load by increasing torso forward lean. This may alter the biomechanics of the activity and also engrain poor movement mechanics, interfering with motor programming.

Now that we have an idea of what is not functional, let's discuss what *is* functional. In simple terms, *function* can be defined as a desired purpose. In relation to human performance, most often *function* refers to the ability to move fluidly at the required speed and using the appropriate amount of force to execute a given task. Therefore, functional training may be defined as any form of training that improves movement quality and enhances a performance outcome (Siff 2003).

Rather than thinking of exercises as either completely functional or completely nonfunctional, we can think of all exercises as on a continuum. The functionality of an exercise is largely determined by the amount of carryover, or transfer, it has to a given activity. For example, if a training goal is to improve performance in the pull-up, the exercise with the highest likelihood of meeting this goal would be the exercise itself. However, performing other exercises for the back, such as a suspension row, lat pull-down, seated row, or bent-over dumbbell row, may improve performance in the pull-up because they develop similar muscle groups. Even the biceps curl, which is normally considered a nonfunctional isolation exercise, can improve pull-up performance because the biceps are secondary movers in this action. Another example is the glute bridge. Although this exercise does not appear to have a direct relationship to any athletic movements, it strengthens the glutes, which are essential for controlling the hips during movements such as running and jumping. Poor glute strength may also contribute to valgus collapse (i.e., the knees moving inward while running, sprinting, and jumping), making an athlete more prone to injury.

In general terms, exercises that require stability through increased synergy have increased functional value (Orr 1999). Most activities, whether in sport or daily life, require us to move effectively and to manipulate our bodies to produce, reduce, and stabilize forces (see figure 2.1). This requires a combination of both stability (i.e., resistance to movement) and mobility (i.e., the ability to move). Although these concepts appear to be diametrically opposed, without one the other suffers. Producing efficient movements at the joints requires a base of stability (i.e., proximal stability) that allows the arms and legs to move fluidly through their intended ranges of motion (i.e., distal mobility). Consequently, inadequate mobility or stability may compromise movement. This is the reason for emphasizing proximal stability and motor control of the trunk first in the training program. Doing so optimizes distal mobility.

When using a Suspension Trainer, one or both limbs of either the upper or lower body are supported in handles or foot cradles. At the other end of the Suspension Trainer is an anchor point. The design of this device increases the demands on the user to control their body weight in multiple planes of movement and at multiple joints, while adding varying and progressive degrees of instability. Thus, the user must often recruit more muscles to remain stable while performing a movement. This improves what is referred to as top-down stability. Other devices, such as gymnastics rings, also develop top-down stability. However, unlike rings, most Suspension Trainers use a single anchor point with a limited-slip locking loop. This allows the user to add progressive amounts

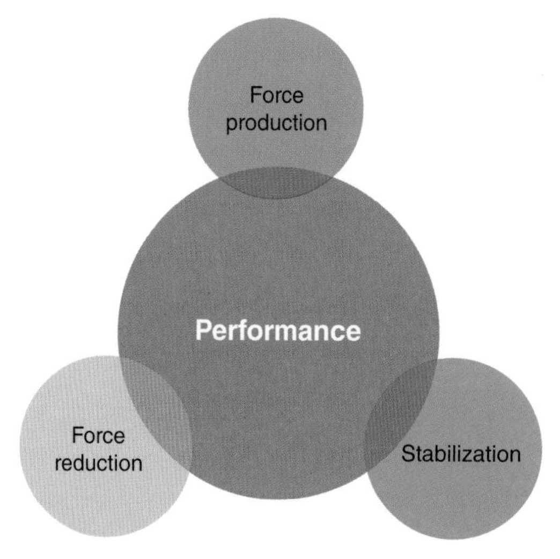

FIGURE 2.1 Essential elements of performance.

of instability to the training programs, which may improve joint stability and body awareness and increase the muscular activity of the core.

Although instability may hinder the total amount of force produced by the prime movers when compared to training in a stable environment, the stabilizer muscles around the joints and the trunk may become more active to resist unwanted motion. Therefore, Suspension Training can be particularly useful for athletes in overhead sports (e.g., baseball, softball, volleyball, and handball players, and quarterbacks in American football) because it may improve scapular control and strength in the muscles of the serratus anterior and those surrounding the shoulder. These improvements may help prevent both acute and chronic shoulder injuries. Suspension Training may also improve kinesthetic awareness and proprioception. This is simply a greater awareness of where the body and joints are in time and space. Enhancing these qualities may have a positive impact on performance as well as aid in reducing injury risk. Furthermore, shoulder injuries are very common in the general population because this ball-and-socket joint can be compromised during overhead lifting and lowering activities. Therefore, top-down instability training may also improve performance in activities of daily living and in recreational sports and resistance training, and reduce injury in the general population.

From a functional perspective, Suspension Training may challenge the trunk stabilizer muscles. Since Suspension Training increases the stability challenges of the trunk and the joints, these exercises may be well suited as preparation to lift heavier resistance. As one attempts to stabilize the joints, contractions of the agonist and antagonist muscle groups that surround the joints may contribute to a greater neuromuscular activation. Because a base of stability is required to produce and reduce force, Suspension Training exercises may be performed as a dynamic warm-up prior to more traditional and complex exercises. For example, a suspension push-up or chest press may be performed prior to a bench press to stimulate, or activate, the stabilizer muscles surrounding the shoulder prior to overloading the prime movers (e.g., pectoralis major, anterior deltoids, and triceps). Additionally, the Suspension Trainer can turn traditional single-joint isolation exercises, such as the biceps curl, into total-body exercises by increasing the demand for core stabilization. Given that the ability to resist unwanted motion in the trunk, or core, is essential in many activities of daily living and sport, this variation may be considered more functional than a similar exercise performed while seated or using a machine with a fixed movement path.

Fitness and Performance

Suspension Training has been shown to improve a variety of fitness and performance measures in recreationally active populations. Janot and colleagues (2013) found that younger (19 to 25 years) adults experienced significant improvements in flexibility, balance, core endurance, and lower-body strength when performing exercises twice a week for seven weeks using a Suspension Trainer. In this same study, the researchers also discovered that middle-aged (44 to 64 years) adults using Suspension Training experienced significant improvements in both core endurance and lower-body strength as well as improved, yet not statistically significant, increases in balance and flexibility. These improvements were similar to those of people performing traditional resistance training in all but one area, lower-body strength. Those in the resistance training group experienced greater overall improvements in lower-body strength than did those in the Suspension Training group. This was most likely due to heavier training loads being used in the traditional resistance training group. However, this should not be seen as a negative finding in the support of Suspension Training. Rather, it supports the use of multiple training modalities to elicit specific adaptations.

Garnacho-Castaño and colleagues (2014) found that untrained men who performed a circuit training program that included both a domed training device (BOSU) and a Suspension Trainer (TRX) three days a week for seven weeks experienced significant improvements in maximal strength, average and peak velocity, and average peak power during both the bench press and back squat exercises. Significant improvements were also seen in vertical jump height when performing the squat jump and countermovement jump exercises. Although this is compelling evidence that instability training using a Suspension Trainer can improve these variables during the early stages of a resistance training program, advanced athletes may not experience similar results. Rather, advanced athletes would likely be better served by using Suspension Training as part of a comprehensive strength training program aimed at preventing injury, encouraging core development, and preventing monotony and boredom from stagnant training programs.

Suspension Training can be used to improve strength or endurance, or both. The attribute best developed may depend on initial strength levels. Individuals who already have a great deal of muscle size and strength may not increase their size and strength significantly with Suspension Training because they will not be moving as much weight when then use the Suspension Trainer in comparison to their normal training routines. These individuals may want to emphasize muscular endurance in working with Suspension Training, which they can still gain. For those who aren't very strong, Suspension Training may increase their muscle size, strength, and endurance because they have a higher training ceiling than those who are experienced in strength training. As a general rule of thumb, those who can perform no more than 10 repetitions of a given exercise should emphasize muscle size and strength rather than endurance. In contrast, those who can perform significantly more than 10 repetitions of a particular Suspension Training exercise would be best suited by using that exercise to develop muscular endurance. In order to shift a training program's focus between these attributes, exercise resistance may need to decrease to train endurance and increase to train strength. This can be done easily by selecting different exercises that change the total amount of body weight that must be lifted, by adding external resistance (such as a weighted vest), or by manipulating body position in relation to the anchor point.

Both strength and endurance exercises should be performed as part of a strength training program. Therefore, the current level of strength in a particular exercise or movement often dictates the most appropriate places in which to incorporate Suspension Training exercises into a training program to achieve the best training effect. For example, a suspension squat or lunge would be unlikely to improve overall strength in someone who is very strong on the back squat. However, it could be used to improve mobility by unloading the body while keeping some stress on the legs to prevent detraining, as part of a compound set during a hypertrophy cycle to increase the density of a training session, or to isolate the stabilizer muscles of the hip to reduce the risk of injury or improve neuromuscular control or balance.

Injury Reduction and Rehabilitation

Previous injuries, habitual movement patterns, and repetitive stress may lead to a variety of anatomical constraints. These constraints may decrease the ability to produce efficient movement by creating compensatory movement patterns. When these patterns are performed chronically, neuromuscular inefficiency and tissue breakdown are common. This may lead to pain or increased injury risk.

Core stability, or the effective recruitment of the muscles surrounding the trunk and pelvis, is essential to produce, reduce, stabilize, and transfer forces through the spine, as well as to control the muscles that surround the lower back and pelvis (Mok et al. 2015). Thus, the ability to maintain core stability has a profound effect on injury prevention. Given that training with suspension has been shown to result in improvements and progress in core stability exercises (Byrne et al. 2014; Mok et al. 2015; Snarr and Esco 2014), incorporating this modality into a training program seems intuitive if injury prevention is a concern. Performing a push-up using suspension may also strengthen the rectus abdominis just as effectively as performing abdominal crunches. Because Suspension Training results in less shortening of the psoas, it may be preferred for people with low back pain (Snarr et al. 2013).

Ease and Adjustability

The configuration of the Suspension Trainer allows the user to adjust the working angle to manipulate body angle and either increase or decrease the training load for each exercise. Melrose and Dawes (2015) conducted a study to evaluate the percentages of body mass people using Suspension Training were required to move with their torsos at angles of approximately 30, 45, 60, and 75 degrees and with their feet directly under the anchor point. Not surprisingly, they found that as people leaned back and their torsos became less vertical, resistance increased (37.44 ± 1.45 percent of body mass at 30 degrees, 52.88 ± 0.59 percent at 45 degrees, 68.08 ± 1.95 percent at 60 degrees, and 79.38 ± 2.14 percent at 75 degrees). Making these small adjustments in body position is significantly easier than changing weights between exercises, which is beneficial in a group training session in which multiple users of varying fitness levels are using the same equipment. In addition, manipulating the base of support (e.g., lifting one leg) can introduce additional balance and stabilization challenges to meet the task-specific demands and current physiological abilities of individual exercisers.

Affordability and Portability

One of the major benefits of Suspension Training is the ability to perform a wide variety of exercises in a small space. This makes it ideal for home gyms and for those who travel frequently. Furthermore, Suspension Training equipment is significantly less expensive than gym memberships. Because the device can be packed and transported easily, Suspension Training is frequently used by military and first responder personnel, especially during deployment.

Suspension Training is unique in its ability to strengthen the intrinsic stabilizing muscles and joint structures. Its benefits include adaptability, portability, and versatility, making it ideal for maintaining muscular strength and endurance anywhere. Integrating Suspension Training into a workout program may also develop accessory muscles, assisting in overall strength development.

Using Suspension Training in a rehabilitation program may also develop the body's core region, lending support to many other structures. Moreover, incorporating it into a daily program requires minimal instruction and supervision by professional staff.

CHAPTER 3

Setup, Safety, and Success

Setting up the Suspension Trainer properly results in effective exercises. The system must also be secured appropriately to avoid injury. As with any exercise program, consultation with a health care provider is recommended, especially for those who have had muscle or joint injuries. Although Suspension Training exercises involve the use of body weight, due to the intensity generated when muscles are under tension for extended periods, as well as the instability of the primary platform, Suspension Training exercises can increase stress on joints and ligaments.

Suspension Trainer Anatomy

A general understanding of the anatomy of the Suspension Trainer is helpful. Figure 3.1 identifies the parts.

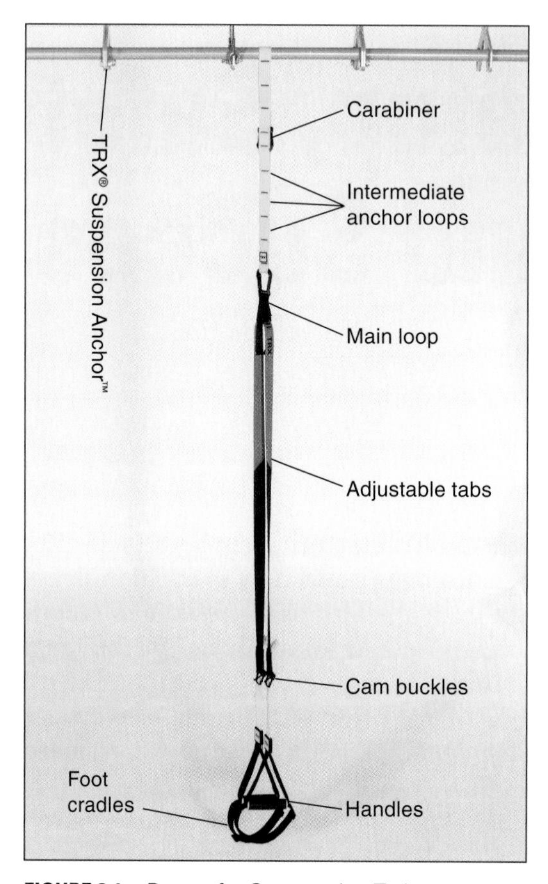

FIGURE 3.1 Parts of a Suspension Trainer.

Anchoring the Suspension Training System

Anchoring the Suspension Trainer requires a sturdy structure that can support the user's weight, such as a beam, bar, or tree limb. The area around it must free of debris to provide enough space to perform the exercises safely. A door can be used as long as the Suspension Trainer has a door anchor attachment.

Hang the Suspension Trainer by wrapping the anchor strap around the structure (see figure 3.2*a*); then, secure it by fastening the carabiner to the appropriate loop (see figure 3.2*b*) so that it hangs straight (see figure 3.2*c*). Be sure to test the weight before using it by pulling firmly on the straps and then gradually shifting weight to the Suspension Trainer.

If using a door, be sure to clip the strap into the loop of the door anchor (see figure 3.3*a*). Place the door anchor over the top of the door (see figure 3.3*b*); then close the door securely (see figure 3.3*c*). Note that the door should open away from the user, allowing the doorjamb to provide extra support during the exercises.

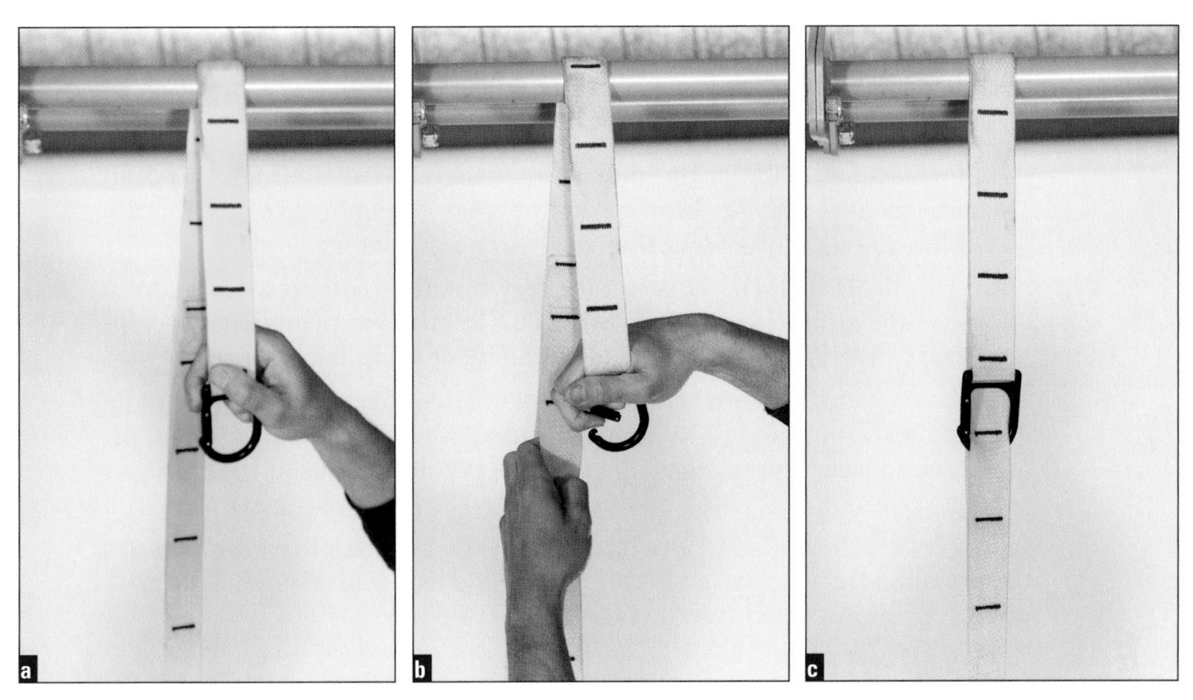

FIGURE 3.2 Anchoring a Suspension Trainer around a beam.

FIGURE 3.3 Anchoring a Suspension Trainer around a door.

Adjusting the Suspension Trainer Length

Adjusting the Suspension Trainer to the appropriate length before each exercise is important to ensure an appropriate training load. The following are typical lengths and positions:

- *Fully shortened*—Adjust the tabs so that they are at the highest point; that is, closest to the anchor (see figure 3.4*a*). This position is primarily used for exercises involving the back, such as row exercises.
- *Mid-length*—Adjust the tabs so that they are approximately at the midpoint of the straps (see figure 3.4*b*). This position is primarily used for exercises involving standing such as the biceps and triceps press.
- *Mid-calf*—Adjust the tabs so that the foot cradles are even with the middle of the user's shin or calf, which is approximately 12 inches (30 cm) off the ground (see figure 3.4*c*). This position is primarily used for exercises involving prone and plank positions.
- *Fully lengthened*—Adjust the tabs so that the bottom of the handles are approximately 3 inches (8 cm) off the ground (see figure 3.4*d*). This position is primarily used for all chest press exercises.

Gripping the Suspension Trainer

There are several ways to grasp the handles during Suspension Training exercises. Some require a specific grip, whereas others use a variety of grips to increase difficulty. The following are the three basic grips:

- *Supinated*—Palms facing up. This grip places a greater demand on the biceps and wrist flexors.
- *Pronated*—Palms facing down. This grip places a greater demand on the rhomboids and wrist extensors.
- *Neutral*—Thumbs facing up or palms facing inward. This grip reduces stress to the shoulder joint and can be used as a modification in any exercise.

Practicing Suspension Training Safely

When using a Suspension Trainer, check and recheck the anchor system prior to use to ensure that it can support weight. Generally, the issue is not related to the system itself (it is designed to support weight); rather, the issue is often related to what the system is anchored to. For instance, when anchoring the Suspension Trainer to a door, a heavy exterior door is much safer than a hollow door usually found between rooms. Use a deadbolt when anchoring to an external door to reduce the risk of the door opening during an exercise. Also, if using the Suspension Trainer in the single-handle configuration, check and recheck the handles to be sure they are secured together prior to use.

The location around the Suspension Trainer should be clear of debris, and the ground should be level and dry. If using the system outside, clear the training area of any loose debris. Do not use electrical poles for anchor attachment, and ensure that there are no electrical wires near the anchor system.

The following are other important guidelines to follow to ensure safe training:

- Never stand in the handles or foot cradles.
- Do not use the Suspension Trainer as a swing.
- Wipe any sweat off the ground, handles, and foot cradles to avoid slipping.

FIGURE 3.4 Suspension Trainer strap lengths: *(a)* fully-shortened, *(b)* mid-length, *(c)* mid-calf, *(d)* fully lengthened.

- Periodically spray the straps, handles, and foot cradles with an antibacterial spray to reduce the risk of transmitting illnesses or disease (such as MRSA), especially if used in a group setting.
- Be cautious about using hand lotion prior to training because it can increase the risk of slipping off the handles.
- Perform all exercises on resilient flooring with a nonslip surface to reduce the risk of slips and falls and to reduce joint stress.
- Make sure the Suspension Trainer is not rubbing against any skin during use to avoid skin abrasions.
- Wear lightweight and nonrestrictive clothing designed for exercise; other types may restrict or hinder movement.
- Perform exercises in an open area free of debris and sharp objects.
- Avoid exercises that may aggravate current or previous injuries.
- Be familiar with, and practice and master, basic exercises prior to performing more advanced variations.
- Perform Suspension Training exercises with caution if you have major orthopedic limitations or are morbidly obese. Do not perform exercise variations that require greater balance challenges (e.g., single-leg variations), at least in the initial stages of training, if you have these conditions.
- Perform a 5- to 10-minute general warm-up prior to training.

When setting up and using a Suspension Trainer, safety is paramount. Following the general guidelines in this chapter will help ensure safe and effective Suspension Training. However, it is the user's responsibility to be aware of the surroundings and make any appropriate adjustments to maximize safety.

CHAPTER 4

Physical Assessment

Periodic physical assessments help determine whether training adjustments are needed and when to increase exercise intensity. This chapter addresses the nuts and bolts of physical assessment and it provides suggestions for testing exercises when using the Suspension Trainer.

Considerations Before Testing

Before undertaking a physical assessment, people need to be familiar with the exercises they will use in the assessment. Moreover, the assessment itself must be both valid and reliable in order to provide accurate and helpful information. These issues are addressed in greater detail in the following section.

Preparedness

Practicing the exercises before the assessment itself reduces the likelihood of using a less-than-optimal technique during the assessment. A 5- to 10-minute general warm-up prior to testing is also recommended. This general warm-up should include movements that will progressively increase your heart rate, respiration rate, and perspiration rate. Walking or jogging for 3 to 5 minutes followed by some light weight exercises performed on the Suspension Trainer would be an appropriate warm-up. Special attention should be given to make certain that the exercises selected and the intensity of the exercises related to the warm-up do not negatively affect the testing process. If fatigue is accumulated during this portion of the testing process, it may have a negative impact when performing the actual test.

Validity

Validity refers to the ability of a test to accurately measure a specific outcome or attribute. For example, for determining lower-body strength, a test that measures strength in this area, such as the rear-foot elevated split squat, would be ideal. In contrast, to measure upper-body strength, a test such as a push-up or row would be most appropriate. To determine strength gains in the biceps, the biceps curl would be the best option for isolating this area. Test selection is largely based on the targeted attributes. The more specific the selection is, the more helpful the results will be.

Reliability

Reliability refers to the consistency of the results. The following are guidelines for improving the reliability of an assessment:

- Perform all tests indoors in a consistent environment (i.e., temperature, humidity, training surface) to reduce variability.
- Adjust the handles and foot cradles to the same length during every test, and place the feet the same distance from the hanging point. Based on the nature of this training device, these small alterations can create significant changes in the testing load. Failure to be consistent with the setup will not allow accurate comparisons.
- Consider body mass. Significant increases or decreases in weight may alter the results because more or less weight is being moved. This is a particularly misleading factor for those who accrue a large amount of muscle mass. Although they may be significantly stronger, they still must move more mass than in their original test. Therefore, the overall amount of weight moved is greater. This may result in a net zero gain in the number of repetitions performed or in the amount of time holding an isometric position. In reality, improvement has occurred because they are moving or stabilizing a higher load.
- Do not perform tests when significantly fatigued or when experiencing muscle soreness; these conditions can affect results. As a general rule, perform testing 48 to 72 hours after the last exercise session to reduce the effects of soreness and fatigue.
- Reassess every four to six weeks.
- Always give your best effort.

Suggested Testing Exercises

This section presents basic testing exercises for gauging fitness progress. Although any of the exercises in this book can be used as a test, these provide a good general assessment of current fitness level. If you experience pain during any of these exercises, obtain medical clearance prior to beginning a training program.

Elbow Plank

Lie facedown with forearms facing away from the anchor point. Place one foot in each stirrup. From the facedown position, lift the hips and torso until the elbows are directly under the shoulders and the upper arms are perpendicular to the ground using one continuous movement (see figure). Measure this test by tracking the time spent holding the plank position with perfect form and technique. As soon as technique breaks, the test should be terminated. This should be the first test performed in the series. If unable to perform this exercise, substitute the standing plank (see pg. 140).

Suspended Push-Up

Face away from the anchor point and place the feet in the foot cradles. Place the hands on the ground approximately shoulder-width apart. Set the body in a straight line, or plank position. While bracing the trunk and keeping the arms straight, pull the shoulder blades down and together (see figure *a*). Bend at the elbows to lower the body to the ground, keeping the torso flat and rigid, until reaching a 90-degree angle at the elbows (see figure *b*). Push the body back up to the starting position. This test is measured by counting the number of repetitions performed within a set period of time (e.g., one or two minutes), or by counting the number of repetitions performed with good technique or until volitional fatigue. During this test, one may rest in the starting position. If the individual is unable to maintain a proper plank position (i.e., hips drop or rise), the test should be terminated and the number of repetitions to this point should be recorded.

a

b

Inverted Row

Face toward the anchor point and grab the handles (one in each hand) using a neutral grip. While keeping the arms completely straight, position your feet directly underneath the anchor point and lean back until the torso is at approximately a 45-degree angle to the ground (see figure *a*). Pull the shoulder blades together and downward. Pull the body toward the anchor point by bending the arms and extending the shoulders (see figure *b*). Slowly extend the arms and allow the shoulders to flex to return to the starting position. This test is measured by counting the number of repetitions performed within a set period of time (e.g., one or two minutes), or by counting the number of repetitions performed with good technique or until volitional fatigue. During the test, one may rest in the starting position. If the individual is unable to maintain a proper plank position (i.e., hips drop or rise), the test should be terminated and the number of repetitions to this point should be recorded.

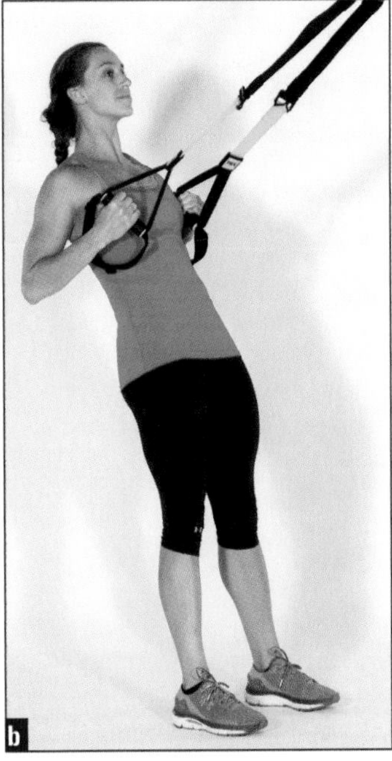

Reverse Lunge

Face away from the anchor point with the hands on the hips and place one foot in the cradles (see figure *a*). The other foot should be firmly planted on the ground with your weight evenly distributed between your big toe, your little toe, and your heel. While maintaining a rigid torso, allow the lead leg, ankle, knee, and hip to bend until the top of the thigh is parallel to the ground (see figure *b*). Extend the lead leg and bring the back foot forward until back in the starting position. This test is measured by counting the number of repetitions performed within a set period of time (e.g., one or two minutes), or by counting the number of repetitions performed with good technique or until volitional fatigue. During this test, one may rest in the starting position. If the individual is unable to maintain balance, the test should be terminated and the number of repetitions to this point should be recorded. After completing this, place the opposite foot in the stirrups, and then repeat this procedure using the opposite leg.

a

b

How to Use the Results

The information gathered from testing can be used in several ways. This section explains how to use this information to determine how effective the training program is and how to adjust it to continue making progress.

Tracking Progress

Figure 4.1 is a blank Suspension Training assessment tracking sheet for measuring fitness progress.

FIGURE 4.1 Suspension Training Assessment Tracking Sheet

	Date: ________	Date: ________	Date: ________
Suspended push-up			
Inverted row			
Reverse lunge (left foot on ground)			
Reverse lunge (right foot on ground)			
Elbow plank			

From J. Dawes, 2017, *Complete guide to TRX® suspension training™* (Champaign, IL: Human Kinetics).

Measuring Change

One way to gauge fitness progress is to simply look at the amount, or percentage, of change from testing date to testing date. To calculate the amount of change, subtract the value of the previous test from the value of the current test. Take a look at the completed tracking sheet in figure 4.2. If the athlete was able to perform 20 push-ups during the first test, and 12 weeks later was able to perform 30 push-ups, this would be a net change of 10 push-ups. The percentage of change could also be calculated as follows:

1. Subtract the old value from the new value:

   30 push-ups (current test) – 20 push-ups (previous test) = 10 push-ups

2. Divide the amount of change by the old value:

   10 push-ups (amount of change) / 20 push-ups (previous test) = 0.50

3. Convert to a percentage by multiplying the decimal number by 100:

   $0.50 \times 100 = 50\%$ increase

FIGURE 4.2 Suspension Training Assessment Tracking Sheet for Sample Athlete

	Date: September 11	Date: October 10	Date: November 12
Suspended push-up	20	25	30
Inverted row	12	15	18
Reverse lunge (left foot on ground)	10	13	15
Reverse lunge (right foot on ground)	8	11	14
Elbow plank	35 sec	50 sec	75 sec

Improving Symmetry

Asymmetry refers to the differences between the right side and left side of the body when performing certain exercises. The sample athlete's results in figure 4.2 reveal a right versus left asymmetry of 20 percent on the rear-foot suspended reverse lunge in the first test. After approximately 8 weeks of training, this asymmetry decreased to approximately 8 percent difference. Although this is subject to some debate, a bilateral deficit greater than 10 percent may present a risk of injury. As shown, after 12 weeks of training, injury risk was reduced significantly as a result of the athlete's developing greater symmetry between the limbs.

Adjusting the Training Load

Test exercises provide an idea of the current fitness level. Meeting the goals of a training program requires adjusting the resistance by progressing or altering the demands of the exercises to stay in the desired repetition ranges (see table 8.1).

Testing is an important step in the design of a training program. Periodically assessing progress provides the best opportunity to achieve the desired results from a training program.

PART II

Suspension Training Exercises

Chapters 5 through 7 present Suspension Training exercises divided into three categories: beginner, intermediate, and advanced. All of the beginner exercises should be mastered before progressing to the intermediate and advanced exercises. Keep in mind that not every variation (e.g., changes in foot position, base of support, or angle of pull) is displayed because the options are limitless. Chapters 1 and 2 describe ways to adjust exercises based on individual constraints and capabilities.

CHAPTER 5

Upper-Body Exercises

This chapter presents exercises to develop upper-body muscular strength and endurance, flexibility, and mobility. A major benefit of using Suspension Training to perform upper-body exercises is that the intensity can easily be adjusted simply by stepping closer to or farther from the anchor point. Additionally, advanced lifters can safely increase the intensity of many exercises by adding external resistance, such as weight vests.

Standing Push-Up Plus

PURPOSE

To develop the serratus anterior muscles. These muscles help actively stabilize the shoulders at the scapulae. This is an excellent prehabilitation exercise for those involved in overhead throwing sports. It is also great for improving posture for those who spend a lot of time sitting (e.g., have desk jobs). This very subtle movement can reduce the injury and pain associated with poor posture.

PREREQUISITES

The ability to maintain a plank position throughout the exercise, and no shoulder or back pain while performing the exercise.

ADJUSTMENT

Fully lengthen the straps of the Suspension Trainer.

STARTING POSITION

Stand facing away from the anchor point and grab a handle with each hand, placing them shoulder-width apart. Set the body in a straight line, or plank position, with the feet hip-width apart.

DESCRIPTION

- Brace the trunk, keep the arms straight, and slowly step backward until there is tension on the straps and the body is at an incline. Simultaneously pull the shoulder blades down and together (see figure *a*).
- Keeping the arms straight, push the shoulder blades apart without rounding the shoulders (see figure *b*).
- Return to the starting position, and repeat for the desired number of repetitions.

TEACHING CUES

- Envision placing the edges of the scapulae in the back hip pockets.
- Brace the trunk as if getting ready to take a punch to the abdomen.

a

b

Chest Press

PURPOSE
To develop upper-body muscular endurance in the chest, shoulders, and triceps, as well as trunk and shoulder strength and stability.

PREREQUISITES
The ability to maintain a plank position throughout the exercise, and no shoulder or back pain while performing the exercise.

ADJUSTMENT
Fully lengthen the straps of the Suspension Trainer.

STARTING POSITION
Face away from the anchor point, and grab a handle with each hand. Extend the arms and position the hands shoulder-width apart. Place the feet hip- to shoulder-width apart. Set the body in a straight line, or in plank position.

DESCRIPTION

- Brace the trunk and slowly step backward until there is tension on the straps and the body is at an incline (see figure *a*).
- Bend the arms and lower the chest between the handles, similar to performing a push-up (see figure *b*).
- Extend the arms to return to the starting position.

TEACHING CUES

- Brace the trunk as if getting ready to take a punch to the abdomen.
- Keep the torso as stiff as a board from the head to the heels.
- Lower the body toward the handles in a slow, controlled manner.
- If you are unable to achieve a full range of motion, perform the exercise through a partial range of motion until the requisite strength and stability are developed.

a

b

Standing Overhead Triceps Extension

PURPOSE
To isolate and develop the triceps and develop isometric trunk strength and stability. Using the Suspension Trainer results in greater total-body development than using traditional barbell and dumbbell versions of this exercise.

PREREQUISITE
The ability to maintain a rigid torso throughout the exercise.

ADJUSTMENT
Adjust the straps of the Suspension Trainer to mid-length.

STARTING POSITION
Stand facing away from the anchor point. Grab a handle with each hand, and lean forward so the torso is at an angle of at least 45 degrees to the ground.

DESCRIPTION

- Bend the elbows to 90 degrees. At this point, the hands should be at the forehead height (see figure *a*).
- While keeping the balls of the feet in contact with the ground and the trunk rigid, extend the arms down in front of the body (see figure *b*).
- Bend the elbows and return to the starting position.

TEACHING CUES

- Maintain a rigid torso throughout the exercise.
- Move only at the elbows.

a

b

Single-Leg Chest Press

PURPOSE
To enhance muscular endurance of the upper-body pushing muscles, and to train trunk antirotation and stability.

PREREQUISITES
The ability to balance on a single leg and maintain a plank position.

ADJUSTMENT
Fully lengthen the straps of the Suspension Trainer.

STARTING POSITION
Face away from the anchor point, and grab a handle with each hand. Extend the arms and position the hands shoulder-width apart. Set the body in a straight line, or in plank position, with the feet close together.

DESCRIPTION
- Brace the trunk and slowly step backward until there is tension on the straps and the body is at an incline.
- While stabilizing the trunk, lift one foot 6 to 12 inches (15 to 30 cm) off the ground (see figure *a*).
- Bend the arms and lower the chest between the handles, similar to performing a push-up (see figure *b*).
- Extend the arms to return to the starting position.

TEACHING CUES
- Brace the trunk as if ready to take a punch to the abdomen.
- Keep the torso as stiff as a board from the head to the heels.
- Lower the body toward the handles in a slow, controlled manner.
- If unable to achieve a full range of motion, perform through a partial range of motion until the requisite strength and stability are developed.

a

b

Push-Up Plus

PURPOSE

To develop the serratus anterior muscles. These muscles help actively stabilize the shoulders at the scapulae. This exercise is a more advanced progression of the standing push-up plus. This variation requires the ability to stabilize a larger portion of the overall body mass.

PREREQUISITES

The ability to maintain a plank position throughout the exercise, and no shoulder or back pain while performing the exercise.

ADJUSTMENT

Adjust the straps of the Suspension Trainer to mid-calf length.

STARTING POSITION

Place the feet in the stirrups, and then roll over onto the abdomen. Place the hands shoulder-width apart on the ground. Set the body in a straight line, or in plank position.

DESCRIPTION

- Brace the trunk and keep the arms straight while pulling the shoulder blades down and together (see figure *a*).
- Keeping the arms straight, push the shoulder blades apart without rounding the shoulders (see figure *b*).
- Return to the starting position, and repeat for the desired number of repetitions.

a

TEACHING CUES

- Envision placing the edges of the scapulae in the back hip pockets.
- Push the shoulder blades up to the ceiling.
- Brace the trunk as if ready to take a punch to the abdomen.

b

Prone Iron Cross

PURPOSE
To develop shoulder and core strength and stability.

PREREQUISITES
The ability to maintain a plank position throughout the exercise, and no shoulder or back pain while performing the exercise.

ADJUSTMENT
Fully lengthen the straps of the Suspension Trainer.

STARTING POSITION
Grab a handle with each hand, and face away from the anchor point. Position the hands against the torso, just below the underarms. Set the body in a straight line, or in plank position.

DESCRIPTION
- Brace the trunk and slowly step backward until there is tension on the straps and the body is at an incline (see figure *a*).
- Slowly extend the arms, pushing them out to the sides, similar to a T position (see figure *b*).
- Return the arms to the starting position against the torso.

VARIATION
Instead of extending the arms simultaneously, extend one arm, maintain the posture, and then extend the other arm, moving in a unilateral fashion.

TEACHING CUES
- Brace the trunk as if ready to take a punch to the abdomen.
- Keep the torso as stiff as a board from the head to the heels.

a

b

Sprinter Chest Press

PURPOSE

To develop upper-body muscular endurance in the chest, shoulders, and triceps. Additionally, this drill helps develop stability in the hip of the stance leg, as well as hip mobility on the drive-leg side. The ability to stabilize the lower body in these positions is essential during acceleration in sports.

PREREQUISITES

The ability to balance on a single leg and maintain a plank position.

ADJUSTMENT

Fully lengthen the straps of the Suspension Trainer.

STARTING POSITION

Face away from the anchor point, and grab a handle with each hand. Extend the arms and position the hands shoulder width-apart. Position the feet hip- to shoulder-width apart. Set the body in a straight line, or in plank position.

DESCRIPTION

- Brace the trunk and slowly step backward until there is tension on the straps and the body is at an incline (see figure *a*).
- Bend the arms and lower the chest between the handles, similar to performing a push-up (see figure *b*).
- Extend the arms and, keeping the left leg straight, drive the right knee forward while keeping the right ankle in a dorsiflexed position. At the peak of the knee drive, extend the ankle of the left leg (see figure *c*).
- Return the right foot to the starting position.
- Repeat using the left leg as the drive leg and the right leg as the stance leg.

TEACHING CUES

- Toe up, knee up on the drive leg.
- Stay stiff as a board from the head through the heels.

Suspended Push-Up

PURPOSE

To develop muscular endurance and stability of the chest, shoulders, and triceps.

PREREQUISITES

The ability to maintain a plank position throughout the exercise, and no shoulder or back pain while performing the exercise.

ADJUSTMENT

Adjust the straps of the Suspension Trainer to mid-calf length.

STARTING POSITION

Face away from the anchor point, and place the feet in the stirrups. Place the hands on the ground shoulder-width apart. Set the body in a straight line, or in plank position.

DESCRIPTION

- Brace the trunk and keep the arms straight while pulling the shoulder blades down and together (see figure *a*).
- Bend at the elbows to lower the body to the ground, keeping the torso flat and rigid, until attaining at least a 90-degree angle at the elbows (see figure *b*).
- Push back up to the starting position.

a

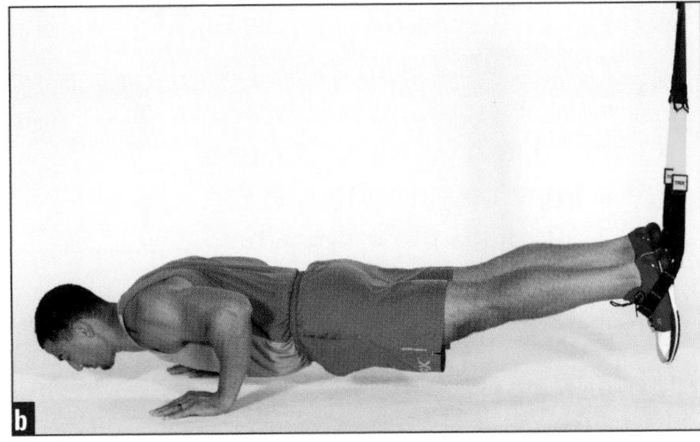
b

TEACHING CUES

- Envision placing the edges of the scapulae in the back hip pockets.
- Stay stiff as a board from the head through the heels.
- Slightly tuck the chin.

Push-Up With Reverse Crunch

PURPOSE

To develop muscular endurance and stability of the chest, shoulders, triceps, and rectus abdominis.

PREREQUISITES

The ability to maintain a plank position, and no shoulder or back pain while performing the exercise.

ADJUSTMENT

Adjust the straps of the Suspension Trainer to mid-calf length.

STARTING POSITION

Face away from the anchor point, and place the feet in the stirrups. Place the hands on the ground shoulder-width apart. Set the body in a straight line, or in plank position.

a

DESCRIPTION

- Brace the trunk and keep the arms straight while pulling the shoulder blades down and together (see figure *a*).
- Bend at the elbows to lower the body to the ground (see figure *b*).
- Extend the arms and push the body back to the starting position, and drive the knees toward the chest (see figure *c*).
- Return to the starting position.

b

TEACHING CUES

- Maintain a plank position.
- Stay stiff as a board from the head to heels.
- Drive the knees to the chest.

c

Chest Fly

PURPOSE

This isolation exercise develops the pectoralis major, which is responsible for horizontal adduction of the arms.

PREREQUISITES

The ability to maintain a rigid torso throughout the exercise, and no shoulder pain or injury.

ADJUSTMENT

Fully lengthen the straps of the Suspension Trainer.

STARTING POSITION

Face away from the anchor point, and grab a handle with each hand. Place the feet hip- to shoulder-width apart. Set the body in a straight line, or in plank position.

DESCRIPTION

- Brace the trunk and keep the arms straight.
- Internally rotate the shoulders so the elbows point out to the sides (see figure *a*).
- Keeping the arms locked in this position, slowly push the hands away from each other while pulling the shoulder blades down and together.
- Attempt to move the hands outward until they are almost directly aligned with the torso, or until a large stretch is felt in the chest (see figure *b*).
- In this position, bring the hands back to the starting position.

TEACHING CUES

- When returning to the starting position, act as if wrapping the hands around a tree trunk.
- Maintain a rigid torso throughout the exercise.

a

b

Kneeling Skull Crusher

PURPOSE

To isolate and develop the triceps and develop isometric trunk stability. Using the Suspension Trainer for this exercise results in greater total-body development than traditional barbell and dumbbell versions of this exercise.

PREREQUISITE

The ability to maintain a rigid torso throughout the exercise.

ADJUSTMENT

Fully lengthen the straps of the Suspension Trainer.

STARTING POSITION

Begin with both knees on the ground facing away from the anchor point. Grab a handle in each hand, and lean forward so the torso is at an angle of at least 45 degrees to the ground.

DESCRIPTION

- Position the upper arms perpendicular to the torso, and bend the elbows to 90 degrees. At this point, the hands should be at forehead height (see figure *a*).
- While keeping the lower leg and knees in contact with the ground, and the trunk rigid, extend the elbows (see figure *b*).
- Slowly allow the elbows to bend to return to the starting position.

TEACHING CUES

- Maintain a rigid torso throughout the exercise.
- Move only at the elbows.

a

b

Kneeling Overhead Triceps Extension

PURPOSE

To isolate and develop the triceps and develop isometric trunk stability. The Suspension Trainer results in greater total-body development than traditional barbell and dumbbell versions of this exercise.

PREREQUISITE

The ability to maintain a rigid torso throughout the exercise.

ADJUSTMENT

Fully lengthen the straps of the Suspension Trainer.

STARTING POSITION

Begin by kneeling and facing away from the anchor point. Grab a handle with each hand, and lean forward so the torso is at an angle of at least 45 degrees to the ground.

DESCRIPTION

- Extend the arms overhead with the upper arms beside the ears (see figure *a*).
- Bend the elbows to 90 degrees. At this point, the hands should be behind the head with a neutral grip (see figure *b*).
- While keeping the lower legs and knees in contact with the ground, and the trunk rigid, extend the elbows to return to the starting position.

TEACHING CUES

- Maintain a rigid torso throughout the exercise.
- Move only at the elbows.

a

b

Clock Press

PURPOSE
To develop shoulder and trunk stability.

PREREQUISITES
The ability to maintain a plank position throughout the exercise, and no shoulder or back pain while performing the exercise.

ADJUSTMENT
Adjust the straps of the Suspension Trainer to mid-length.

STARTING POSITION
Grab a handle with each hand, and face away from the anchor point with the feet hip- to shoulder-width apart. Position the hands against the torso just below the underarms. Set the body in a straight line, or in plank position.

DESCRIPTION

- Brace the trunk and step backward slowly until there is tension on the straps and the body is at an incline (see figure *a*).
- Slowly extend the arms, pushing them out to the sides, similar to a T position.
- Return the arms to the starting position against the torso; then, repeat this movement while pressing the left hand to the 2 o'clock position and the right hand to the 8 o'clock position (see figure *b*).
- Return the arms to the starting position against the torso; then, repeat this movement pressing the left hand to the 4 o'clock position and the right hand to the 10 o'clock position.
- Return to the starting position, and repeat this series three or four times.

TEACHING CUES

- Brace the trunk as if ready to take a punch to the abdomen.
- Keep the torso as stiff as a board from the head to the heels.
- If unable to fully extend the arms, use a partial range of motion until the requisite strength and stability are developed.

a

b

Off-Center Chest Press

PURPOSE
To develop upper-body muscular endurance in the chest, shoulders, and triceps, as well as trunk, hip, and shoulder stability during weight shifts.

PREREQUISITES
The ability to balance on a single leg and maintain a plank position.

ADJUSTMENT
Adjust the straps of the Suspension Trainer to mid-calf length.

STARTING POSITION
Face away from the anchor point, and grab a handle with each hand. Extend the arms and position the hands shoulder-width apart. Set the body in a straight line, or in plank position, with the feet hip-width apart.

DESCRIPTION
- Brace the trunk and slowly step backward until there is tension on the straps and the body is at an incline.
- While stabilizing the trunk, lift the left foot 6 to 12 inches (15 to 30 cm) off the ground and position it at 7 or 8 o'clock (see figure *a*).
- Bend the arms and lower the chest between the handles, similar to performing a push-up (see figure *b*).
- Extend the arms to return to the starting position.
- After performing the desired number of repetitions, lift the right foot out to 4 or 5 o'clock and repeat the exercise.

TEACHING CUE
Perform the same number of repetitions on the right and left legs.

a

b

Single-Arm Chest Press

PURPOSE

To enhance muscular endurance of the chest, shoulders, and triceps while resisting trunk rotation.

PREREQUISITES

The ability to maintain a plank position and resist hip and torso rotation.

ADJUSTMENT

Fully lengthen the straps of the Suspension Trainer.

STARTING POSITION

Face away from the anchor point, grab the handles with one hand, and extend the arm. Place the other hand on the hip or hold it in the same position as if performing the exercise. Set the body in a straight line, or in plank position, and position the feet in an offset stance (easier) or a shoulder-width stance (harder).

DESCRIPTION

- Brace the trunk and slowly step backward until there is tension on the straps and the body is at an incline (see figure *a*).
- Bend the working arm and lower the chest between the handles, similar to performing a push-up (see figure *b*).
- Extend the working arm to return to the starting position.

TEACHING CUES

- Stay stiff as a board from the head through the heels.
- In the offset stance, push the body into the handles to increase the stability of the movement and the training load. Note: The load can also be increased in this exercise by assuming a tandem stance and shifting more of one's body weight into the strap.

a

b

Incline Push-Up

PURPOSE
To develop muscular strength and endurance and stability of the chest, shoulders, and triceps.

PREREQUISITES
The ability to maintain a plank position throughout the exercise, and no shoulder or back pain while performing the exercise.

ADJUSTMENT
Adjust the straps of the Suspension Trainer to mid-calf length.

STARTING POSITION
Face away from the anchor point, and place one foot in both foot cradles. Position the hands on the ground shoulder-width apart. Set the body in a straight line, or in plank position.

DESCRIPTION
- Brace the trunk and keep the arms straight while pulling the shoulder blades down and together.
- Raise the support leg off the ground and position it parallel to the foot in the foot cradles (see figure *a*).
- Bend at the elbows to lower the body to the ground, keeping the torso flat and rigid (see figure *b*).
- Push back to the starting position.

TEACHING CUES
- Envision placing the edges of the scapulae in the back hip pockets.
- Do not perform with both feet in separate stirrups; doing so makes achieving the proper body position more difficult and may increase injury risk. Note: Be sure to switch legs in order to make certain that isometric strength and muscular symmetry are developed uniformly on both sides.

a

b

Inverted Shoulder Press

PURPOSE

To develop strength, stability, and muscular endurance in the shoulders.

PREREQUISITES

No preexisting shoulder pain or injuries, and sufficient strength and mobility to perform a pike.

ADJUSTMENT

Adjust the straps of the Suspension Trainer to mid-calf length.

STARTING POSITION

Face away from the anchor point, and place one foot in both foot cradles. The hands are on the ground shoulder-width apart. Set the body in a straight line, or in plank position.

DESCRIPTION

- Brace the trunk and keep the arms straight.
- Bend the hips until the torso is nearly vertical (see figure *a*).
- Bend at the elbows to lower the head to the ground until attaining a 90-degree angle at the elbows (see figure *b*).
- Push back to the starting position.

TEACHING CUES

- Use a partial range of motion for this exercise until the strength and stability in the trunk and shoulders are sufficient to achieve a 90-degree angle at the elbows.
- Maintain a stiff torso. Note: Be sure to switch legs in order to make certain that isometric strength and muscular symmetry are developed uniformly on both sides.

a

b

Push-Up With Oblique Crunch

PURPOSE

To develop muscular endurance and stability of the chest, shoulders, and triceps, and improve thoracic mobility.

PREREQUISITES

The ability to maintain a plank position, and no shoulder or back pain while performing the exercise.

ADJUSTMENT

Adjust the straps of the Suspension Trainer to mid-calf length.

STARTING POSITION

Face away from the anchor point, and place the feet in the stirrups. Place the hands on the ground shoulder-width apart. Set the body in a straight line, or in plank position, with the feet hip- to shoulder-width apart.

DESCRIPTION

- Brace the trunk and keep the arms straight while pulling the shoulder blades down and together (see figure *a*).
- Bend at the elbows to lower the body to the ground (see figure *b*).
- Extend the arms and push back to the starting position while rotating the hips (see figure *c*).

TEACHING CUES

- Stay stiff as a board from the head through the heels.
- Slightly tuck the chin.
- Try to use as little momentum as possible to execute the movement.

a

b

c

Drop Push-Up

PURPOSE

This exercise accentuates eccentric loading of the chest, shoulders, and triceps. It can be used to teach proper landing technique prior to performing explosive, plyo, or depth drop plyo push-ups.

PREREQUISITES

The ability to maintain a plank position throughout the exercise, no shoulder or back pain while performing the exercise, and the ability to bench press 1.5 times body weight.

ADJUSTMENT

Adjust the straps of the Suspension Trainer to mid-calf length.

STARTING POSITION

Face away from the anchor point, and place the feet in the stirrups. Position the hands on the ground shoulder-width apart with the elbows lower than the shoulders. Set the body in a straight line, or in plank position.

a

DESCRIPTION

- Brace the trunk and keep the arms straight while pulling the shoulder blades down and together (see figure *a*).
- Jump the hands to the sides slightly wider than shoulder width (see figure *b*), bending the elbows to absorb the landing (see figure *c*).
- Push back up to the starting position.

b

TEACHING CUES

- Absorb the landing softly, and land as quietly as possible.
- Maintain a rigid torso throughout the exercise.

c

Single-Leg Chest Fly

PURPOSE

This isolation exercise develops the pectoralis major, which is responsible for horizontal adduction of the arms, and challenges balance and stability on the stance leg.

PREREQUISITES

The ability to maintain a rigid torso throughout the exercise, and no shoulder pain or injury.

ADJUSTMENT

Fully lengthen the straps of the Suspension Trainer.

STARTING POSITION

Face away from the anchor point, and grab a handle with each hand. Place the feet hip- to shoulder width apart. Set the body in a straight line, or in plank position.

DESCRIPTION

- Brace the trunk and keep the arms straight.
- Internally rotate the shoulders so the elbows point out to the sides, and lift one foot 6 inches (15 cm) off the ground (see figure *a*).
- While keeping the arms locked in this position, slowly push the hands away from each other while pulling the shoulder blades down and together.
- Attempt to move the hands outward until they are almost directly aligned with the torso, or until a large stretch is felt in the chest (see figure *b*).
- In this position, bring the hands back to the starting position.

TEACHING CUES

- When returning to the starting position, act as though wrapping the hands around a tree trunk.
- Maintain a rigid torso throughout the exercise.

a

b

Explosive Push-Up

PURPOSE

To develop power in the upper body. This exercise minimizes the effects of the stretch–shortening cycle and focuses on concentric force production. This variation of the traditional explosive push-up (in which the feet are on the ground) increases the load.

PREREQUISITES

The ability to maintain a plank position throughout the exercise, no shoulder or back pain while performing the exercise, and the ability to bench press 1.5 times body weight.

ADJUSTMENT

Adjust the straps of the Suspension Trainer to mid-calf length.

STARTING POSITION

Face away from the anchor point, and place the feet in the stirrups. Position the hands on the ground shoulder-width apart. Set the body in a straight line, or in plank position.

DESCRIPTION

- Brace the trunk and keep the arms straight while pulling the shoulder blades down and together (see figure *a*).
- Bend at the elbows to lower the body to the ground, while keeping the torso flat and rigid, until creating a 90-degree angle at the elbows (see figure *b*).
- Hold this position for one or two seconds; then, push off the ground as rapidly as possible so the hands lose contract with the ground (see figure *c*).
- Upon landing, bend the elbows and extend the shoulders slightly to absorb the landing (see figure *d*).

TEACHING CUES

- Absorb the landing softly, and land as quietly as possible.
- Maintain a rigid torso throughout the exercise.

a

b

c

d

Plyo Push-Up

PURPOSE

To develop power in the upper body. This exercise maximizes the effects of the stretch–shortening cycle and focuses on the use of stored elastic energy within the muscle tissue and tendons to produce explosive force and power. This variation of the traditional plyo push-up (in which the feet are on the ground) increases the load.

PREREQUISITES

The ability to maintain a plank position throughout the exercise, no shoulder or back pain while performing the exercise, and the ability to bench press 1.5 times body weight.

ADJUSTMENT

Adjust the straps of the Suspension Trainer to mid-calf length.

STARTING POSITION

Face away from the anchor point, and place the feet in the stirrups. Position the hands on the ground shoulder-width apart. Set the body in a straight line, or in plank position.

DESCRIPTION

- Brace the trunk and keep the arms straight while pulling the shoulder blades down and together (see figure *a*).
- Rapidly bend at the elbows to lower the body to the ground, while keeping the torso flat and rigid (see figure *b*).
- Once a 90-degree angle at the elbows is attained, immediately push off the ground as fast as possible so the hands lose contract with the ground (see figure *c*). Note: It is not necessary to clap the hands when performing this exercise.
- Upon landing, bend the elbows and extend the shoulders slightly to absorb the landing (see figure *d*).

TEACHING CUES

- Absorb the landing softly, and land as quietly as possible.
- Maintain a rigid torso throughout the exercise.

a

b

c

d

Single-Arm Chest Fly

PURPOSE

This isolation exercise develops the pectoralis major, which is responsible for horizontal adduction of the arms.

PREREQUISITES

The ability to maintain a rigid torso throughout the exercise, and no shoulder pain or injury.

ADJUSTMENT

Fully lengthen the straps of the Suspension Trainer.

STARTING POSITION

Stand sideways and assume an offset stance. Grab the handles with the hand that is closer to the anchor point, and place the other hand on the hip. Set the body in a straight line, or in a side plank position.

DESCRIPTION

- Brace the trunk and keep the arm straight.
- Internally rotate the shoulder of the working arm so the elbow points out to the side (see figure *a*).
- While keeping the arm locked in this position, slowly push the hand against the handle, or away from the anchor point.
- Attempt to move the hand inward until it is almost directly aligned with the torso, or until a large stretch is felt in the chest (see figure *b*).
- Bring the hand back to the starting position.

TEACHING CUES

- Maintain a slight bend in the elbow throughout so as not to hyperextend this joint.
- Keep the hips stacked under the shoulders, and do not let them drop while lowering to the starting position.

a

b

Standing Skull Crusher

PURPOSE

To isolate and develop the triceps and develop isometric trunk stability. The Suspension Trainer results in greater total-body development than traditional barbell and dumbbell versions of this exercise.

PREREQUISITE

The ability to maintain a rigid torso throughout the exercise.

ADJUSTMENT

Adjust the straps of the Suspension Trainer to mid-length.

STARTING POSITION

Begin by facing away from the anchor point. Grab a handle in each hand, and lean forward so the torso is at an angle of at least 45 degrees to the ground.

DESCRIPTION

- Position the upper arms perpendicular to the torso, and bend the elbows to 90 degrees. At this point, the hands should be at forehead height (see figure *a*).
- While keeping the feet in contact with the ground, and the trunk rigid, extend the elbows (see figure *b*).
- Slowly bend the elbows to return to the starting position.

TEACHING CUES

- Maintain a rigid torso throughout the exercise (i.e., stiff as a board from the head to the heels).
- For an advanced version of the exercise, move only at the elbows.

a

b

Scapular Retraction

PURPOSE

To develop strength in the rhomboids and upper and lower trapezius muscles, which surround the scapulae.

PREREQUISITE

The ability to maintain a rigid torso throughout the exercise.

ADJUSTMENT

Fully shorten the straps of the Suspension Trainer.

STARTING POSITION

Face the anchor point, and grab a handle with each hand. Position the feet about hip- to shoulder-width apart, and lean back until the torso is at a 45-degree angle to the ground (see figure *a*).

DESCRIPTION

- Pull the shoulder blades together and downward (see figure *b*).
- Without shrugging the shoulders, slowly allow the shoulder blades to separate and return to the starting position.

TEACHING CUES

- Envision placing the edges of the scapulae in the back hip pockets.
- Brace the core.

a

b

Inverted Row

PURPOSE
To develop the muscles of the back.

PREREQUISITE
The ability to maintain a rigid torso throughout the exercise.

ADJUSTMENT
Adjust the straps of the Suspension Trainer to mid-length.

STARTING POSITION
Face the anchor point, and grab a handle with each hand using a neutral, overhand, or supinated grip. Lean back until the torso is at a 45-degree angle to the ground.

DESCRIPTION

- Pull the shoulder blades together and downward (see figure *a*).
- Pull the body toward the anchor point by bending the arms and extending the shoulders (see figure *b*).
- Slowly extend the arms and allow the shoulders to flex to return to the starting position.

TEACHING CUES

- Maintain a braced core throughout the exercise, and squeeze the glutes.
- Pull the straps to the chest.

a

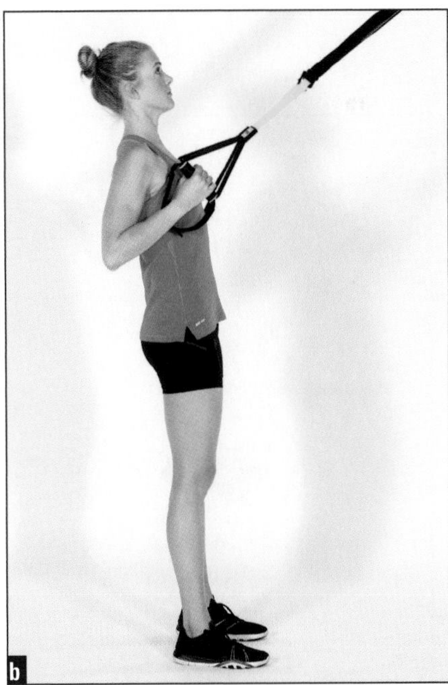
b

Rear Deltoid Row

PURPOSE
To develop the muscles of the upper back and shoulders.

PREREQUISITE
The ability to maintain a rigid torso throughout the exercise.

ADJUSTMENT
Fully shorten the straps of the Suspension Trainer.

STARTING POSITION
Face the anchor point, and grab a handle with each hand using a neutral, overhand, or supinated grip. Position the feet hip- to shoulder-width apart. While keeping the arms completely straight, lean back until the torso is at a 45-degree angle to the ground while pulling the shoulder blades together and downward (see figure *a*).

DESCRIPTION
- While keeping the elbows in line with the center of the breastbone, pull the body toward the anchor point by bending the arms and pulling the handles toward the underarms. At this point the hands and the elbows should be in line with one another (see figure *b*).
- Slowly extend the arms and allow the shoulders to flex to return to the starting position.

TEACHING CUES
- Do not lift the elbows above the shoulders.
- Keep the core braced and squeeze the glutes.

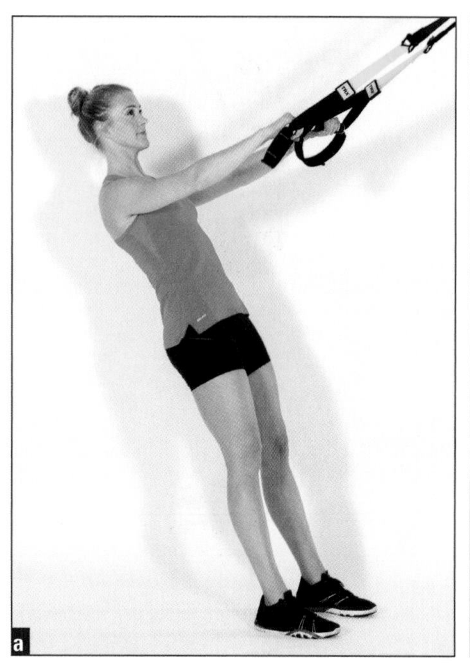
a

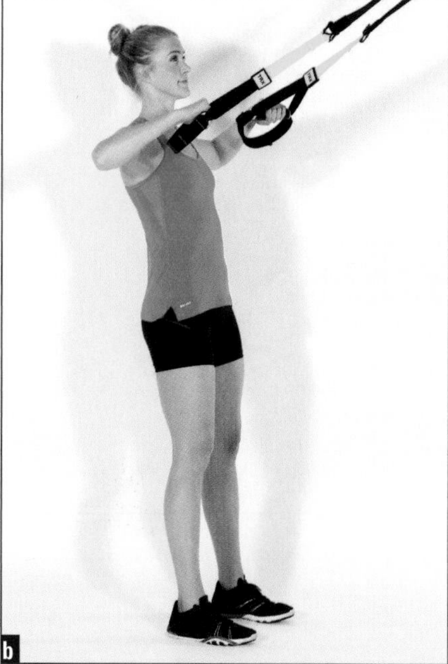
b

Biceps Curl

PURPOSE

To develop the biceps.

PREREQUISITE

The ability to maintain a rigid torso throughout the exercise.

ADJUSTMENT

Fully shorten the straps of the Suspension Trainer.

STARTING POSITION

Face the anchor point, and grab a handle with each hand using an underhand or supinated grip. Position the feet hip- to shoulder-width apart. Keeping the arms completely straight, lean back until the torso is at a 45-degree angle to the ground (see figure *a*).

DESCRIPTION

- Pull the shoulder blades together and downward, bend the elbows, and bring the hands toward the face (see figure *b*).
- Extend the elbows and return to the starting position.

TEACHING CUES

- Move only at the elbows.
- Brace the trunk and squeeze the glutes.

a

b

Wrist Flexion

PURPOSE
To develop the wrist flexors.

PREREQUISITE
The ability to maintain a rigid torso throughout the exercise.

ADJUSTMENT
Adjust the straps of the Suspension Trainer to mid-length.

STARTING POSITION
Face the anchor point, and grab a handle with each hand using an underhand or supinated grip. Position the feet hip- to shoulder width apart. Keep the arms completely straight while leaning back until the torso is at a 45-degree angle to the ground (see figure *a*).

DESCRIPTION
- Pull the shoulder blades together and downward; then, bend the wrists toward the body (see figure *b*).
- Extend the wrists and return to the starting position.

TEACHING CUES
- Move only at the wrists.
- Brace the trunk and squeeze the glutes.

a

b

Dual-Arm External Rotation

PURPOSE
To strengthen the rotator cuff and develop the deltoids.

PREREQUISITE
The ability to maintain a rigid torso throughout the exercise.

ADJUSTMENT
Fully shorten the straps of the Suspension Trainer.

STARTING POSITION
Face the anchor point, and grab a handle with each hand using a neutral grip. Stagger the feet. Bend the elbows at 90 degrees, and hold them and the upper arms against the body (see figure *a*).

DESCRIPTION

- While keeping the body rigid and elbows bent, externally rotate at the shoulders by pushing the hands away from the body (see figure *b*).
- Return to the starting position, and perform the desired number of repetitions.

TEACHING CUES

- Keep the elbows locked in to the torso.
- Brace the core.

a

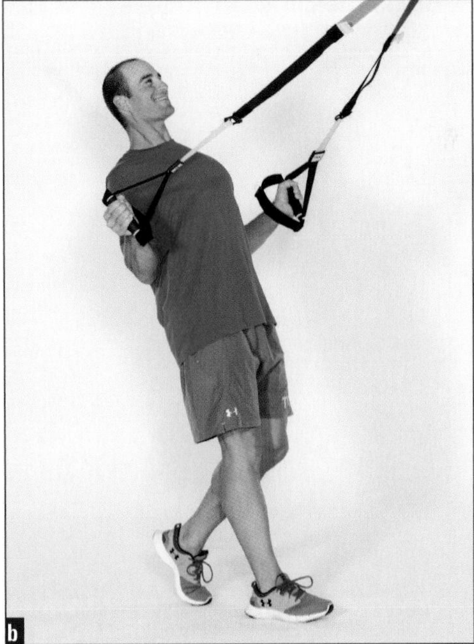
b

Field Goal

PURPOSE
To strengthen the upper back, deltoids, and the rotator cuff muscles.

PREREQUISITE
The ability to maintain a rigid torso throughout the exercise.

ADJUSTMENT
Fully shorten the straps of the Suspension Trainer.

STARTING POSITION
Face the anchor point, and grab a handle with each hand using a neutral, overhand, or supinated grip. Position the feet hip- to shoulder-width apart. Keep the arms bent at 90 degrees while leaning back until the torso is at a 45-degree angle to the ground and pulling the shoulder blades together and downward (see figure *a*).

DESCRIPTION

- Keep the elbows in line with the center of the breastbone, and pull the handles toward the ears, using only the shoulders to rotate them up (see figure *b*). At this point, the hands and the elbows should be in line with the ears.
- Slowly lower the arms to the starting position.

TEACHING CUES

- Rotate only at the shoulders.
- Brace the core.

a

b

Supine Iron Cross

PURPOSE

To develop the muscles of the rear deltoids, as well as trunk stability.

PREREQUISITES

The ability to maintain a plank position throughout the exercise, and no shoulder or back pain while performing the exercise.

ADJUSTMENT

Adjust the straps of the Suspension Trainer to mid-length.

STARTING POSITION

Face toward the anchor point, and grab a handle with each hand. Position the hands against the torso just below the underarms. The feet should be hip- to shoulder width-apart. Set the body in a straight line, or in plank position.

DESCRIPTION

- Brace the trunk and slowly step forward until there is tension on the straps and the body is at an incline (see figure *a*).
- Slowly extend the arms, pushing them out to the sides, similar to a T position (see figure *b*).
- Return to the starting position.

TEACHING CUES

- Push the hands straight out to the sides.
- Squeeze the shoulder blades together, and put them in the back hip pockets.

a

b

Low Row

PURPOSE

To develop the muscles of the back.

PREREQUISITE

The ability to maintain a rigid torso throughout the exercise.

ADJUSTMENT

Fully shorten the straps of the Suspension Trainer.

STARTING POSITION

Face the anchor point, and grab a handle in each hand using a neutral, overhand, or supinated grip. Position the feet hip- to shoulder-width apart. While keeping the arms completely straight, slowly bend the knees and lean back until the torso is parallel to the ground and the knees are bent at a 90-degree angle.

DESCRIPTION

- Pull the shoulder blades together and downward (see figure *a*).
- Pull the body toward the anchor point by bending the arms and extending the shoulders while allowing the knees to extend to 110 to 120 degrees at the apex of the pull (see figure *b*).
- Extend the arms and allow the shoulders to flex to return to the starting position.
- The intensity of this exercise can be increased by slowly lowering the body back to the starting position (i.e., a 1:3; 1:4 count).

a

b

TEACHING CUES

- Maintain a braced core throughout the exercise, and squeeze the glutes.
- Pull the straps to the chest.

Rear Deltoid Row to Y

PURPOSE

To strengthen the rhomboids, upper and lower trapezius, and rotator cuff muscles.

PREREQUISITE

The ability to maintain a rigid torso throughout the exercise.

ADJUSTMENT

Adjust the straps of the Suspension Trainer to mid-length.

STARTING POSITION

Face the anchor point, and grab a handle with each hand using a neutral, overhand, or supinated grip. Assume a staggered stance (or place the feet hip-width apart for more of a challenge). Lean back until the torso is at a 45-degree angle to the ground while pulling the shoulder blades together and downward and keeping the arms completely straight (see figure *a*).

DESCRIPTION

- Perform a rear deltoid row as previously described on page 64. At this point, the hands and the elbows should be in line with one another (see figure *b*).
- Move the arms outward, rotate the shoulders, and extend the arms to form a Y (see figure *c*).
- Now, slowly lower the arms back to the T position; then, extend them and return to the starting position.

TEACHING CUES

- Do not lift the elbows above the shoulders during the rear deltoid row portion of the exercise.
- Brace the core.

a

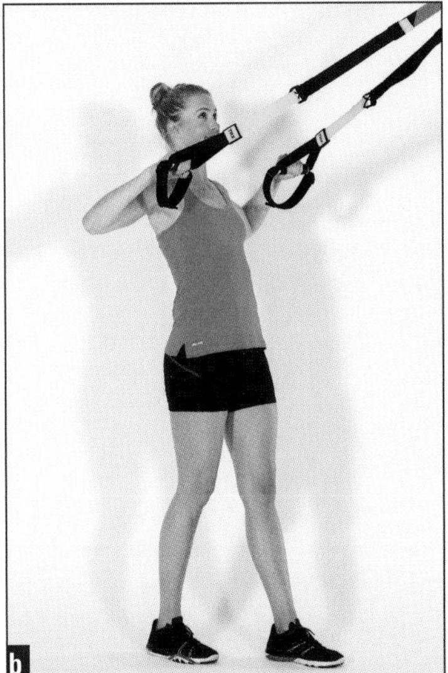
b

c

I, Y, T

PURPOSE

To strengthen the rhomboids, upper and lower trapezius, and rotator cuff muscles.

PREREQUISITE

The ability to maintain a rigid torso throughout the exercise.

ADJUSTMENT

Adjust the straps of the Suspension Trainer to mid-length.

STARTING POSITION

Face the anchor point, and grab a handle with each hand. Assume a staggered stance. Lean back until the torso is at a 45-degree angle to the ground while pulling the shoulder blades together and downward and keeping the arms completely straight (see figure *a*).

DESCRIPTION

- Moving only at the shoulders, rotate the arms and position them directly overhead to form an I (see figure *b*), at a 45-degree angle over the head to form a Y (see figure *c*), and finally directly out to the sides to form a T (see figure *d*).
- Return to the starting position prior to performing each movement.

TEACHING CUES

- Maintain a stiff torso.
- Pause at the top of each movement for one second before returning to the starting position.

T Fly

PURPOSE
To strengthen the rhomboids, upper and lower trapezius, and rotator cuff muscles.

PREREQUISITE
The ability to maintain a rigid torso throughout the exercise.

ADJUSTMENT
Adjust the straps of the Suspension Trainer to mid-length.

STARTING POSITION
Face the anchor point, and grab a handle with each hand using a neutral grip. Position the feet hip- to shoulder-width apart. Keep the arms slightly bent. Lean back until the torso is at a 45-degree angle to the ground while pulling the shoulder blades together and downward (see figure *a*).

DESCRIPTION

- Maintain a slight bend in the elbow, and internally rotate the shoulders so the elbows point out to the sides.
- While keeping the arms locked in this position, slowly push the hands away from each other while pulling the shoulder blades down and together.
- Attempt to move the hands outward until they are almost directly aligned with the torso (see figure *b*).
- Bring the hands back to the starting position.

TEACHING CUES

- Keep the elbows slightly bent throughout the exercise, and lock them in this position.
- Brace the core.
- Do not shrug the shoulders during the movement.

a

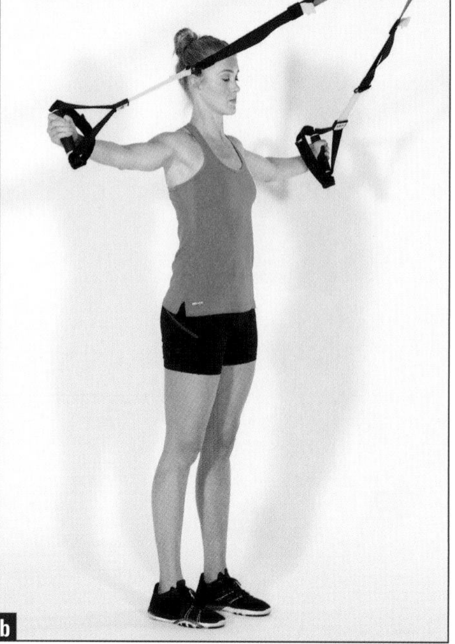
b

Reverse Biceps Curl

PURPOSE
To develop the biceps and wrist extensors.

PREREQUISITE
The ability to maintain a rigid torso throughout the exercise.

ADJUSTMENT
Adjust the straps of the Suspension Trainer to mid-length.

STARTING POSITION
Face the anchor point, and grab a handle with each hand using an overhand or pronated grip. Position the feet hip- to shoulder-width apart. While keeping the arms completely straight, lean back until the torso is at a 45-degree angle to the ground (see figure *a*).

DESCRIPTION

- Pull the shoulder blades together and downward, bend the elbows, and bring the hands toward the face (see figure *b*).
- Extend the elbows and return to the starting position.

TEACHING CUES

- Move only at the elbows.
- Brace the trunk and squeeze the glutes.

a

b

Dual-Arm Internal Rotation

PURPOSE

To strengthen the rotator cuff muscles, deltoids, and pectoralis major.

PREREQUISITE

The ability to maintain a rigid torso throughout the exercise.

ADJUSTMENT

Adjust the straps of the Suspension Trainer to mid-length.

STARTING POSITION

Face the anchor point, and grab a handle with each hand using a neutral grip. Position the feet hip- to shoulder-width apart, and lean back until the torso is at a 45-degree angle to the ground. Bend the elbows at 90 degrees, and hold them and the upper arms against the body (see figure *a*).

DESCRIPTION

- While keeping the body rigid, bend the elbows and internally rotate at the shoulders by pulling the hands toward the opposite elbows (see figure *b*).
- With each repetition, switch the arm that is on top.

TEACHING CUES

- Keep the elbows locked in to the torso.
- Brace the core.

a

b

Single-Arm Inverted Row

PURPOSE
To develop the muscles of the back.

PREREQUISITE
The ability to maintain a rigid torso throughout the exercise.

ADJUSTMENT
Fully shorten the straps of the Suspension Trainer.

STARTING POSITION
Face the anchor point, and grab both handles with one hand using a neutral, overhand, or supinated grip. Place the opposite hand on the hip or at the side. Position the feet hip- to shoulder-width apart. While keeping the working arm completely straight, lean back until the torso is at a 45-degree angle (or more if too difficult) to the ground (see figure *a*).

DESCRIPTION
- Pull the body toward the anchor point by bending the elbow and extending the shoulder of the working arm (see figure *b*).
- Slowly extend the working arm and allow the shoulder to flex to return to the starting position.

TEACHING CUES
- Do not allow the hips or torso to rotate.
- Pull the straps to the chest.

a

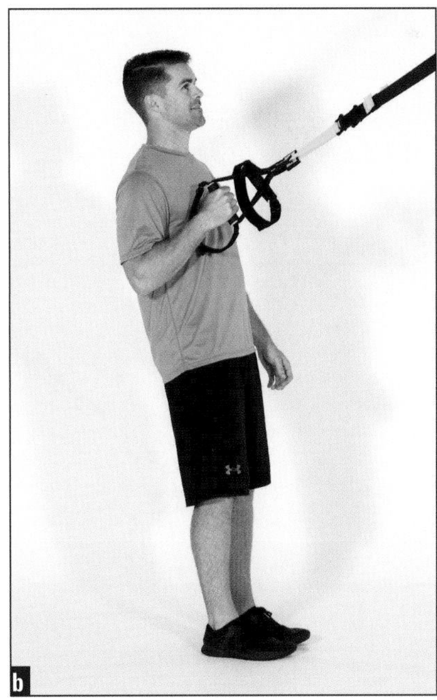
b

Split Fly

PURPOSE
To strengthen the rhomboids, upper and lower trapezius, and rotator cuff muscles.

PREREQUISITE
The ability to maintain a rigid torso throughout the exercise.

ADJUSTMENT
Adjust the straps of the Suspension Trainer to mid-length.

STARTING POSITION
Face the anchor point, and grab a handle with each hand using a neutral grip. Position the feet hip- to shoulder-width apart. While keeping the arms slightly bent, lean back until the torso is at a 45-degree angle to the ground while pulling the shoulder blades together and downward (see figure *a*).

DESCRIPTION

- Maintain a slight bend in the elbow; while keeping the arms locked in this position, slowly push the hands away from each other while pulling the shoulder blades down and together.
- Attempt to move the hands outward until they are almost directly aligned with the torso (i.e., 3 o'clock and 9 o'clock positions) (see figure *b*).
- Now, bring the hands back to the starting position.
- Repeat this action by moving the hands in the following combinations:
  - Right hand to the 1 o'clock position, and left hand to the 7 o'clock position.
  - Right hand to the 5 o'clock position, and left hand to the 10 o'clock position.

TEACHING CUES

- Keep the elbows slightly bent throughout the exercise, and lock them in this position.
- Brace the core.
- Do not shrug the shoulders during the movement.

a

b

Single-Arm Biceps Curl

PURPOSE
To develop the biceps.

PREREQUISITE
The ability to maintain a rigid torso throughout the exercise.

ADJUSTMENT
Adjust the straps of the Suspension Trainer to mid-length.

STARTING POSITION
Put the straps into the single-handle mode. Face the anchor point, and grab the handle with one hand using an underhand grip. Position the feet hip- to shoulder-width apart. While keeping the arm completely straight, lean back until the torso is at a 45-degree angle to the ground (see figure *a*).

DESCRIPTION

- Pull the shoulder blades together and downward, bend the elbow, and bring the hand toward the face (see figure *b*).
- Extend the elbow and return to the starting position.

TEACHING CUES

- Move only at the elbow.
- Brace the trunk and squeeze the glutes.
- Do not allow the trunk or hips to rotate.

a

b

Single-Arm Reverse Biceps Curl

PURPOSE
To develop the biceps and wrist extensors.

PREREQUISITE
The ability to maintain a rigid torso (plank position) throughout the exercise.

ADJUSTMENT
Adjust the straps of the Suspension Trainer to mid-length.

STARTING POSITION
Put the straps into the single-handle mode. Face the anchor point, and grab the handle with one hand using an overhand grip. Position the feet hip- to shoulder width apart. While keeping the arm completely straight, lean back until the torso is at a 45-degree angle to the ground (see figure *a*).

DESCRIPTION

- Pull the shoulder blades together and downward, bend the arm at the elbow, and bring the hand toward the face (see figure *b*).
- Extend the elbow and return to the starting position.

TEACHING CUES

- Move only at the elbow.
- Brace the trunk and squeeze the glutes.
- Do not allow the trunk or hips to rotate.

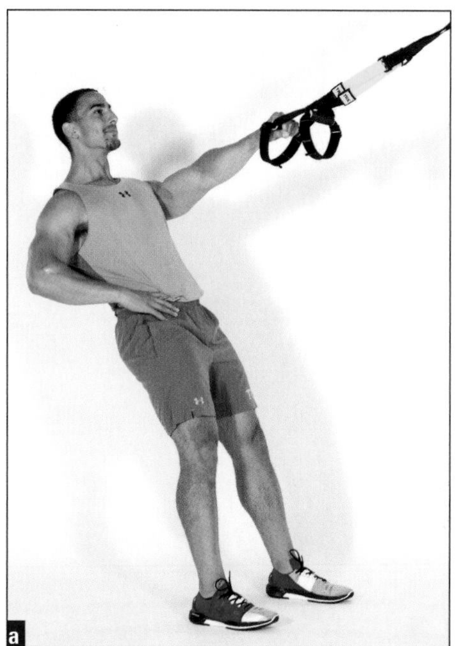
a

b

Pec Stretch

PURPOSE

To improve pectoral muscle flexibility and shoulder joint mobility.

PREREQUISITES

The ability to maintain a rigid torso throughout the exercise, and no shoulder pain or injury.

ADJUSTMENT

Adjust the straps of the Suspension Trainer to mid-length.

STARTING POSITION

Face away from the anchor point, and grab a handle with each hand. Assume a staggered stance. Set the body in a straight line, or in plank position.

DESCRIPTION

- Brace the trunk, slightly bend the elbows, and extend the arms out to the sides.
- While keeping the arms locked in this position, slowly push the hands away from each other and pull the shoulder blades down and together.
- Lean forward and move the hands outward until a large stretch is felt in the chest (see figure).
- Bring the hands back to the starting position.

TEACHING CUES

- Stretch to the point of mild tension.
- Do not stretch to the point of pain.

Single-Arm Pec Stretch

PURPOSE
To improve pectoral muscle flexibility and shoulder joint mobility.

PREREQUISITES
The ability to maintain a rigid torso throughout the exercise, and no shoulder pain or injury.

ADJUSTMENT
Adjust the straps of the Suspension Trainer to mid-length.

STARTING POSITION
Face sideways and grab the handles with the hand that is closer to the anchor point. Set the body in a straight line, or in plank position.

DESCRIPTION

- Brace the trunk with the working arm straight and the non-working arm to the side of the body or on the hip.
- Rotate the hips while repositioning the feet to the 6 o'clock position, or until a large stretch is felt in the chest (see figure).
- Hold this position for 10 to 30 seconds; then, repeat on the other side.

TEACHING CUES

- Stretch to the point of mild tension.
- Do not stretch to the point of pain.

Single-Arm Kneeling Pec Stretch

PURPOSE
To improve pectoral muscle flexibility and shoulder joint mobility.

PREREQUISITES
The ability to maintain a rigid torso throughout the exercise, and no shoulder pain or injury.

ADJUSTMENT
Adjust the straps of the Suspension Trainer to mid-length.

STARTING POSITION
In a kneeling position, face sideways, extend the arm that is closer to the anchor point, and grab both handles.

DESCRIPTION
- Brace the trunk with the working arm straight and the non-working arm to the side of the body or on the hip.
- Lean forward and rotate the torso away from the extended arm while pushing the hand downward (see figure).
- Hold this position for 10 to 30 seconds; then, repeat on the other side.

TEACHING CUES
- Stretch to the point of mild tension.
- Do not stretch to the point of pain.

Overhead Lat Stretch

PURPOSE

To improve latissimus dorsi flexibility and shoulder joint mobility.

PREREQUISITES

The ability to maintain a rigid torso throughout the exercise, and no shoulder pain or injury.

ADJUSTMENT

Adjust the straps of the Suspension Trainer to mid-length.

STARTING POSITION

Face away from the anchor point (or stand sideways to stretch the obliques), and grab a handle with each hand. Assume a staggered stance. Set the body in a straight line, or in plank position.

DESCRIPTION

- Brace the trunk and keep the arms straight.
- Lunge forward until the hands are behind the head, and lean away from the anchor point until a stretch is felt through the latissimus dorsi (see figure).
- Hold this position for 10 to 30 seconds.

TEACHING CUES

- Stretch to the point of mild tension.
- Do not stretch to the point of pain.

Rear Deltoid Stretch

PURPOSE
To improve shoulder joint flexibility and mobility.

PREREQUISITE
No shoulder pain or injury.

ADJUSTMENT
Adjust the straps of the Suspension Trainer to mid-length.

STARTING POSITION
Stand sideways and hold both straps in the hand that is farther from the anchor point.

DESCRIPTION
- Step laterally, away from the anchor point, until the strap is taught.
- While keeping the arm extended at chest height, lean away from the anchor point until a stretch is felt through the back of the shoulder (see figure).
- Hold this position for 10 to 30 seconds; then, repeat on the opposite side.

TEACHING CUES
- For a greater stretch, step farther from the anchor point.
- Stretch to the point of mild tension.
- Do not stretch to the point of pain.

Bent-Over Rear Deltoid Stretch

PURPOSE
To improve shoulder joint flexibility and mobility.

PREREQUISITE
No shoulder pain or injury.

ADJUSTMENT
Adjust the straps of the Suspension Trainer to mid-length.

STARTING POSITION
Stand sideways and hold both straps in the hand that is farther from the anchor point.

DESCRIPTION
- Step laterally away from the anchor point until the strap is taught.
- Hinge forward at the hips (similar to performing a Romanian deadlift), keep the arm extended, and press the hand toward the ground until a stretch is felt in the back of the shoulder (see figure).
- Hold this position for 10 to 30 seconds; then, repeat on the other side.

TEACHING CUES
- For a greater stretch, step farther from the anchor point.
- Stretch to the point of mild tension.
- Do not stretch to the point of pain.

Lower-Body Exercises

The chapter presents exercises to develop lower-body endurance, strength, mobility, and power. For advanced lifters, adding external resistance such as dumbbells, kettlebells, and weight vests can increase the intensity of many of the exercises.

Excursions

PURPOSE
To develop single-leg balance and hip stability.

PREREQUISITE
The ability to maintain balance on a single leg.

ADJUSTMENT
Fully shorten the straps of the Suspension Trainer.

STARTING POSITION
Stand facing the anchor point. Grasp the handles, bend the arms, and step back until there is no slack in the straps.

DESCRIPTION

- Assume a single-leg stance with the support foot maintaining full contact with the ground and the free foot about 3 inches (8 cm) off the ground (see figure *a*).
- Point the toe downward, and slide the foot forward as far as possible, as if reaching to the 3 o'clock position (see figure *b*).
- Return to the starting position; then repeat at the 12 o'clock position.

TEACHING CUES

- Do not move the support knee forward past the toes of the support foot.
- Make sure the big toe, little toe, and heel remain in contact with the ground on the stance foot throughout the movement.

a

b

Single-Leg Reaching Romanian Deadlift

PURPOSE
To develop single-leg balance and hip stability while stretching the hamstring of the stance leg as well as the latissimus dorsi.

PREREQUISITE
The ability to maintain balance on a single leg.

ADJUSTMENT
Adjust the straps of the Suspension Trainer to mid-calf length.

STARTING POSITION
Stand facing the anchor point. Grasp the handles, extend the arms with hands at chest level, and step back until there is no slack in the straps.

DESCRIPTION

- Assume a single-leg stance with the support foot maintaining full contact with the ground and the free foot lifted off the ground (see figure *a*).
- Bend at the hip while extending the free leg (see figure *b*).
- Keep the arms straight and, while holding the handles, reach out as far as possible.
- Return to the starting position, and repeat for the desired number of repetitions.

TEACHING CUES

- Keep the hips neutral and the toes of the free foot pointed downward.
- Turn the toes of the lead leg slightly inward. This typically puts the hip in the appropriate position and prevents rotation. When the hip rotates the hamstring, the stance leg shortens and the stretch is less effective.

a

b

Reverse Lunge With Knee Drive

PURPOSE
To develop single-leg balance, hip stability, and proper lower-body mechanics for the acceleration phase of a sprint.

PREREQUISITE
The ability to maintain balance on a single leg.

ADJUSTMENT
Fully lengthen the straps of the Suspension Trainer.

STARTING POSITION
Face toward the anchor point. Position the hands at underarm level, and lean forward until the torso is at a 45-degree angle.

DESCRIPTION

- Take a step back so that the legs are in alignment with the torso, and perform a reverse lunge (see figure *a*).
- Drive the rear knee forward while extending the ankle, knee, and hip of the lead leg. The ankle of the drive leg should remain in a cast position, or with the toes pulled back toward the shin (see figure *b*).
- Maintain balance on the standing foot for a count of 2.
- Return to the starting position, and repeat on the opposite leg.

TEACHING CUES

- Stay straight as a board from the head through the heels.
- Keep the toes and knee up on the free leg.

a

b

Deep Squat

PURPOSE

To improve mobility at the ankles, knees, and hips, as well as lower-body muscular endurance.

PREREQUISITE

No lower-body joint pain or injury.

ADJUSTMENT

Adjust the straps of the Suspension Trainer to mid-length.

STARTING POSITION

Stand facing the anchor point. Grasp the handles with elbows bent and step back until there is no slack in the straps.

DESCRIPTION

- Point the toes outward slightly (see figure *a*).
- Squat until the knees are bent at or more than 90 degrees. The knees should remain behind, or directly over, the toes (see figure *b*). Maintain a tall, neutral spine.
- Extend the hips, knees, and ankles, and return to the starting position.

TEACHING CUES

- Imagine standing in the center of a square, and drop the hips to the middle of the square.
- Keep the weight evenly distributed among the big toe, little toe, and heel.

a

b

Iso Squat

PURPOSE
To improve ankle, knee, and hip mobility, as well as lower-body muscular endurance and joint stability.

PREREQUISITE
No lower-body joint pain or injury.

ADJUSTMENT
Adjust the straps of the Suspension Trainer to mid-length.

STARTING POSITION
Stand facing the anchor point. Grasp the handles with elbows bent and step back until there is no slack in the straps.

DESCRIPTION

- Point the toes outward slightly (see figure *a*).
- Squat until the top of the knees are bent at or more than 90 degrees. The knees should remain behind, or directly over, the toes (see figure *b*). Maintain a tall, neutral spine.
- Hold this position for three to five seconds; then extend the hips, knees, and ankles, and return to the starting position.

TEACHING CUES

- Imagine standing in the center of a square, and drop the buttocks to the middle of the square.
- Keep the weight evenly distributed among the big toe, little toe, and heel.

a

b

Split Squat

PURPOSE

To improve ankle, knee, and hip mobility, as well as lower-body muscular endurance.

PREREQUISITE

No lower-body pain or injury.

ADJUSTMENT

Adjust the straps of the Suspension Trainer to mid-length.

STARTING POSITION

Stand facing the anchor point. Grasp the handles with elbows bent and step back until there is no slack in the straps.

DESCRIPTION

- Stagger the feet front and back with the toes facing straight ahead. The front foot should be flat on the ground (see figure *a*).
- The heel of the back foot should be up, and the weight should be on the ball of the foot.
- Lower the body by allowing the front knee to flex until the back knee is just above the ground (see figure *b*).
- Push through the front heel, and extend the ankle, knee, and hip to return to the starting position.
- Repeat for the desired number of repetitions; then, switch legs and repeat.

TEACHING CUES

- Drop the back knee straight down.
- Drive off the lead foot.

a

b

Overhead Squat

PURPOSE
To improve ankle, knee, and hip mobility, as well as lower-body muscular endurance. This exercise also strengthens the muscles of the upper back.

PREREQUISITE
No lower-body joint pain or injury.

ADJUSTMENT
Adjust the straps of the Suspension Trainer to mid-length.

STARTING POSITION
Stand facing the anchor point. Grasp the handles, extend the arms overhead, and step back until there is no slack in the straps.

DESCRIPTION

- Point the toes outward slightly (see figure *a*).
- Squat until the knees are bent more than 90 degrees. The knees should remain behind, or directly over, the toes (see figure *b*).
- Extend the hips, knees, and ankles, and return to the starting position.

TEACHING CUES

- Imagine standing in the center of a square, and drop the buttocks to the middle of the square.
- Squeeze the shoulder blades together.
- Keep the weight evenly distributed among the big toe, little toe, and heel.

a

b

Lateral Squat

PURPOSE
To improve ankle, knee, and hip mobility, as well as lower-body muscular endurance.

PREREQUISITE
No lower-body pain or injury.

ADJUSTMENT
Adjust the straps of the Suspension Trainer to mid-length.

STARTING POSITION
Stand facing the anchor point. Grasp the handles with elbows bent and step back until there is no slack in the straps.

DESCRIPTION:

- Position the feet wider than shoulder width, with the heels in contact with the ground (see figure *a*).
- Keep both feet in position and shift the body weight to one side while bending the knee and pushing the hips back. At this point, the same-side glute and shoulder should be directly aligned with the heel (see figure *b*).
- The lead knee should be at 90 degrees, and the nonsquatting leg should be fully extended at the side.
- Push off the lead foot, return to the starting position, and then shift the weight to the opposite leg.

TEACHING CUES

- Keep the big toe, little toe, and heel in contact with the ground at all times.
- Keep the lead ankle, knee, and hip aligned.

a

b

Iso Lateral Squat

PURPOSE
To improve ankle, knee, and hip mobility, as well as lower-body muscular endurance.

PREREQUISITE
No lower-body pain or injury

ADJUSTMENT
Adjust the straps of the Suspension Trainer to mid-length.

STARTING POSITION
Stand facing the anchor point. Grasp the handles with elbows bent and step back until there is no slack in the straps.

DESCRIPTION
- Position the feet wider than shoulder width, with the heels in contact with the ground (see figure *a*).
- Keep both feet in position and shift the body weight to one side while bending the knee and pushing the hips back. At this point, the same-side glute and shoulder should be directly aligned with the heel (see figure *b*).
- The lead knee should be at 90 degrees, and the nonworking leg should be fully extended at the side.
- Hold this position for three to five seconds; then, push off the lead foot and return to the starting position.
- Shift the weight to the opposite leg and repeat.

TEACHING CUES
- Keep the big toe, little toe, and heel in contact with the ground at all times.
- Keep the lead ankle, knee, and hip aligned.

a

b

Lateral Lunge

PURPOSE
To improve ankle, knee, and hip mobility, as well as lower-body muscular endurance.

PREREQUISITE
No lower-body pain or injury.

ADJUSTMENT
Adjust the straps of the Suspension Trainer to mid-length.

STARTING POSITION
Stand facing the anchor point. Grasp the handles with elbows bent and step back until there is no slack in the straps.

DESCRIPTION

- Position the feet together (see figure *a*).
- Step one foot to the side so that the feet are slightly wider than shoulder width. The heel of the stepping-leg foot should be in full contact with the ground.
- Shift the body weight toward the stepping leg, bend the knee, and drop the hips. At this point, the same-side glute and shoulder should be directly aligned with the heel of the stepping-leg foot (see figure *b*).
- The stepping-leg knee should be at 90 degrees, and the nonworking leg should be fully extended at the side.
- Push off the stepping-leg foot and return to the starting position; then, step to the opposite side and repeat.

TEACHING CUES

- Make certain the lead-leg big toe, little toe, and heel are in contact with the ground before descending into the lunge position.
- Drive off the lead leg to return to the starting position.

a

b

Sprinter Lunge

PURPOSE

To improve lower-body muscular endurance and coordination.

PREREQUISITES

Good balance and coordination, and no lower-body pain or injuries.

ADJUSTMENT

Fully lengthen the straps of the Suspension Trainer.

STARTING POSITION

Stand facing the anchor point, and put one foot in the stirrups.

DESCRIPTION

- While maintaining a 90-degree bend at the elbow of the arm opposite the lead leg, take the hand toward the cheek and move the lead-leg-side hand toward the back hip pocket. Then, drop into a reverse lunge position. Allow the lead ankle, knee, and hip to bend until the thigh is parallel to the ground (see figure a).
- Simultaneously extend the lead leg and bring the back foot forward until the left side heel is in contact with the buttocks (see figure b).
- Swing the left arm back so that the left hand is touching the back hip pocket, and swing the right hand forward so that it is just to the side of the right cheek.
- Return to the starting position and repeat for the desired number of repetitions.

TEACHING CUES

- Make certain the lead knee stays aligned with the second toe of the lead foot.
- Swing the arms from lips to hips or from eye socket to hip pocket.
- Kick the heel to the buttocks.

a

b

Leg Sweep

PURPOSE

To develop balance, hip stability, strength, and endurance on a single leg.

PREREQUISITES

The ability to maintain balance on a single leg, and no pain or lower-body injury.

ADJUSTMENT

Adjust the straps of the Suspension Trainer to mid-length.

STARTING POSITION

Stand facing the anchor point. Grasp the handles, bend the arms, and step back until there is no slack in the straps.

DESCRIPTION

- Stand on the right leg with the right foot in full contact with the ground and the left foot about 3 inches (8 cm) off the ground (see figure *a*).
- Bend the right leg until the thigh is at a 110- to 130-degree angle; then reach the left foot toward the 4 o'clock position (see figure *b*).
- Repeat for the desired number of repetitions; then, switch legs.

TEACHING CUES

- Do not move the support knee forward past the toes of the support foot.
- Reach back as far as possible while maintaining balance and proper body alignment.

a

b

Calf Raise

PURPOSE
To develop the muscles on the posterior side of the lower leg.

PREREQUISITES
The ability to maintain balance, and no lower-leg injuries.

ADJUSTMENT
Fully shorten the straps of the Suspension Trainer.

STARTING POSITION
Stand facing away from the anchor point. Grasp the handles, bend the arms, and step forward until there is no slack in the straps.

DESCRIPTION

- Begin with the feet in full contact with the ground and the weight evenly distributed between the big toe and little toe (see figure *a*).
- Lift the heels and rise up on the toes (see figure *b*).
- Lower the heels to the ground and repeat.

TEACHING CUES

- Stand tall.
- Pause at the top for a count of 2.

a

b

Suspended Reverse Lunge

PURPOSE

To improve ankle, knee, and hip mobility; lower-body strength and muscular endurance; trunk stability; and shoulder endurance.

PREREQUISITES

The ability to maintain balance, and no lower-body or shoulder pain or injury.

ADJUSTMENT

Adjust the straps of the Suspension Trainer to mid-calf length.

STARTING POSITION

Stand facing away from the anchor point. Place the trail foot in both foot cradles, and adjust the position until the straps are at a 110- to 130-degree angle to the ground (see figure *a*).

DESCRIPTION

- Lower the body by allowing the front knee to flex until it is at 90 degrees and the thigh is parallel to the ground (see figure *b*).
- Simultaneously push the suspended foot back.
- Push through the front heel, and extend the front knee and hip to return to the starting position.
- Repeat for the desired number of repetitions; then switch legs and repeat.

TEACHING CUES

- This exercise can be performed while holding the weight on the same side as the free leg.
- Drop the back knee straight down.
- Drive off the lead foot.

a

b

Lying Leg Curl

PURPOSE

To develop hamstring strength and endurance.

PREREQUISITE

The ability to maintain a plank position.

ADJUSTMENT

Adjust the straps of the Suspension Trainer to mid-calf length.

STARTING POSITION

Lie face up with the heels of each foot in the foot cradles. Place the hands to the sides of the torso with the palms down.

DESCRIPTION

- Extend the legs and lift the hips so that the trunk, legs, and shoulders are aligned (see figure *a*).
- Slowly bend the hips and knees while pulling the heels toward the buttocks (see figure *b*).
- Extend the hips and knees, and return to the starting position.
- To make this exercise more challenging, do not allow the hips to bend; rather, bend only at the knees. Note: the number of sets and reps should be equalized between limbs (i.e. sets × reps).

a

b

TEACHING CUES

- Brace the core.
- Keep in mind that control is more important than speed.
- Squeeze the hamstrings at the top of the movement.

Triangle Squat

PURPOSE
To develop hip mobility and stretch the adductors of the inner thigh.

PREREQUISITE
No lower-body pain or injury.

ADJUSTMENT
Adjust the straps of the Suspension Trainer to mid-length.

STARTING POSITION
Stand facing the anchor point with the feet wider than shoulder width. Grasp the handles, bend the arms, and step back until there is no slack in the straps (see figure *a*).

DESCRIPTION

- Drop the hips down and back toward the right while keeping the chest up (see figure *b*).
- Once in the lateral squat position, shift the weight until it is all the way to the left (see figure *c*).
- Ascend to the beginning position; then repeat moving from left to right.
- Repeat for the desired number of repetitions.

TEACHING CUES

- Imagine scooting the buttocks across a park bench.
- Keep the hips low, chest up, and eyes focused straight ahead.

a

b

c

Pigeon Stretch

PURPOSE
To improve hip mobility and low back flexibility.

PREREQUISITES
No lower-body or back pain or injury.

ADJUSTMENT
Adjust the straps of the Suspension Trainer to mid-calf length.

STARTING POSITION
Facing the anchor point, sit on the ground with one leg outstretched behind and the other bent at the knee in front. Grasp a handle with each hand (see figure *a*).

DESCRIPTION

- Lean forward, pushing the chest toward the ground.
- Stretch to the point of mild discomfort, hold for 5 to 10 seconds, and then return to the starting position (see figure *b*).
- Repeat for 30 to 60 seconds; then, perform on the opposite side.

TEACHING CUES

- Maintain a big chest position.
- Breathe out while reaching forward.

a

b

Figure-Four Stretch

PURPOSE
To stretch the piriformis muscle and improve single-leg balance.

PREREQUISITE
No lower-body pain or injury.

ADJUSTMENT
Adjust the straps of the Suspension Trainer to mid-length.

STARTING POSITION
Facing the anchor point, stand on one foot with the ankle of the other foot crossed over the knee of the standing leg. Grasp a handle with each hand (see figure *a*).

DESCRIPTION

- Squat until the lead knee is at 90 degrees.
- Stretch to the point of mild discomfort, hold for 5 to 10 seconds, and then return to the starting position (see figure *b*).
- Repeat for 30 to 60 seconds; then, perform on the other side.

TEACHING CUES

- Maintain a big chest position.
- Breathe out while descending into the squat position.
- To increase the intensity, descend deeper into the squat position.

a

b

Reaching Hip Flexor Stretch

PURPOSE
To stretch the hip flexor muscles.

PREREQUISITE
No lower-body pain or injury.

ADJUSTMENT
Adjust the straps of the Suspension Trainer to mid-length.

STARTING POSITION
Stand on the left foot, grab the handles with the left hand, grab the right ankle with the right hand, and pull it back toward the buttock (see figure *a*).

DESCRIPTION

- While keeping the hips facing forward, bend forward at the waist (see figure *b*).
- Pull the right ankle back while pushing the right hip toward the ground.
- Stretch to the point of mild discomfort, hold for 5 to 10 seconds, and then return to the starting position.
- Repeat for 30 to 60 seconds; then, perform on the opposite side.

TEACHING CUES

- Keep the hips pointed toward the ground when leaning forward; do not let them rotate.
- Maintain an open chest.
- Breathe out on the descent.

a

b

Reverse Lunge

PURPOSE
To improve lower-body muscular endurance and coordination.

PREREQUISITES
Good balance and coordination, and no lower-body pain or injuries.

ADJUSTMENT
Adjust the straps of the Suspension Trainer to mid-length.

STARTING POSITION
Stand facing away from the anchor point, place one foot in both foot cradles, and place your hands on your hips (see figure *a*).

DESCRIPTION

- While maintaining a rigid torso, drop down until the lead-leg thigh is parallel to the ground (see figure *b*).
- Extend the lead leg and bring the back foot forward until back in the starting position; then, repeat with the other leg.

TEACHING CUES

- Keep the lead knee aligned with the second toe of lead foot.
- Drive up on the lead leg as if pushing the ground away.

a

b

Single-Leg Calf Raise

PURPOSE
To develop the muscles on the back of the lower leg.

PREREQUISITES
The ability to maintain balance, and no lower-leg injuries.

ADJUSTMENT
Fully shorten the straps of the Suspension Trainer.

STARTING POSITION
Stand facing the anchor point. Grasp the handles, extend the arms, and step back until there is no slack in the straps.

DESCRIPTION
- Position one foot behind the other (see figure *a*).
- Lift the heel of the working leg, and rise up on the toes (see figure *b*).
- Lower the heel to the ground and repeat for the desired number of repetitions; then, switch legs.

TEACHING CUES
- Stand tall.
- Pause at the top for a count of 2.

a

b

Reverse Lunge With Chop and Lift

PURPOSE

To improve ankle, knee, and hip mobility, as well as lower-body strength and muscular endurance. This exercise can also be used to improve trunk stability and shoulder endurance. It also teaches upper- and lower-body dissociation, which may be important in sports in which players use implements, such as hockey and lacrosse.

PREREQUISITES

The ability to maintain balance, and no lower-body or shoulder pain or injury.

ADJUSTMENT

Adjust the straps of the Suspension Trainer to mid-calf length.

STARTING POSITION

Stand facing away from the anchor point. Place one foot in both foot cradles, and adjust the position until the straps are roughly perpendicular to the ground. Grasp a medicine ball in both hands, and position it at hip level.

DESCRIPTION

- Push the suspended foot back until the feet are staggered; the toes should face straight ahead, and the lead foot should be flat on the ground (see figure *a*).
- Lower the body by flexing the front knee until it is at 90 degrees and the thigh is parallel to the ground. At the same time, while keeping the arms completely straight, lift the medicine ball overhead (see figure *b*).
- Push through the front heel, and extend the knee and hip to return to the starting position.
- Repeat for the desired number of repetitions; then, switch legs and repeat.

TEACHING CUES

- Drop the back knee straight down.
- Drive off the lead foot.
- Maintain a rigid torso throughout the exercise.

a

b

Reverse Lunge With Horizontal Push

PURPOSE
To improve ankle, knee, and hip mobility; lower-body strength and muscular endurance; trunk stability; and shoulder endurance.

PREREQUISITES
The ability to maintain balance, and no lower-body or shoulder pain or injury.

ADJUSTMENT
Adjust the straps of the Suspension Trainer to mid-calf length.

STARTING POSITION
Stand facing away from the anchor point. Place one foot in both foot cradles, and adjust the position until the straps are roughly perpendicular to the ground. Grasp a medicine ball in both hands, and position it across the chest.

DESCRIPTION
- Push the suspended foot back until the feet are staggered; the toes should face straight ahead, and the lead foot should be flat on the ground (see figure *a*).
- Lower the body by allowing the front knee to flex until the knee is at 90 degrees and the thigh is parallel to the ground. At the same time, while keeping the arms completely straight, press the medicine ball straight out in front of the body (see figure *b*).
- Push through the front heel and extend the knee and hip to return to the starting position.
- Repeat for the desired number of repetitions; then, switch legs and repeat.

TEACHING CUES
- Drop the back knee straight down.
- Drive off the lead foot.
- Maintain a rigid torso throughout the exercise.
- Keep the ball at shoulder height; if unable, use a lighter weight.

a

b

Suspended Single-Leg Deadlift

PURPOSE
To improve ankle, knee, and hip mobility; lower-body strength and muscular endurance; trunk stability; and shoulder endurance.

PREREQUISITES
The ability to maintain balance, and no lower-body or shoulder pain or injury.

ADJUSTMENT
Adjust the straps of the Suspension Trainer to mid-calf length.

STARTING POSITION
Stand facing away from the anchor point. Place one foot in both foot cradles, and adjust the position until the straps are at a 110- to 130-degree angle to the ground. Grasp a pair of dumbbells or kettlebells, and hold them at either side of the lead leg (see figure *a*).

DESCRIPTION
- Lower the body by allowing the front knee to flex until it is at 90 degrees and the thigh is parallel to the ground (see figure *b*).
- Simultaneously push the suspended foot back.
- Push through the front heel and extend the knee and hip to return to the starting position.
- Extend the arms and return the dumbbells to the starting position.
- Repeat for the desired number of repetitions; then, switch legs and repeat.

TEACHING CUES
- Drive off the lead foot.
- Push the ground away.
- Maintain a rigid torso throughout the exercise.

a

b

Suspended Knee Extension

PURPOSE
To develop quadriceps strength and endurance.

PREREQUISITE
The ability to maintain a plank position.

ADJUSTMENT
Adjust the straps of the Suspension Trainer to mid-calf length.

STARTING POSITION
Lie face down and place the feet in the foot cradles. Place the elbows directly under the shoulders; the hands should be in full contact with the ground.

DESCRIPTION
- Extend the arms and legs and lift the hips so that the trunk, the shoulders, and the hips are aligned (see figure *a*).
- Bend the knees and hips to 90 degrees (see figure *b*).
- Extend the knees and return to the starting position.

TEACHING CUES
- Move only at the knees.
- Brace the trunk.

a

b

Drop Squat

PURPOSE
To develop eccentric strength and stability while learning proper landing mechanics.

PREREQUISITES
No pain or lower-body injury, and the ability to perform a squat.

ADJUSTMENT
Fully lengthen the straps of the Suspension Trainer.

STARTING POSITION
Stand facing the anchor point. Grasp the handles with elbows bent and step back until there is no slack in the straps.

DESCRIPTION

- Stand tall with the feet hip-width apart (see figure *a*).
- Rise up on the toes, and then rapidly split the feet to the side and land in the universal athletic position with the chest up, shoulders back, and a slight bend in the ankles, knees, and hips (see figure *b*).
- Land softly in a squat position (see figure *c*).
- Rise to return to the starting position.

TEACHING CUES

- Make sure the knees stay aligned with the first and second toes.
- Land with the knees just behind the toes and both feet in full contact with the ground.
- Land quietly, like a cat.
- Stick the landing.

Drop Split Squat

PURPOSE
To develop eccentric strength and stability in a staggered stance, as well as proper landing mechanics.

PREREQUISITE
No lower body pain or injury.

ADJUSTMENT
Adjust the straps of the Suspension Trainer to mid-length.

STARTING POSITION
Stand facing the anchor point. Grasp the handles with elbows bent and step back until there is no slack in the straps.

DESCRIPTION

- Stand tall with the feet hip-width apart.
- Rise up on the balls of the feet (see figure *a*).
- Rapidly drop and split the feet (see figure *b*), and land in a staggered position (see figure *c*).
- Push through the front heel, and extend the ankle, knees, and hips to return to the starting position.
- Repeat for the desired number of repetitions; then, switch legs and repeat.

TEACHING CUES

- Land quietly, like a cat.
- Stick the landing.

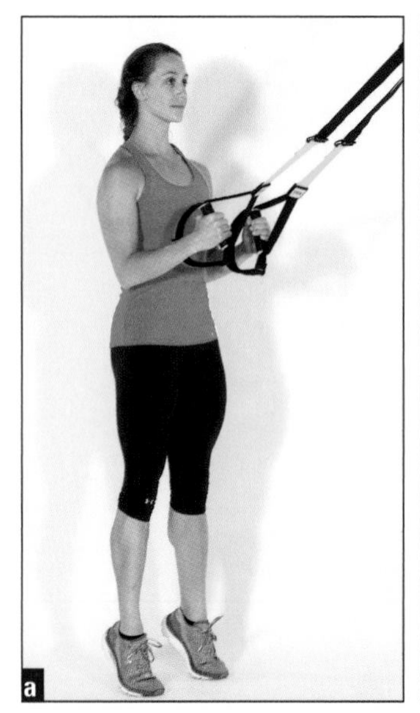
a

b

c

Squat Jump

PURPOSE
To develop concentric power of the lower body and proper landing mechanics.

PREREQUISITES
The ability to perform a proper squat and drop squat.

ADJUSTMENT
Adjust the straps of the Suspension Trainer to mid-length.

STARTING POSITION
Stand facing the anchor point with the feet about hip-width apart. Grasp the handles, bend the arms, and step back until there is no slack in the straps.

DESCRIPTION
- Flex the hips, knees, and ankles, and lower the body into a half-squat position (see figure *a*).
- Before coming to a complete stop, extend the knees and hips, jumping as high as possible off both feet (see figure *b*).
- Land in the takeoff position (see figure *c*).
- Hold this position for two or three seconds; then, perform the next jump.

TEACHING CUES
- Take off like a rocket.
- Land softly.

a

b

c

Countermovement Jump to Stick

PURPOSE
To develop lower-body power and proper landing mechanics.

PREREQUISITES
The ability to perform a proper squat and drop squat.

ADJUSTMENT
Adjust the straps of the Suspension Trainer to mid-length.

STARTING POSITION
Stand facing the anchor point with the feet about hip-width apart. Grasp the handles with elbows bent and step back until there is no slack in the straps.

DESCRIPTION

- Flex the hips, knees, and ankles, and lower the body into a full squat (see figure *a*).
- Before coming to a complete stop, extend the knees and hips and jump as high as possible off both feet (see figure *b*).
- Land softly in the takeoff position, and stick the landing (see figure *c*).

TEACHING CUES

- Take off like a rocket.
- Land softly.

a

b

c

Lateral Skater With Stick

PURPOSE
To develop concentric power of the lower body, as well as knee and hip stability.

PREREQUISITE
No lower-body pain or injury.

ADJUSTMENT
Adjust the straps of the Suspension Trainer to mid-length.

STARTING POSITION
Stand facing the anchor point with the feet about hip-width apart. Grasp the handles with elbows bent and step back until there is no slack in the straps.

DESCRIPTION
- With the feet hip-width apart, shift the weight to the left foot while lifting the right leg and bringing it behind the left leg (see figure *a*).
- Drive the right leg laterally, jumping to the right and landing on the right foot, with the left leg bent and crossing behind the right leg (see figure *b*).
- Stick the landing, pause for one or two seconds, and then bound back to the left side and stick the landing on the left foot.

TEACHING CUES
- Take off quickly, like a rubber ball bouncing off the ground.
- Land softly.

a

b

Split Squat Jump to Stick

PURPOSE
To develop eccentric strength and proper landing mechanics.

PREREQUISITE
No lower-body pain or injury.

ADJUSTMENT
Adjust the straps of the Suspension Trainer to mid-length.

STARTING POSITION
Stand facing the anchor point. Grasp the handles with elbows bent and step back until there is no slack in the straps.

DESCRIPTION

- Stagger the feet front and back with the toes facing straight ahead (see figure *a*). The front foot should be flat on the ground. The heel of the back foot should be up, and the weight should be on the ball of the foot.
- Drop rapidly by flexing the front knee until it reaches 100 to 120 degrees (see figure *b*).
- Push through the front heel, and extend the ankles, knees, and hips to jump as high as possible (see figure *c*).
- Land softly in the starting position and stick the landing.
- Repeat for the desired number of repetitions; then, switch legs and repeat.

TEACHING CUES

- Land softly.
- Take off like a rocket.

a

b

c

Pistol Squat

PURPOSE

To develop lower-body strength, endurance, stability, and mobility.

PREREQUISITES

No lower-body pain or injury, and the ability to maintain single-leg balance.

ADJUSTMENT

Adjust the straps of the Suspension Trainer to mid-length.

STARTING POSITION

Stand on one foot while facing the anchor point (see figure *a*). Grasp the handles with the elbows bent, and step back until there is no slack in the straps.

DESCRIPTION

- Squat and extend the free leg out in front (see figure *b*).
- Return to the starting position, and repeat for the desired number of repetitions; then, switch and perform the same number of repetitions on the opposite leg.

TEACHING CUES

- Brace the trunk.
- Lift the free leg while descending into the squat.

a

b

Alternated Split Squat Jump to Stick

PURPOSE
To learn proper landing mechanics and improve lower-body coordination.

PREREQUISITE
No lower-body pain or injury.

ADJUSTMENT
Adjust the straps of the Suspension Trainer to mid-length.

STARTING POSITION
Stand facing the anchor point. Grasp the handles with elbows bent and step back until there is no slack in the straps.

DESCRIPTION

- Stagger the feet front and back in a lunge position with the toes facing straight ahead. The front foot should be flat on the ground. The heel of the back foot should be up, and the weight should be on the ball of the foot.
- Quickly perform a small countermovement by flexing the front knee until it reaches 90 degrees (see figure *a*).
- Immediately push through the front heel; extend the ankles, knees, and hips; and jump as high as possible (see figure *b*).
- At the top of the jump, rapidly scissor the legs so that they switch positions (see figure *c*).
- Land softly and stick the landing (see figure *d*).
- Repeat for the desired number of repetitions, switching legs with each jump.

TEACHING CUES

- Land softly.
- Take off like a rocket.

a
b
c
d

Kettlebell Reverse Lunge

PURPOSE
To improve ankle, knee, and hip mobility, as well as lower-body muscular endurance and strength.

PREREQUISITES
The ability to maintain balance, and no lower-body pain or injury.

ADJUSTMENT
Adjust the straps of the Suspension Trainer to mid-calf length.

STARTING POSITION
While holding two kettlebells or dumbbells at the sides (or in front of the shoulders), stand facing away from the anchor point. Place one foot in both foot cradles.

DESCRIPTION

- While holding the kettlebells or dumbbells, push the suspended foot back until the feet are staggered; the toes should face straight ahead, and the lead foot should be flat on the ground (see figure *a*).
- Flex the front knee until it is at 90 degrees and the thigh is parallel to the ground (see figure *b*).
- Push through the front heel, and extend the knee and hip to return to the starting position.
- Repeat for the desired number of repetitions; then, switch legs and repeat.

TEACHING CUES

- Drop the back knee straight down.
- Drive off the lead foot.

a

b

Suitcase Reverse Lunge

PURPOSE
To improve ankle, knee, and hip mobility; lower-body strength and muscular endurance; trunk stability; and trunk musculature (the trunk must flex laterally to resist the weight in the opposite hand).

PREREQUISITES
The ability to maintain balance, and no lower-body pain or injury.

ADJUSTMENT
Adjust the straps of the Suspension Trainer to mid-calf length.

STARTING POSITION
Stand facing away from the anchor point. Place one foot in both foot cradles, and adjust the position until the straps are roughly perpendicular to the ground. Grasp a weight (e.g., dumbbell, kettlebell, handled medicine ball) in the hand opposite the stance leg.

DESCRIPTION
- Push the suspended foot back until the feet are in a staggered position; the toes should face straight ahead, and the lead foot should be flat on the ground (see figure *a*).
- Lower the body by flexing the front knee until it is at 90 degrees and the thigh is parallel to the ground (see figure *b*).
- Push through the front heel and extend the knee and hip to return to the starting position.
- Repeat for the desired number of repetitions; then switch legs.

TEACHING CUES
- Do not allow the trunk to dip or flex in the direction of the weighted implement.
- Drop the back knee straight down.
- Drive off the lead foot.
- Maintain a rigid torso throughout the exercise.

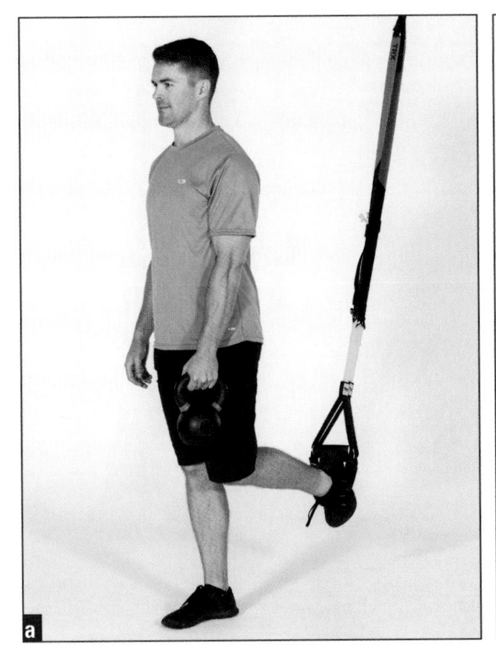
a

b

Reverse Lunge With Overhead Press

PURPOSE

To improve ankle, knee, and hip mobility; lower-body strength and muscular endurance; trunk stability; and shoulder endurance.

PREREQUISITES

The ability to maintain balance, and no lower-body or shoulder pain or injury.

ADJUSTMENT

Adjust the straps of the Suspension Trainer to mid-calf length.

STARTING POSITION

Stand facing away from the anchor point. Place one foot in both foot cradles, and adjust the position until the straps are roughly perpendicular to the ground. Grasp a medicine ball in both hands, and position it at the chest.

DESCRIPTION

- Push the suspended foot back until the feet are in a staggered position; the toes should face straight ahead, and the lead foot should be flat on the ground (see figure *a*).
- Lower the body by flexing the front knee until it is at 90 degrees and the thigh is parallel to the ground. At the same time, press the medicine ball overhead while keeping the arms completely straight (see figure *b*).
- Push through the front heel, and extend the knee and hip to return to the starting position.
- Repeat for the desired number of repetitions; then, switch legs and repeat.

TEACHING CUES

- Drop the back knee straight down.
- Drive off the lead foot.
- Maintain a rigid torso throughout the exercise.
- Press the ball directly overhead.

a

b

Reverse Lunge With Single-Arm Overhead Press

PURPOSE

To improve ankle, knee, and hip mobility; lower-body strength and muscular endurance; trunk stability; and shoulder endurance.

PREREQUISITES

The ability to maintain balance, and no lower-body or shoulder pain or injury.

ADJUSTMENT

Adjust the straps of the Suspension Trainer to mid-calf length.

STARTING POSITION

Stand facing away from the anchor point. Place one foot in both foot cradles, and adjust the position until the straps are roughly perpendicular to the ground. Grasp a weight (e.g., dumbbell, kettlebell, handled medicine ball) in the hand opposite the stance leg, and position it over the same-side shoulder.

DESCRIPTION

- Push the suspended foot back until the feet are in a staggered position; the toes should face straight ahead, and the lead foot should be flat on the ground (see figure *a*).
- Lower the body by flexing the front knee until it is at 90 degrees and the thigh is parallel to the ground (see figure *b*).
- Push through the front heel and extend the knee and hip to rise up; simultaneously, press the weight overhead while keeping the arm completely straight (see figure *c*).
- Repeat for the desired number of repetitions; then switch legs and repeat.
- To make this exercise more challenging, press the weight up while descending into the lunge position. This teaches upper- and lower-body dissociation and coordination.

TEACHING CUES

- Drop the back knee straight down.
- Drive off the lead foot.
- Maintain a rigid torso throughout the exercise.

a

b

c

Deadlift to Press

PURPOSE
To improve ankle, knee, and hip mobility; lower-body strength and muscular endurance; trunk stability; and shoulder endurance.

PREREQUISITES
The ability to maintain balance, and no lower-body or shoulder pain or injury.

ADJUSTMENT
Adjust the straps of the Suspension Trainer to mid-calf length.

STARTING POSITION
Stand facing away from the anchor point. Place one foot in both foot cradles, and adjust the position until the straps are at a 110- to 130-degree angle to the ground. Grasp a pair of dumbbells, and hold them down at each side of the working leg.

DESCRIPTION

- Lower the body by flexing the front knee until it is at 90 degrees and the thigh is parallel to the ground; simultaneously, push the suspended foot back (see figure *a*).
- Push through the front heel and extend the knee and hip to rise up while bending the arms to lift the dumbbells to shoulder level. At this point, the upper arms should be parallel to the ground (see figure *b*).
- Push the dumbbells overhead (see figure *c*).
- Slowly return the dumbbells to the shoulders; then, extend the arms to return the dumbbells to the starting position.
- Repeat for the desired number of repetitions; then, switch legs and repeat.

TEACHING CUES

- Drive off the lead foot.
- Maintain a rigid torso throughout the exercise.

a

b

c

Rear-Foot Elevated Overhead Squat

PURPOSE

To improve ankle, knee, and hip mobility; lower-body strength and muscular endurance; and trunk stability.

PREREQUISITES

The ability to maintain balance, and no lower-body or shoulder pain or injury.

ADJUSTMENT

Adjust the straps of the Suspension Trainer to mid-calf length.

STARTING POSITION

Stand facing away from the anchor point. Place one foot in both foot cradles, and adjust the position until the straps are roughly perpendicular to the ground. Grasp a pair of dumbbells and hold them overhead.

DESCRIPTION

- Push the suspended foot back until the feet are in a staggered position; the toes should face straight ahead, and the lead foot should be flat on the ground (see figure *a*).
- Lower the body by flexing the front knee until it is at 90 degrees and the thigh is parallel to the ground; simultaneously, press the arms overhead while keeping them completely straight (see figure *b*).
- Push through the front heel, and extend the knee and hip to return to the starting position.
- Repeat for the desired number of repetitions; then, switch legs and repeat.

TEACHING CUES

- Drop the back knee straight down.
- Drive off the lead foot.
- Maintain a rigid torso throughout the exercise.
- Keep the upper arms lined up with the ears.

a

b

Rear-Foot Elevated Muscle Clean to Press

PURPOSE

To improve ankle, knee, and hip mobility; lower-body strength and muscular endurance; trunk stability; and shoulder endurance. This drill is not performed for power the way a clean normally is; rather, it is for developing basic coordination.

PREREQUISITES

The ability to maintain balance, and no lower-body or shoulder pain or injury.

ADJUSTMENT

Adjust the straps of the Suspension Trainer to mid-calf length.

STARTING POSITION

Stand facing away from the anchor point. Place one foot in both foot cradles, and adjust the position until the straps are roughly perpendicular to the ground. Grasp a pair of weights (e.g., dumbbells, kettlebells, handled medicine balls) in each hand and hold them down to each side.

DESCRIPTION

- Push the suspended foot back until the feet are staggered; the toes should face straight ahead, and the lead foot should be flat on the ground.
- Lower the body by flexing the front knee until it is at 90 degrees and the thigh is parallel to the ground (see figure *a*); in this position, perform a clean (see figure *b*).
- Extend the lead knee and hip to rise up. Slowly extend the left arm overhead until it is in an overhead squat position (see figure *c*).
- Lower the arms to return to the starting position.
- Repeat for the desired number of repetitions; then, switch both legs and arms and repeat.

TEACHING CUES

- Maintain a rigid torso throughout the exercise.
- Perform a slight dip to create momentum for the overhead press (i.e., dip and drive).

a

b

c

Single-Leg Lying Leg Curl

PURPOSE
To develop hamstring strength and endurance.

PREREQUISITE
The ability to maintain a plank position.

ADJUSTMENT
Adjust the straps of the Suspension Trainer to mid-calf length.

STARTING POSITION
Lie face up, and place one heel in both foot cradles. Place the hands to the sides with the palms down.

DESCRIPTION:

- Extend both legs and lift the hips so that the trunk, legs, and shoulders are aligned (see figure *a*).
- The free leg and hip should remain parallel to the working leg.
- Slowly bend the knee of the working leg and pull the heel toward the buttock (see figure *b*). The free leg can move next to the working leg.
- Extend the knee of the working leg, and return to the starting position.
- To make this exercise more challenging, cross the feet and do not allow the hips to bend; rather, bend only at the knees.

a

b

TEACHING CUES

- Brace the core.
- Keep in mind that control is more important than speed.
- Squeeze the hamstrings at the top of the movement.

Single-Leg Suspended Knee Extension

PURPOSE
To develop quadriceps strength and endurance.

PREREQUISITE
The ability to maintain a plank position.

ADJUSTMENT
Adjust the straps of the Suspension Trainer to mid-calf length.

STARTING POSITION
Lie face down and place one foot in both foot cradles. Extend the arms and place the hands directly under the shoulders. Once this has been accomplished, bend the knees and the hips to 90-degree angles (see figure *a*).

DESCRIPTION

- Extend the legs and lift the hips so that the trunk, the hips, and the shoulders are aligned (see figure *b*).
- Slowly bend the knees and lower yourself back to the starting position.

TEACHING CUES

- Maintain a rigid torso throughout the exercise.
- Push your hips and your glutes toward the ceiling.

a

b

Rear-Foot Elevated Drop Squat

PURPOSE
To develop eccentric strength and stability on a single leg while learning proper landing mechanics.

PREREQUISITES
No pain or lower-body injury, and the ability to perform a squat.

ADJUSTMENT
Adjust the straps of the Suspension Trainer to mid-length.

STARTING POSITION
Stand facing away from the anchor point. Place one foot in a foot cradle, and adjust the position until the straps are at a 120- to 130-degree angle to the ground.

DESCRIPTION

- Rise up on the toes of the stance leg (see figure *a*).
- Rapidly drop the center of mass and, on landing, keep the chest up, shoulders back, and a slight bend in the ankles, knees, and hips (see figure *b*). The lead ankle should be 110 to 130 degrees on landing (see figure *c*).
- Extend the ankles, knees, and hips; hop back; and return to the starting position.

TEACHING CUES

- Drop the rear knee down and back, and make sure the lead knee stays aligned with the first and second toes.
- Land softly.

a

b

c

Repeat Countermovement Jump

PURPOSE

To develop lower-body power.

PREREQUISITES

The ability to perform a proper squat, drop squat, and countermovement jump to stick.

ADJUSTMENT

Adjust the straps of the Suspension Trainer to mid-length.

STARTING POSITION

Stand facing the anchor point with the feet about hip-width apart. Grasp the handles with elbows bent and step back until there is no slack in the straps.

DESCRIPTION

- Flex the hips, knees, and ankles, and lower the body into a full squat (see figure *a*).
- Before coming to a complete stop, extend the knees and hips, jumping as high as possible off both feet (see figure *b*).
- Land in the takeoff position; then, immediately perform the next jump.

TEACHING CUES

- Take off like a rocket.
- Jump off the ground like a rubber ball.
- Land softly.

a

b

Repeat Lateral Skater

PURPOSE
To develop lower-body power.

PREREQUISITE
No lower-body pain or injury.

ADJUSTMENT
Adjust the straps of the Suspension Trainer to mid-length.

STARTING POSITION
Stand facing the anchor point with the feet about hip-width apart. Grasp the handles with elbows bent and step back until there is no slack in the straps.

DESCRIPTION
- Standing with the feet hip-width apart, shift the weight to the left foot while bringing the right leg behind the left leg (see figure *a*).
- Jump to the right, landing on the right foot with the left leg bent and behind the right leg (see figure *b*).
- Immediately bound back to the left side and stick the landing on the left foot.

TEACHING CUES
- Take off quickly like a rubber ball bouncing off the ground.
- Land softly.

a

b

Repeat Split Squat Jump

PURPOSE

To develop lower-body power in a staggered stance, as well as proper landing mechanics.

PREREQUISITE

No lower-body pain or injury.

ADJUSTMENT

Adjust the straps of the Suspension Trainer to mid-length.

STARTING POSITION

Stand facing the anchor point. Grasp the handles with elbows bent and step back until there is no slack in the straps.

DESCRIPTION

- Stagger the feet front and back with the toes facing straight ahead. The front foot should be flat on the ground. The back heel should be up, and the weight should be on the ball of the foot (see figure *a*).
- Quickly perform a small countermovement by flexing the front knee until it reaches 90 degrees (see figure *b*).
- Immediately push through the front heel; extend the ankles, knees, and hips; and jump as high as possible (see figure *c*).
- Repeat for the desired number of repetitions; then switch legs and repeat.

TEACHING CUES

- Take off quickly like a rubber ball bouncing off the ground.
- Land softly.

a

b

c

Alternated Repeat Split Squat Jump

PURPOSE
To learn proper landing mechanics and improve lower-body coordination.

PREREQUISITE
No lower-body pain or injury.

ADJUSTMENT
Adjust the straps of the Suspension Trainer to mid-length.

STARTING POSITION
Stand facing the anchor point. Grasp the handles, extend the arms, and step back until there is no slack in the straps.

DESCRIPTION

- Stagger the feet front and back with the toes facing straight ahead. The front foot should be flat on the ground. The back heel should be up, and the weight should be on the ball of the foot.
- Quickly perform a small countermovement by flexing the front knee until it reaches 90 degrees (see figure *a*).
- Immediately push through the front heel; extend the ankles, knees, and hips; and jump as high as possible (see figure *b*).
- At the top of the jump, rapidly scissor the legs so that they switch places (see figure *c*).
- Without resting between jumps, repeat for the desired number of repetitions, switching legs with each jump.

TEACHING CUES

- Take off quickly like a rubber ball bouncing off the ground.
- Land softly.

a

b

c

CHAPTER 7

Core Exercises

Most of us have heard the parable about the builders that chose to build their house on sand rather than solid rock. Similarly, if we build fitness and performance on a poor foundation it decreases the opportunity for success and increases the risk of injury. Developing effective and efficient movement patterns is a complex process that requires the muscles to work in concert to produce, reduce, and stabilize forces. Quality movement is predicated on the ability to stabilize certain body segments and facilitate more efficient movements at others. Developing the muscles of the trunk, or core, stabilizes the spine against loading forces and creates a solid platform, or anchor point, for movement at the joints.

This chapter presents exercises for developing the trunk. Many can be used to establish a proper foundation of stability and mobility for the more advanced upper- and lower-body exercises in chapters 5 and 6.

Glute Bridge

PURPOSE

To develop hip and trunk stability, strength, and endurance.

PREREQUISITE

No pain while performing the movement.

ADJUSTMENT

Adjust the straps of the Suspension Trainer to mid-calf length.

STARTING POSITION

Lie face up and place the heels in the foot cradles. The hands are to the sides of the torso with the palms up (see figure *a*).

DESCRIPTION

- Begin with one heel in each stirrup. Bend the knees and the hips at a 90-degree angle and lift the hips off the ground (see figure *b*).
- Hold this position for 30 to 60 seconds.
- For an added challenge, slowly lower the hips until they are 1 inch (2.5 cm) from the ground; then, return to the starting position. Repeat for 10 to 12 repetitions and for the desired number of sets.

a

b

TEACHING CUES

- Squeeze the glutes.
- Brace the trunk as if readying for a punch to the abdomen.

Standing Plank

PURPOSE
To develop trunk stability and endurance.

PREREQUISITE
No pain while performing the movement.

ADJUSTMENT
Fully lengthen the straps of the Suspension Trainer.

STARTING POSITION
Face away from the anchor point, and grab a handle with each hand. Position the hands shoulder-width apart.

DESCRIPTION
- Set the body in a straight line. Brace the trunk, keep the arms straight, and slowly step back until there is tension on the straps and the body is at an incline.
- Simultaneously pull the shoulder blades down and together (see figure).
- While keeping the arms straight, attempt to hold this position for 30 to 60 seconds.

TEACHING CUES
- Put the edges of the scapulae in the back hip pockets.
- Stay straight as a board from the head through the heels.

Elbow Plank

PURPOSE
To develop trunk stability and endurance.

PREREQUISITE
No pain while performing the movement.

ADJUSTMENT
Adjust the straps of the Suspension Trainer to mid-calf length.

STARTING POSITION
Lie face down with the forearms on the ground and facing away from the anchor point. Place the feet in the stirrups.

DESCRIPTION
- In one continuous movement, lift the hips and torso until the elbows are directly under the shoulders and the upper arms are perpendicular to the ground (see figure).
- Attempt to hold this position for 30 to 60 seconds.

TEACHING CUES
- Put the edges of the scapulae in the back hip pocket.
- Stay straight as a board from the head through the heels.

Supine Plank

PURPOSE

To develop hip and trunk stability, strength, and endurance.

PREREQUISITE

No pain while performing the movement.

ADJUSTMENT

Adjust the straps of the Suspension Trainer to mid-calf length.

STARTING POSITION

Lie face up and place the heels in the stirrups. Place the hands to the sides of the torso with the palms up.

DESCRIPTION

- Extend the legs and lift the hips so that the trunk, legs, and shoulders are aligned (see figure).
- Hold this position for 30 to 60 seconds.
- For an added challenge, slowly lower the hips until they are 1 inch (2.5 cm) from the ground; then, return to the starting position. Repeat for 10 to 12 repetitions and for the desired number of sets.

TEACHING CUES

- Squeeze the glutes
- Brace the trunk as if readying for a punch to the abdomen.

Single-Leg Plank

PURPOSE

To develop hip and trunk stability, strength, and endurance.

PREREQUISITES

No pain while performing the movement, and the ability to stabilize the pelvis and resist hip rotation.

ADJUSTMENT

Adjust the straps of the Suspension Trainer to mid-calf length.

STARTING POSITION

Lie face up and place one heel into a stirrup. The hands are to the sides of the torso with the palms up

DESCRIPTION

- Extend both legs and lift the hips so that the trunk, legs, and shoulders are aligned (see figure). The free leg and hip should remain parallel to the working leg.
- Hold this position for 30 to 60 seconds.
- For an added challenge, slowly lower the hips until they are 1 inch (2.5 cm) from the ground; then, return to the starting position. Repeat for 10 to 12 repetitions and for the desired number of sets. Note: The number of sets and reps should be equalized between limbs. In other words, be sure to perform the same volume (sets × reps × time using each foot in the stirrup. Cluster sets may also be used to accomplish this (see chapter 8).

TEACHING CUES

- Squeeze the glutes.
- Brace the trunk as if readying for a punch to the abdomen.
- Do not allow the hips to rotate.

Extended-Arm Plank

PURPOSE

To develop trunk stability and endurance.

PREREQUISITES

No pain while performing the movement.

ADJUSTMENT

Adjust the straps of the Suspension Trainer to mid-calf length.

STARTING POSITION

Face away from the anchor point, and place the feet in the stirrups. Place the hands on the ground shoulder-width apart.

DESCRIPTION

- Set the body in a straight line, brace the trunk, and keep the arms straight (see figure).
- Simultaneously pull the shoulder blades down and together.
- Attempt to hold this position for 30 to 60 seconds.

TEACHING CUES

- Put the edges of the scapulae in the back hip pockets.
- Stay straight as a board from the head through the heels.

Sprinter Plank

PURPOSE

To develop hip and trunk stability and endurance.

PREREQUISITE

No pain while performing the movement.

ADJUSTMENT

Adjust the straps of the Suspension Trainer to mid-calf length.

STARTING POSITION

Face away from the anchor point, and place one foot in both stirrups. Place the hands on the ground shoulder-width apart.

DESCRIPTION

- Set the body in a straight line, brace the trunk, and keep the arms straight (see figure *a*).
- Simultaneously pull the shoulder blades down and together.
- While keeping the arms and torso straight, drive the free knee up toward the chest until the knee and hip are at 90-degree angles (see figure *b*). The ankle should remain flexed.
- Hold this position for 15 to 30 seconds; then repeat on the opposite side.

a

b

TEACHING CUES

- Put the edges of the scapulae in the back hip pockets.
- Stay straight as a board from the head through the heels.
- Keep the toe up, heel up, and knee up on the free leg.

Side Plank

PURPOSE
To develop trunk and hip stability and endurance.

PREREQUISITE
No pain while performing the movement.

ADJUSTMENT
Adjust the straps of the Suspension Trainer to mid-calf length.

STARTING POSITION
Face away from the anchor point, and place the feet in the stirrups.

DESCRIPTION

- Lie on the right side with the right forearm in contact with the ground, the elbow directly under the shoulder, and the right foot behind the left.
- Place the left hand on the left hip, and then lift the hips until the torso is parallel to the ground (see figure).
- Hold this position for the desired amount of time, and then repeat on the opposite side.
- For an added challenge to core stability, extend the top arm and reach toward the ceiling, or lower the hip until it is 6 inches (15 cm) from the ground; then, return to the starting position.

TEACHING CUES

- Put the edges of the scapulae in the back hip pockets.
- Stay straight as a board from the head through the heels.

Rotational Side Plank

PURPOSE
To develop trunk stability, mobility, and endurance.

PREREQUISITE
No pain while performing the movement.

ADJUSTMENT
Adjust the straps of the Suspension Trainer to mid-calf length.

STARTING POSITION
Face away from the anchor point, and place the feet in the stirrups.

DESCRIPTION

- Lie on the right side with the right forearm in contact with the ground, the elbow directly under the shoulder, and the right foot behind the left.
- Place the left hand on the left side of the thigh; then, lift the hips until the torso is parallel to the ground.
- Extend the top arm and reach toward the ceiling (see figure *a*).
- Rotate the torso and then reach the hand down and back behind the body (see figure *b*).
- Hold this position for the desired amount of time, and then repeat on the opposite side.

a

b

TEACHING CUES

- Put the edges of the scapulae in the back hip pockets.
- Stay straight as a board from the head through the heels.
- For more of a challenge, extend the bracing arm.

Palov Press

PURPOSE
To develop trunk and shoulder stability and endurance.

PREREQUISITES
No pain while performing the movement, and no preexisting shoulder injuries.

ADJUSTMENT
Adjust the straps of the Suspension Trainer to mid-length.

STARTING POSITION
Face to the side of the anchor point, and grasp the handles in both hands using a neutral grip.

DESCRIPTION
- Stagger the feet front and back. The foot farther from the anchor point should be the lead foot.
- While keeping the hands close to the chest, lean laterally so that the torso is at 30 to 45 degrees to the ground (see figure *a*).
- While keeping the torso rigid, press the hands away from the body and extend the arms (see figure *b*).
- Slowly bend the arms and return to the starting position.
- Perform for the desired number of repetitions, turn 180 degrees, and repeat.

TEACHING CUES
- Squeeze the glutes
- Brace the trunk as if readying for a punch to the abdomen.
- If unable to fully extend the arms, walk farther from the anchor point to reduce the amount of lean and lighten the resistance, or extend the arms as far as possible and progress over time until able to fully extend the arms (i.e., use a partial to whole range of motion).

a

b

Reverse Crunch

PURPOSE

To develop muscular endurance and stability of the trunk.

PREREQUISITE

No pain while performing the movement.

ADJUSTMENT

Adjust the straps of the Suspension Trainer to mid-calf length.

STARTING POSITION

Face away from the anchor point, and place the feet in the stirrups. Place the hands on the ground shoulder-width apart.

DESCRIPTION

- Set the body in a straight line, or plank position, brace the trunk, and keep the arms straight (see figure *a*).
- Pull the shoulder blades down and together while pulling both knees toward the chest (see figure *b*).
- Return to the starting position, and continue this movement for the desired number of repetitions.

a

b

TEACHING CUES

- Brace the core first; then drive the knees toward the chest.
- Control the movement. Perform at an even tempo (e.g., a count of 2 for the crunch and a count of 2 to return to the fully extended position).

Bicycle Crunch

PURPOSE
To develop muscular endurance and stability of the trunk.

PREREQUISITE
No pain while performing the movement.

ADJUSTMENT
Adjust the straps of the Suspension Trainer to mid-calf length.

STARTING POSITION
Face away from the anchor point, and place the feet in the stirrups. Place the hands on the ground shoulder-width apart.

DESCRIPTION

- Set the body in a straight line, or plank position, brace the trunk, and keep the arms straight (see figure *a*).
- Simultaneously pull the shoulder blades down and together and bring the right knee up toward the chest (see figure *b*).
- While the right leg returns to the starting position, bring the left leg toward the chest in the same manner.
- Continue this movement, alternating between right and left sides as if pedaling a bike.

a

b

TEACHING CUES

- Brace the core first; then drive the knee toward the chest.
- Control the movement. Perform at an even tempo (e.g., a count of 2 for the crunch and a count of 2 to return to the fully extended position).

Rotational Crunch

PURPOSE
To develop muscular endurance, mobility, and stability of the trunk.

PREREQUISITE
No pain while performing the movement.

ADJUSTMENT
Adjust the straps of the Suspension Trainer to mid-calf length.

STARTING POSITION
Face away from the anchor point, and place the feet in the stirrups. Place the hands on the ground shoulder-width apart.

DESCRIPTION
- Set the body in a straight line, or plank position, brace the trunk, and keep the arms straight (see figure *a*).
- Simultaneously pull the shoulder blades down and together and bring the right knee up toward the left shoulder (see figure *b*).
- While the right leg returns to the starting position, bring the left leg toward the right shoulder in the same manner; then, return to the starting position.
- Continue this movement, alternating between right and left sides as if pedaling a bike.

TEACHING CUES
- Brace the core before moving the lower body.
- Control the movement. Use an even tempo when lifting the knees and returning to the starting position.

a

b

Kneeling Rollout

PURPOSE
To develop muscular endurance, eccentric strength, and stability of the trunk.

PREREQUISITES
No pain while performing the movement, and the ability to perform a plank.

ADJUSTMENT
Fully lengthen the straps of the Suspension Trainer.

STARTING POSITION
Kneel facing the anchor point and back up until the straps are at a 45-degree angle. Grasp the handles with an overhand, shoulder-width grip.

DESCRIPTION

- Pull the toes back toward the shins (see figure *a*). While keeping the knees and toes fixed on the ground, arms taut, and torso stiff, lean forward as far as possible without touching the ground (see figure *b*).
- Return to the starting position by contracting the abdominal muscles, and then return along the same path to the starting position.
- Perform the desired number of repetitions.

TEACHING CUES

- Keep the back flat.
- Brace the trunk.
- Control the movement. Use an even tempo during the lowering phase and on the return to the starting position.

a

b

Standing Lateral Twist

PURPOSE
To develop muscular endurance, eccentric strength, mobility, and stability of the trunk.

PREREQUISITES
No pain while performing the movement, and the ability to perform a plank.

ADJUSTMENT
Fully lengthen the straps of the Suspension Trainer.

STARTING POSITION
Face sideways to the anchor point, and grasp the handles in both hands using a neutral grip. Stagger the stance so that one foot is closer to the anchor point.

DESCRIPTION

- While keeping the arms slightly bent, lean laterally until the torso is at a 30- to 45-degree angle to the ground (see figure *a*).
- While keeping the arms locked in the starting position and the torso rigid, rotate the shoulders toward the anchor point (see figure *b*).
- Perform the desired number of repetitions; then, repeat turning toward the right.

TEACHING CUES

- Brace the core.
- Pull the strap toward the midline of the body.

a

b

Standing Russian Twist

PURPOSE
To develop muscular endurance, eccentric strength, mobility, and stability of the trunk.

PREREQUISITES
No pain while performing the movement, and the ability to perform a plank.

ADJUSTMENT
Fully lengthen the straps of the Suspension trainer.

STARTING POSITION
Face the anchor point, and grasp the handles in both hands using a neutral grip.

DESCRIPTION

- While keeping the arms slightly bent, lean back until the torso is at a 45-degree angle to the ground (see figure *a*).
- Pull the shoulder blades together and downward while rotating the torso to the right. Keep the feet planted in the starting position (see figure *b*).
- Perform the desired number of repetitions; then, repeat turning toward the left.

TEACHING CUES

- Brace the core.
- Pull the straps toward the midline of the body.

a

b

Power Pull

PURPOSE
To develop muscular endurance, eccentric strength, mobility, and stability of the trunk.

PREREQUISITES
No pain while performing the movement, and the ability to perform a plank.

ADJUSTMENT
Adjust the straps of the Suspension Trainer to mid-length.

STARTING POSITION
Face the anchor point, grasp the handles with one hand using a neutral grip, and touch the handle with the palm of the free hand.

DESCRIPTION

- While keeping the arms straight, lean back until the torso is at a 45-degree angle to the ground.
- Rotate the torso toward the free-hand side, and reach back as far as possible (see figure *a*).
- Pull the strap to bring the working elbow into the rib cage while pivoting on the toes and reaching with the free arm toward the straps (see figure *b*).
- Once balanced, slowly return to the starting position.
- Perform the desired number of repetitions; then, repeat turning toward the right.

TEACHING CUES

- Reach for the ground; then reach for the ceiling.
- Keep the eyes on the lead hand.

a

b

Standing Oblique Crunch

PURPOSE

To develop muscular endurance, eccentric strength, mobility, and stability of the trunk.

PREREQUISITES

No pain while performing the movement, and the ability to perform a plank.

ADJUSTMENT

Fully shorten the straps of the Suspension Trainer.

STARTING POSITION

Face sideways to the anchor point and grasp the handles in both hands using a neutral grip.

DESCRIPTION

- Facing sideways (see figure *a*), keep the arms slightly bent and lean away from the anchor point by allowing the trunk to flex laterally toward the anchor point and the hips to shift in the opposite direction (see figure *b*).
- To return to the starting position, contract the obliques on the side furthest from the anchor point until the trunk is in a neutral position.

TEACHING CUES

- On the descent, drop the hips toward the ground.
- On the ascent, push the hips toward the anchor point and the hands toward the ground.

a

b

Extended-Arm Side Plank

PURPOSE

To develop hip, trunk, and shoulder stability and endurance.

PREREQUISITES

No pain while performing the movement, and no preexisting shoulder injuries.

ADJUSTMENT

Adjust the straps of the Suspension Trainer to mid-calf length.

STARTING POSITION

Face away from the anchor point, and place the feet in the stirrups.

DESCRIPTION

- Perform a side plank with the arm fully extended (see figure).
- Hold this position for the desired amount of time, and then repeat on the opposite side.

TEACHING CUES

- Place the scapulae in the back hip pockets.
- Stay straight as a board from the head through the heels.
- For more of a challenge, lower the hip until it is 6 inches (15 cm) from the ground; then, return to the side plank position.

Crab Plank

PURPOSE

To develop trunk and shoulder stability, mobility, and endurance.

PREREQUISITES

No pain while performing the movement, and no preexisting shoulder injuries.

ADJUSTMENT

Adjust the straps of the Suspension Trainer to mid-calf length.

STARTING POSITION

From a seated position, place the heels in the stirrups with the arms extended to the sides and the hands in contact with the ground.

DESCRIPTION

- Walk the hands back until the shoulders are in a hyperextended position (see figure *a*).
- Extend the legs and lift the hips so that the trunk, legs, and shoulders are aligned (see figure *b*).
- Hold this position for 30 to 60 seconds.
- For an added challenge, slowly lower the hips until they are 1 inch (2.5 cm) from the ground; then, return to the starting position. Perform 10 to 12 repetitions for the desired number of sets.

a

b

TEACHING CUES

- Squeeze the glutes.
- Brace the trunk as if readying for a punch to the abdomen.

Pike

PURPOSE

To develop muscular endurance, mobility, and stability of the trunk, as well as improve hamstring flexibility.

PREREQUISITES

No pain while performing the movement, good hip mobility, and the ability to perform a plank.

ADJUSTMENT

Adjust the straps of the Suspension Trainer to mid-calf length.

STARTING POSITION

Face away from the anchor point, and place the feet in the stirrups. Place the hands on the ground shoulder-width apart.

DESCRIPTION

- Set the body in a straight line, or plank position, brace the trunk, and keep the arms straight (see figure *a*).
- Simultaneously pull the shoulder blades down and together while flexing the hips and pushing the buttocks up. Keep the legs completely straight while bringing the feet toward the chest (see figure *b*).
- At the end of the movement, the shoulders and back should be as close to perpendicular to the ground as possible.
- Return to the starting position, and repeat for the desired number of repetitions.

a

b

TEACHING CUES

- Brace the core before moving the lower body.
- Control the movement. Use an even tempo when lifting the knees and returning to the starting position.
- Place the head between the upper arms, and push the buttocks to the ceiling.

Standing Rollout

PURPOSE
To develop muscular endurance, eccentric strength, and stability of the trunk.

PREREQUISITES
No pain while performing the movement, and the ability to perform a plank.

ADJUSTMENT
Fully lengthen the straps of the Suspension Trainer.

STARTING POSITION
Face the anchor point, and grab a handle in each hand.

DESCRIPTION

- Set the body in a straight line, or plank position, brace the trunk, and keep the arms straight out in front at shoulder height (see figure *a*).
- While keeping the arms completely straight, lean the torso forward and flex the shoulder so that the arms are extended overhead (see figure *b*).
- Contract the abs and the lats to return to the starting position.

TEACHING CUES

- Keep the back flat.
- Brace the trunk.
- Control the movement. Use an even tempo during the lowering phase and on the return to the starting position.

a

b

Suspension Training Programs

Part III shows how to use the exercises and apply the science covered in parts I and II to develop Suspension Training programs. The sample programs can be used as stand-alone modalities or as part of comprehensive strength and conditioning programs that include other forms of resistance training (e.g., barbells, dumbbells, resistance training machines).

CHAPTER 8

Foundations of Program Design

Dumping a bunch of random ingredients into a bowl would be highly unlikely to result in a gourmet meal. Training, too, requires a systematic rather than random approach to maximize results. Excellence does not occur by chance; it requires planning, focused effort, and consistency. This chapter presents the foundations of a comprehensive fitness program as well as principles to guide decision making when developing a training plan.

Principles of Training and Conditioning

Regardless of the training goal, six key principles should be followed when developing a training program. Progressive overload, load variation, specificity, individuality, diminishing returns, and reversibility must all be addressed to maximize progress and ensure long-term improvements.

Progressive Overload

Stress is often perceived as a negative experience or state. However, when presented with the right types of stress in the proper amounts, the body can transform in miraculous ways. The principle of progressive overload states that applying a stressor beyond what the body is accustomed to, in a systematic and progressive way, results in an adaptation to the new demands. Too much stress, or stress applied too frequently, may increase injury risk or cause maladaptation. Too little stress, or stress applied too infrequently, will result in no progress or adaptations. For this reason, some consider the stress induced via exercise to be like medicine: we need the right dose in the right amount to get the best results.

Load Variation

Progressive overload is paramount to success, but the load applied to the body should not progress in a strictly linear way. People can't lift or train hard all the time. Without some variation in the training cycle, the body cannot realize fitness gains because of the accumulation of fatigue. To realize fitness gains, the body must be allowed to recover. This is one reason for using a periodized strength and conditioning program, which provides small fluctuations in intensity and volume in the short term. In a periodized program, short-term variations occur, but the overall trend is toward increasing fitness.

Numerous forms of periodization can be used to improve health, fitness, and performance. The design selected is based on a variety of factor such as goals, time constraints, and equipment availability. Several forms of periodization, with examples, are presented in the sidebar, Basics of Periodization.

Specificity

In the most simplistic terms, the specificity principle states that you get what you train for. This relates to improving the quality of specific muscles (e.g., quadriceps, biceps), overall muscle qualities (e.g., endurance, strength, power), movements (e.g., pushing, pulling, squatting), muscle actions (i.e., concentric, eccentric, isometric), and conditioning (i.e., anaerobic or aerobic). Receiving the greatest benefit from a training program requires setting goals and then determining which variables to consider to reach those goals.

One critical aspect of specificity that is often overlooked is that some exercises look nothing like the movements they improve. For example, lying face up and performing a hip bridge may look nothing like high-speed running. However, this exercise is excellent for strengthening the glutes and the muscles surrounding the hips, which may contribute to greater stability on the stance leg during gait, a reduced risk of injury from biomechanical inefficiencies, and better force production at ground contact. Because this exercise isolates muscles that may contribute to improved performance, it is deemed functional for improving running speed. Specificity does not mean mimicry. Some exercises develop the parts that contribute to improving the whole.

Individuality

Although for the most part we are fairly similar physiologically, we respond to training programs differently based on our fitness levels, genetics, and anthropometrics (e.g., body size, limb and torso length). A beginner who takes part in a training program designed for an elite athlete may very well overtrain. Similarly, an advanced athlete in a beginner's program would likely detrain and experience reductions in performance.

Tall people may experience less increases in muscle size than shorter people because longer limbs, or levers, tend to favor speed, whereas shorter levers tend to favor strength. Additionally, when performing a push-up, someone with longer arms has to do more mechanical work than someone with shorter arms because of the need to cover a greater distance to perform the same task. The shorter person may appear to increase muscle size to a greater extent, whereas the taller person may accrue just as much lean mass, but it may look less bulky because of the length of the muscle. Although a training program may affect some factors, some are genetic and cannot be altered.

Basics of Periodization

Periodization can be a very confusing topic. To simplify it, I define it as planning change over time to maximize results. Essentially, periodization is a systematic approach to altering the training variables to ensure continued progress and to minimize overtraining injuries. Of the numerous variations of periodization, I focus on the two major types: linear and nonlinear.

Linear Periodization

Linear periodization, also referred to as classic periodization, uses training blocks that enhance specific physical attributes. Each phase supports the subsequent phase. These phases consist of the following cycles:

- *Macrocycle*—A macrocycle is the big picture. Typically, it consists of a full year of training. However, it may also be a four-year cycle for athletes such as Olympians who are looking to peak for Olympic trials or competitions. A macrocycle is made up of a series of mesocycles.
- *Mesocycle*—A mesocycle is a block of training that generally lasts between six and eight weeks. A mesocycle consists of a series of microcycles.
- *Microcycle*—A microcycle is typically a one- to two-week block of training. At the beginning of a linear periodization program, the emphasis is generally on improving movement proficiency, improving muscular endurance, and increasing muscle size. During this phase, strength also improves, although this is not the main focus. At this stage, Suspension Training can be used extensively to improve muscular endurance, improve movement quality, and facilitate rehabilitation. Most beginners experience rapid changes in coordination and strength as a result of a variety of neurological influences (e.g., greater rate coding and synchronization).

After about 6 to 12 weeks of training, the focus starts to shift from increasing general muscular fitness to increasing muscular size and strength. Increasing size increases force-generating capacity by increasing muscle cross-sectional area. In addition, neurological changes occur as a result of lifting heavier loads, allowing for greater loads to be lifted than before. Suspension Training plays a critical role in this phase. Suspension Training exercises can increase the overall density of a training session (i.e., more work in less time), unload muscles and muscle groups to enhance recovery while minimizing losses, and to help reduce and minimize potential injury.

The last phase of a linear periodization cycle tends to focus on maximizing strength and power. During this phase, Suspension Training is very useful during the dynamic warm-up to wake up stabilizer muscles while taking the emphasis off the prime movers. During this stage, Suspension Training can be a very effective method of periodically unloading and reducing fatigue that has been accrued via heavy or very intense training. This may also help reduce the stress on the body to minimize the risk of injury and overtraining.

Nonlinear Periodization

Nonlinear periodization follows a similar pattern to linear periodization, although the training is altered more quickly (i.e., addressing muscular endurance, fitness, strength, and power within a week). For example, a Monday session may focus on muscular endurance; Wednesday, on muscular power; and Friday, on muscle size or strength (or both). Nonlinear periodization tends to work well for those with more experience and a good training foundation. It also works well for those who may not need to peak for a particular competition or event, but rather want to maintain a level of fitness in all muscle qualities year round, such as fitness enthusiasts or tactical athletes (e.g., soldiers, firefighters, law enforcement officers).

Diminishing Returns

Someone new to exercise can generally take part in any training program for six to eight weeks and see significant improvements. However, as the body adapts, new and different stimuli must be applied to keep making progress. As fitness increases, we near our genetic potential, and the gains we experience become more marginal, or slow down. Suspension Training is a fantastic tool for improving muscular strength during the early stages of a training program. However, at a certain point, straps and body positions must be manipulated to increase the load and to keep getting stronger. Eventually, Suspension Training may not be the primary tool used to continue improving strength; rather, it may be used to maintain strength, improve endurance, or prevent injury in addition to a more traditional weight training program that allows heavier loads to be utilized.

Reversibility

The reversibility principle is related to the amount, frequency, and consistency of the stress applied to the body. This principle is summed up in the phrase *Use it or lose it.* Stopping training, or significantly reducing the training load, volume, or frequency long enough will result in regression, potentially to pretraining levels. One benefit of Suspension Training is its portability and convenience at times when keeping up normal training schedules is difficult. Maintaining stress on the body during these times can prevent, or at least slow, the detraining process. For example, soldiers on deployment frequently use Suspension Training to maintain fitness when they do not have access to regular training facilities or traditional weight training equipment such as barbells and dumbbells. Additionally, Suspension Training is great for frequent travelers since the equipment takes up minimal space and can be thrown into a bag or suitcase. This helps travelers reduce the number of training days missed while on the road.

Variables of Training Program Design

When designing a training program, the frequency, intensity, volume, and speed of training must be considered. Equally important are the rest periods between sets in each session as well as between training days.

Frequency

Frequency of training refers to the number of training sessions performed, usually in the context of a week. The frequency of training is predicated on factors such as the initial training level, the time available, and training goals. For example, two or three training sessions per week would likely suffice if the goal is to improve general fitness. To maintain fitness, one session may suffice, although two (at least) are generally recommended. To reach more robust goals, such as significantly increasing muscle mass, anywhere from three to six days per week may be ideal.

Intensity

Intensity, which refers to the training load (i.e., the amount of weight lifted), may be the factor most critical to the outcome of a training program. In general, loads that permit 12 or more repetitions are suited to improving muscular endurance. Loads that permit between 8 and 12 repetitions are suited to improving muscle size or general fitness (depending on the volume, or sets × reps). Finally, a training load that permits 6 or fewer repetitions is best for improving strength. This does not mean that training in a range more suited to improving endurance will not enhance strength, or vice versa; it just would not optimize gains in the targeted area. This is a critical consideration for Suspension Training, especially for already well-trained individuals, and will be further addressed in chapter 11.

Volume

Volume of training can be defined as the number of sets multiplied by the number of repetitions (sets \x\ reps) performed, or as the load multiplied by the number of sets and repetitions. When using traditional equipment such as barbells and dumbbells, volume is typically calculated using the latter equation. However, those using body weight as resistance (i.e., Suspension Training) generally multiply sets by repetitions because the load moved is often difficult to quantify and varies based on body position. Furthermore, when performing isometric work, such as a plank, sets multiplied by time may be used to quantify volume. For many of the exercises that require one foot in a strap, the overall volume can be equalized by making certain that each limb receives the same amount of stress or time under tension. This can be achieved by performing what is commonly known as a cluster set with the weaker limb. To complete a cluster set, perform as many repetitions as possible, take a brief 10- to 15-second rest, and then complete the set. For instance, suppose you can perform 60 seconds of work on the stronger limb and only 50 seconds of work on the weaker limb. When working on the weaker limb, simply take a break at 50 seconds. Then, perform 10 more seconds of work on the weak limb when you can. The cluster set technique helps you to maintain overall training volume and to use good form throughout the set. This is very important for maintaining body symmetry.

Speed

Speed of movement is an often-overlooked variable in resistance training programs. However, it is critical when seeking to develop specific attributes. For example, power is the optimal combination of force and velocity to achieve a specific task; every exercise has its own unique power profile. Therefore, the speed of movement during a rep will either increase or decrease the amount of power produced. Because resistance training exercise is mostly used to improve performance, which is specifically related to power production, speed of movement should be considered in every exercise.

In general, the speed of movement is directly related to and dependent on the load being moved. Maximal loads cannot be moved quickly because creating the appropriate amount of force takes time. Therefore, maximal exercises do not directly improve power. However, this is not to say that maximal lifting does not improve power. Improving overall strength results in being able to move a given load faster because a smaller percentage of maximal strength is required at a submaximal load. For these reasons, using a variety of training loads at different speeds is ideal for improving performance.

Rest

Rest refers to the amount of time between sets and between training sessions. The amount of rest has a significant impact on the quality of the workout and the outcome. To improve muscular endurance, rest periods of 30 to 60 seconds between sets for the same muscles or muscle groups are generally recommended. However, alternating opposing muscle groups (e.g., chest and back) or movements (e.g., push and pull) in the training session creates sufficient rest between muscle groups. This is very beneficial for those with time constraints. To improve muscular fitness or muscle size, rest periods between 30 and 90 seconds are adequate. For strength and power, greater rest periods (three to five minutes) are required to fully replenish energy stores and ensure sufficient effort in subsequent repetitions.

The rest required between training sessions should also be considered. For sufficient recovery, a minimum of 48 hours (and up to 72 hours) should be allowed before muscle groups are trained again. Following a Monday session aimed at training the lower body, the next lower-body training session should be on Wednesday or Thursday to give these muscles time to recover. Table 8.1 provides basic recommendations for each training variable to use when creating plans based on specific training goals.

Training should not be a random process; basic principles of training and conditioning should be followed to maximize results. A periodized program can ensure safe and effective progress and continuing challenge with new stimuli to help with working through training plateaus.

Chapters 9 to 13 describe how to use Suspension Training in the context of periodized training, and provide sample training programs for improving specific aspects of health, fitness, and performance. In these chapters, a detailed explanation of how to integrate Suspension Training into a comprehensive program using a variety of training tools and modalities is also addressed.

TABLE 8.1 Basic Training Guidelines

	Frequency	Intensity	Volume	Speed	Rest between sets
Muscular endurance	2 or 3 days per week	60% of 1RM	1 or 2 exercises per muscle group or movement; 2 or 3 sets for each muscle group or movement; 10-20 reps of each exercise	Variable	30-60 sec between muscle groups
Muscular fitness	3 or 4 days per week	60-75% of 1RM	1 or 2 exercises per muscle group or movement; 3-6 sets for each muscle group or movement; 10-12 reps of each exercise	Moderate	30-90 sec between muscle groups
Muscle size	3-6 days per week	60-75% of 1RM	2 or 3 exercises or muscle group or movement; 3-6 sets for each muscle group or movement; 6-20 reps of each exercise	Slow to moderate	60-90 sec between muscle groups
Muscular strength	3-6 days per week	Basic strength: 80-90% of 1RM Max strength: 93% of 1RM Maintenance: 80-85% of 1RM	1-3 exercises or muscle group or movement Basic strength: 4-8 reps Max strength: 2-6 reps Maintenance: 6-8 reps	Slow	2-5 min between muscle groups
Muscular power	2 or 3 days per week	87-95% of 1RM for a single rep 75-90% for multiple reps Variable when using own body weight	1RM for max efforts 6 for multiple reps 6-10 reps for body weight–based power exercises	Fast	2-5 min between muscle groups

Reprinted, by permission, from D. Wathen, T.R. Baechle, and R.W. Earle, 2008, Periodization. In *Essentials of strength training and conditioning*, 3rd ed., by the National Strength and Conditioning Association, edited by T.R. Baechle and R.W. Earle (Champaign, IL: Human Kinetics), 511.

CHAPTER 9

Total-Body Conditioning

Both muscular and cardiorespiratory conditioning are essential for health, fitness, and performance. Consequently, engaging in total-body conditioning can have a profound impact on overall quality of life. Activities such as walking, running, cycling, and swimming combined with resistance training, such as Suspension Training, develop the body as well as the mind and spirit. This chapter addresses the importance of including total-body conditioning in a training program to achieve long-term success and prevent injuries. Conditioning the entire body requires addressing many factors, such as muscular and cardiorespiratory health and fitness. However, for the purpose of this discussion, I define total-body conditioning as a method of developing overall muscular fitness using Suspension Training.

What Is Total-Body Conditioning?

Developing muscular fitness can be defined as improving several muscle qualities simultaneously—strength, endurance, power, and size. However, based on the intensities and volumes (sets x reps) used, total-body training tends to favor the development of muscular endurance and toning (slight increases in muscle size and reductions in body fat). Depending on the type of program, total-body conditioning is best used for developing general physical preparedness (GPP), maintaining health and fitness, preventing injury, and avoiding overtraining. These goals are addressed in the following sections.

Developing General Physical Preparedness (GPP)

When beginning a fitness program, a good base of overall fitness is important to set the stage for intense training and reduce the risk of injury. The exercises used at the beginning should be basic and aimed at improving fundamental movement mechanics before moving on to heavier, more advanced lifts. Body weight exercises that can be augmented with Suspension Training are ideal at this stage.

Advanced fitness enthusiasts and athletes often begin each macrocycle with a GPP phase. This helps transition into activity after an active rest period (e.g., following a sport season or a yearly training cycle). During this phase, the emphasis is on increasing training volume and accumulating more physical stress to improve general fitness and setting the stage for higher-load, lower-volume training focused on strength and power (see chapter 11).

Maintaining Health and Fitness

Because total-body conditioning improves general muscular fitness, it also helps not only to develop but also to maintain a general level of health and fitness. Although not maximized, strength and power can be improved using a total-body conditioning program while maintaining a good level of muscular endurance and improving muscle size. Improving cardiorespiratory fitness with total-body circuit training can result in both physical and mental health improvements.

Preventing Injury and Avoiding Overtraining

As mentioned, total-body conditioning programs typically involve exercises that can be performed relatively easily with one's own body weight or light external loading. Suspension Training is excellent for making subtle and progressive resistance changes during the initial stages of learning, and for improving the efficiency of certain movement patterns prior to increasing resistance for that movement (e.g., learning how to perform a body weight squat prior to performing a barbell back squat).

Also, total-body conditioning using Suspension Training is an ideal way to unload the stress on the body from several weeks of increasing intensities during a periodized training program. Reducing this stress allows physiological adaptations to take place.

Incorporating Suspension Training Into a Total-Body Conditioning Program

Suspension Training can be used as a stand-alone training modality or as part of a more traditional training program that uses barbells, dumbbells, and machines to improve muscular fitness. In either case, it is a fun and unique method that can make training feel less monotonous, thus increasing motivation and enthusiasm for training sessions or workouts.

Using Suspension Training along with an existing program provides variety to muscles. Although the resistance and load for some exercises seem low compared to traditional resistance or weight training, they can be enough to develop muscle strength. For this reason, it is important to be aware of the contribution of Suspension Training to the overall training volume to avoid overtraining.

Suspension Training is also a great way to warm up the muscles and tendons prior to heavier resistance training. This prepares the muscles surrounding the joints and the core for the increased tension that comes with heavy lifting while also increasing proprioceptor activity at the joints. Performing a Suspension Training exercise as a warm-up to a similar exercise may result in greater force production during the heavier lift.

The use of Suspension Training with an existing training program provides diversity and a greater number of exercises to select from and incorporate into a training program. The challenges that Suspension Training provides also help avoid the plateaus encountered in most traditional programs.

Sample Total-Body Conditioning Programs

The following are sample total-body training circuits. They can be used as stand-alone workouts or as finishers for those at higher fitness levels.

Suspension-Only Total-Body Conditioning Program

INSTRUCTIONS

Perform 8 to 12 repetitions for each of the following exercise. Each exercise should be performed in sequential order before returning to the first exercise. Repeat each exercise as many times as possible for 10 minutes; then, rest for 3 minutes. Perform 1 to 3 rounds.

EXERCISES

1. Chest press (pg. 37)
2. Inverted row (pg. 63)
3. Reverse lunge with knee drive, right (pg. 90)
4. Reverse lunge with knee drive, left (pg. 90)
5. I, Y, T (pg. 72)
6. Triangle squat (pg. 103)

Suspension and Body Weight Total-Body Conditioning Program

INSTRUCTIONS

Perform 8 to 12 repetitions for each of the following exercises. Each exercise should be performed in sequential order before returning to the first exercise. Repeat each exercise as many times as possible for 10 minutes; then, rest for 3 minutes. Perform 1 to 3 rounds.

EXERCISES

1. Deep squat (pg. 91)
2. Squat jump (pg. 115)
3. Chest fly (pg. 45)
4. Lateral squat (pg. 95)
5. Low row (pg. 70)
6. Reverse lunge (pg. 107)

Suspension and Dumbbell or Kettlebell Total-Body Conditioning Program

INSTRUCTIONS

Select a weight you can lift for 20 reps when performing the dumbbell or kettlebell exercises. Perform 6 reps of each exercise for three rounds. Then, rest for 3 minutes.

EXERCISES

1. Romanian deadlift (dumbbell or kettlebell)
2. Pike (pg. 158)
3. Low row (pg. 70)
4. High pull (dumbbell or kettlebell)
5. Bicycle crunch (pg. 149)
6. Overhead press (dumbbell or kettlebell)

Suspension Warrior Total-Body Conditioning Program

This circuit uses a combination of supersets and compound sets to improve muscular fitness and endurance. The amount of work completed is determined by fitness level and the ability to maintain good form and technique throughout the circuit. If unable to maintain good technique and form, slow down or take brief bouts of rest between repetitions or exercises to keep moving for the allotted time.

INSTRUCTIONS

Perform 2 rounds with a 3 to 5-minute rest between them, for a total of 15 minutes. This circuit may be repeated 2 to 3 times in a single training session.

EXERCISES

1. Chest press (pg. 37): 30 seconds
2. Inverted row (pg. 63): 30 seconds
3. Lateral squat, right (pg. 95): 30 seconds
4. Lateral squat, left (pg. 95): 30 seconds
5. Chest fly (pg. 45): 30 seconds
6. Overhead squat (pg. 94): 30 seconds, alternating left and right
7. Rear deltoid row (pg. 64): 30 seconds
8. Lying leg curl (pg. 102): 30 seconds
9. Biceps curl (pg. 65): 30 seconds
10. Standing overhead triceps extension (pg. 38): 30 seconds
11. Standing lateral twist (pg. 152): 30 seconds
12. Suspended reverse lunge, right (pg. 101): 30 seconds
13. Suspended reverse lunge, left (pg. 101): 30 seconds
14. Rotational side plank, right (pg. 146): 30 seconds
15. Rotational side plank, left (pg. 146): 30 seconds
16. Bicycle crunch (pg. 149): 60 seconds

General Total-Body Conditioning Program

This general physical preparedness program was designed for athletes, but it can also be used for those looking to develop general fitness. This program shows how Suspension Training can be used with a more traditional training program to develop a base of fitness for more intense training in subsequent stages (see figure 9.1).

FIGURE 9.1 General Total-Body Conditioning Program

		Week			
Day 1	**Page**	**1**	**2**	**3**	**4**
1a. Back squat		3 x 10	3 x 10	3 x 8	2 x 8
1b. Single-arm dumbbell row (supported)		3 x 10	3 x 10	3 x 8	2 x 8
2a. Dumbbell incline bench press		3 x 10	3 x 10	3 x 8	2 x 8
2b. Dumbbell Romanian deadlift		3 x 10	3 x 10	3 x 8	2 x 8
2c. Sprinter plank	Pg. 144	3 x 10	3 x 10	3 x 12	2 x 10
3a. 90-degree low row		3 x 10	3 x 10	3 x 12	2 x 10
3b. Side plank	Pg. 145	2 x 20 sec	2 x 25 sec	2 x 30 sec	2 x 20 sec
3c. Lying leg curl	Pg. 102	3 x 10	3 x 10	3 x 12	2 x 10
		Week			
Day 2	**Page**	**1**	**2**	**3**	**4**
1a. Clean pull		3 x 6	3 x 6	3 x 6	2 x 6
1b. Push-up plus	Pg. 40	3 x 10	3 x 10	3 x 10	2 x 10
2a. Push press		3 x 6	3 x 6	3 x 6	2 x 6
2b. Deep squat	Pg. 91	3 x 6	3 x 6	3 x 6	2 x 6
3a. Reverse lunge	Pg. 107	3 x 8	3 x 8	3 x 8	2 x 8
3b. Single-leg reaching Romanian deadlift	Pg. 89	3 x 8	3 x 8	3 x 8	2 x 8

Core Strengthening Program

INSTRUCTIONS

Perform exercises 3 days per week for 6 weeks. Perform each exercise for 3 sets of 12 to 15 reps unless otherwise indicated. Rest 90 seconds between sets.

EXERCISES

Day 1

1. Deep squat (pg. 91)
2. Bicycle crunch (pg. 149)
3. Power pull (pg. 154)
4. Pike (pg. 158)
5. Extended-arm plank (pg. 143): 30 seconds

Day 2

1. Overhead squat (pg. 94)
2. I, Y, T (pg. 72)
3. Rotational crunch (pg. 150)
4. Rotational side plank (pg. 146)
5. Glute bridge (pg. 138)
6. Suspended push-up (pg. 43)

Day 3

1. Suspended reverse lunge (pg. 101)
2. Inverted row (pg. 63)
3. Push-up with reverse crunch (pg. 44)
4. Pike (pg. 158)

Trunk-Strengthening Program

INSTRUCTIONS

Perform each of the following routines on non-consecutive days for 6 weeks. Perform 10 to 15 repetitions of each exercise in sequential order without resting, or for the prescribed amount of time listed. Once you have performed each exercise, rest 90 to 120 seconds, then repeat.

EXERCISES

Day 1

1. Single-leg chest fly (pg. 55)
2. Standing Russian twist (pg. 153): 10 to 15 in each direction
3. Bicycle crunch (pg. 149)
4. Pike (pg. 158)
5. Elbow plank (pg. 140): 30 to 90 seconds

Day 2

1. Push-up with reverse crunch (pg. 44)
2. Extended arm plank 30 to 90 seconds (pg. 143)
3. Rotational side plank (pg. 146): 10 to 15 each side
4. Supine plank (pg. 141): 30 to 90 seconds
5. Single-leg lying leg curl (pg. 129): 10 to 15 each side

Day 3

1. Kneeling or standing rollout (pg. 151 or pg. 159)
2. Power pull (pg. 154): 10 to 15 reps each side
3. Pavlov press (pg. 147): 10 to 15 reps each side
4. Sprinter chest press (pg. 42): 10 to 15 reps each leg
5. Standing lateral twist (pg.152): 10 to 15 reps each side

CHAPTER 10

Prehabilitation

Prehabilitation is a proactive approach to avoiding injury. Athletes and physically active people should include some form of prehabilitation into their programs. Muscle imbalances and repetitive motion often lead to injury, and incorporating a few prehabilitation exercises into an existing program greatly reduces the risk. This chapter addresses some of the areas of the body most susceptible to injury, and thus most benefited by a proactive approach.

What Is Prehabilitation?

Prehabilitation is the process of using exercises to strengthen vulnerable areas of the body to avoid injury. Most trainers and therapists working with physically active people and athletes are aware of the value of prehabilitation, sometimes targeting areas that have been injured in the past.

A prehabilitation exercise program is most often used to address muscle imbalances that typically lead to future injury. It should not replace a rehabilitation program, which addresses an injury and should be directed by a rehabilitation expert such as a physical therapist or athletic trainer. Prehabilitation addresses commonly injured areas before they become injured.

Sample Suspension Training Prehabilitation Programs

This section outlines prehabilitation programs for specific joints and body regions. They should be used as part of more comprehensive training programs and not necessarily as stand-alone programs. These programs may benefit those engaged in sports and recreational activities with known injury risks. For instance, overhead throwing sports such as baseball, softball, and volleyball carry an increased risk of shoulder injury. It is well known that strengthening the rotator cuff muscles can reduce this risk. Similarly, in athletes involved in swinging sports such as tennis and golf, strengthening the muscles that surround the elbow joint may reduce the risk of strains in this area. Although no prehabilitation program can guarantee that an injury will not occur, being proactive may reduce the risk and provide more time enjoying recreation and sports and less time on the sidelines.

Checking with a health care provider before attempting any of these exercises is important. Those with existing or previous injuries should consult a physical therapist or physician to learn of any contraindications or necessary modifications. Anyone who experiences pain during any of these exercises should seek the advice of a medical professional.

Shoulder Prehabilitation Program

Shoulder prehabilitation is useful for avoiding common overuse conditions such as tendinitis. The rotator cuff is especially vulnerable during activities that involve throwing or overhead lifting. Strong rotator cuff muscles as well as the other muscles around the shoulder are key to avoiding muscle injury in the shoulder.

INSTRUCTIONS

Perform 2 or 3 sets of 8 to 12 repetitions. Perform 2 or 3 days per week on non-consecutive days.

EXERCISES

1. Scapular retraction (pg. 62)
2. Push-up plus (pg. 40) (may be substituted with standing push-up plus)
3. Rear deltoid row (pg. 64)
4. Dual-arm external rotation (pg. 67)
5. Dual-arm internal rotation (pg. 76)
6. I, Y, T (pg. 72)

Elbow Prehabilitation Program

Elbow prehabilitation targets the structures surrounding the elbow joint. As with the shoulder, overuse is a major cause of elbow tendinitis. Elbow tendinitis is commonly referred to as golfer's elbow when it involves the medial aspect of the elbow and tennis elbow when it involves the lateral aspect of the elbow.

Elbow issues are often a result of overuse symptoms caused by poor technique. Strong extensor muscles in the forearm, as well as in the biceps and triceps, are key to avoiding elbow injury. Exercises that increase the time the muscle is under tension can be beneficial. Exercises must be performed with good technique and form so as not to contribute to elbow pain.

INSTRUCTIONS

Perform 2 or 3 sets of 8 to 12 repetitions. Perform 2 or 3 days per week on non-consecutive days.

EXERCISES

1. Biceps curl (pg. 65)
2. Kneeling overhead triceps extension (pg. 47)
3. Standing skull crusher (pg. 61)
4. Reverse biceps curl (pg. 75)
5. Wrist flexion (pg. 66)
6. Wrist extension (pg. 66)

Knee Prehabilitation Program

Knee prehabilitation is useful for addressing common overuse conditions such as patellar tendinitis, quadriceps tendinitis, and hamstring tendinitis. Having strong quadriceps is key in avoiding knee pain, as is flexibility in both knees and hips. Strong hamstrings are also necessary, but more important is maintaining a good hamstring-to-quadriceps strength ratio.

INSTRUCTIONS

Perform 2 or 3 sets of 8 to 12 repetitions. Perform 2 or 3 days per week on non-consecutive days.

EXERCISES

1. Deep squat (pg. 91)
2. Pistol squat (pg. 119)
3. Lying leg curl (pg. 102)
4. Bicycle crunch (pg. 149)
5. Glute bridge (pg. 138)

Low Back Prehabilitation Program

Low back prehabilitation is important in most physical activities. The causes of low back pain are many and varied; regardless of the cause, strengthening the muscles around the spine is often effective. Equally important is strengthening the muscles of the trunk such as the abdominals, as well as strengthening and improving movement patterns.

INSTRUCTIONS

Perform 2 or 3 sets of 8 to 12 repetitions. Perform 2 or 3 days per week on non-consecutive days.

EXERCISES

1. Elbow plank (pg. 140)
2. Reverse crunch (pg. 148)
3. Pike (pg. 158)
4. Rotational side plank (pg. 146)
5. Palov press (pg. 147)
6. Figure-four stretch (pg. 105)
7. Reaching hip flexor stretch (pg. 106)

Hip and Ankle Prehabilitation Program

The major areas of mobility restriction in the lower body are the hips and ankles. Limited dorsiflexion and hip mobility may lead to compensatory movement patterns in the lower extremities that may cause injury and poor biomechanical technique during activities of daily living and sports.

INSTRUCTIONS

Perform 2 or 3 sets of 8 to 12 repetitions. Perform 2 or 3 days per week on non-consecutive days.

EXERCISES

1. Excursions (pg. 88)
2. Deep squat (pg. 91)
3. Triangle squat (pg. 103)
4. Pigeon stretch (pg. 104)
5. Single-leg reaching Romanian deadlift (pg. 89)
6. Lateral lunge (pg. 97)
7. Reverse lunge with knee drive (pg. 90)
8. Leg sweep (pg. 99)

CHAPTER 11

Strength and Power

Strength and power are two highly desirable attributes for athletes. In the sport world, the value of being able to exert high levels of force quickly is evident; however, this ability is also important for improving and maintaining quality of life throughout the life span. Possessing adequate strength and power improves not only the performance of recreational activities and activities of daily living, but also the ability to respond in emergency situations, all while reducing the risk of certain types of injury.

This chapter discusses how to improve strength and power through a combination of traditional training and Suspension Training. Using Suspension Training in combination with traditional training (e.g., velocity-based training) can improve structural integrity in the joints during high-velocity exercises.

What Are Strength and Power?

Strength and power, two muscle qualities essential to high-level performance and activities of daily living, are often lumped together. Although they are strongly linked, they are separate qualities, and they must be trained differently to maximize performance.

Strength can be defined as the ability to exert a maximal (or near maximal) force. The ability to exert this force does not depend on time. In fact, the more time we have to lift the load, the more muscle fibers we can recruit (a.k.a. summation of forces). For example, a powerlifter's main goal is to lift as much weight as possible in three main lifts—the bench press, squat, and deadlift. As the weight increases, the time required to move the weight increases. The amount of force required to lift the weight is very high, and it takes a long time for the muscles to exert near maximum force.

In contrast, power can be defined as the optimal combination of force and velocity to perform a task with skill and efficiency. For example, although similar to the back squat, the vertical jump is performed by generating enough force at a high enough speed to overcome the pull of gravity (32.2 ft/ sec^2 or 9.81 m/sec^2). When not performed quickly, the vertical jump resembles a squat because not enough power is created to generate thrust, or liftoff. When not trying to move a heavy load, just one's own body weight, it is much easier to produce the needed force fast enough to leave the ground. This force–speed trade-off is commonly known as the force–velocity continuum. Essentially, as load increases, the force required to move that load increases and movement velocity decreases. The lighter the load is, the less force is required to move it and the ability to move the load quickly increases. This can be seen in the previous example of using a back squat in contrast to a vertical jump.

Developing strength and power requires a good base of muscular endurance and fitness to support and accommodate higher levels of stress on the musculoskeletal and neurological systems. This is why strength and power training are typically performed during the latter stages of a linear periodization program, after establishing a general fitness base. Strength and power training also require a good level of mobility, stability, and motor control to execute movements correctly. These factors help increase the ability to synergize the joints and joint structures in more biomechanically advantageous positions to generate force while reducing injury risk.

Because power is the optimal combination of force and speed to perform a task, strength is generally considered a precursor to power. In other words, lacking the appropriate level of strength to generate force during explosive movements reduces power potential. Therefore, those seeking to improve power must first dedicate an appropriate amount of time to enhancing strength. For example, in plyometric, or jump-based, training, force is required to jump as high as necessary; however, strength is still required to land in a good biomechanical position to absorb the force of the landing, or to transition to another movement in a sporting activity (e.g., a jump to a sprint).

Incorporating Suspension Training Into a Strength and Power Program

Suspension Training exercises can be used as a primary method of developing strength and power or as an ancillary method depending on strength level and goals. When the primary goal is to develop strength and power for recreational activities, Suspension Training works well as the primary training method. However, if the primary goal is to enhance sport performance, Suspension Training should be used to augment traditional training methods. The following are ways to do so.

Priming for Bigger Exercises

Suspension Training exercises can be used as priming, or neuromuscular activation, exercises to prepare for heavier lifts (e.g., performing a chest fly or chest press a few minutes prior to performing a bench press). Essentially, these exercises force the intrinsic muscles that stabilize the joint during movement to work harder, which takes the emphasis off the prime movers. When the lifter attempts the heavier lift with a barbell or dumbbell, the stabilizers are activated, which may improve inter- and intramuscular coordination when performing heavier lifts.

Improving Lagging Muscles and Muscle Groups

Some people find that smaller and weaker muscles or muscle groups limit their ability to lift heavier weights or break out of a training plateau. Working these smaller muscle groups may improve strength, thereby improving performance on the target exercise. For example, during a chin-up, the biceps are a secondary mover, whereas the latissimus dorsi is the prime mover. Strengthening the biceps may result in the ability to perform more chin-ups.

Improving Training Density

Improving training density means getting in more training in less time. This can be done by inserting Suspension Training exercises aimed at improving mobility, stability, and coordination between heavy lifts in a strength and power program.

Preventing Injury and Overtraining

Suspension Training exercises may challenge the stabilizer muscles to a larger extent than traditional resistance training exercises do. This can improve joint stability and motor control, which enhances coordination and movement economy. Additionally, many of the drop drills can be used to improve dynamic stability, increase joint position sense, and teach proper landing mechanics as a precursor to plyometric training. The ability to decrease the load while increasing the intensity makes Suspension Training a valuable asset to any training program.

Strength is typically developed using low volumes (i.e., sets × reps) and heavy weights. Generally, a training load that can be lifted only six or fewer times is prescribed to optimize strength gains. Thus, developing strength directly from Suspension Training requires the performance of exercises that allow only six or fewer repetitions. For beginners, such exercises may not be hard to find, but for experienced lifters, this becomes more challenging. Adding dumbbells, medicine balls, kettlebells, and weighted vests can increase the load and continue to challenge strength levels. Performing single-leg Suspension Training exercises is another way to increase the workload to enhance strength.

Power exercises often use similar repetition ranges to strength exercises. This is because they are highly neurologically demanding (i.e., performing more than 10 repetitions often leads to significant power reductions as fatigue ensues). Also, as fatigue increases, the risk of injury increases exponentially. Some Suspension Training power exercises are more general and may be great progressions or regressions for those looking for sport-specific plyometric variations.

Developing a Strength Program Using Suspension Training

A sufficient load, or training weight, must be used to optimize strength gains. For some people, especially beginners, body weight exercises provide the challenge necessary for improving strength. This does not mean that working in higher repetition ranges will not improve strength; it just will not optimize strength. To increase strength significantly, a person may need to add weight to some Suspension Training exercises—for example, wearing a weighted vest when doing performing an inverted or low row, holding a pair of dumbbells or kettlebells when performing a reverse lunge, or manipulating body position and angle to increase resistance. Manipulating Suspension Training exercises to keep them in a range of one to eight repetitions before volitional fatigue can result in significant strength improvements.

For the strongest of the strong, such as powerlifters and weightlifters, time under tension (TUT) training in conjunction with more traditional forms of training may be a more appropriate use of Suspension Training, rather than using it as a method of optimizing strength. By increasing the amount of time a muscle is under tension, the amount of time the muscle is under isometric stress is increased. This forces the lifter to use good form and technique, as well as increases the stabilization and metabolic demands of an exercise. For these reasons it is a great addition to training for those seeking to improve maximal strength. The following are explanations of how to implement this style of training.

Time Under Tension (TUT) Method

The Time Under Tension (TUT) method requires slow movements to increase the amount of time the muscle is under stress. This is accomplished by increasing the amount of time spent performing the concentric (lifting and shortening the muscle) portion of the exercise, holding the contraction (isometric muscle action) for a few seconds at the peak, and slowly lowering (eccentric muscle action) back to the starting position. This technique progressively overloads the muscle using volume rather than increased training load. For example, if it normally takes 10 seconds to perform 10 push-ups, using TUT it may take up to 60 seconds (2 seconds in the lowering phase, 2 seconds holding the body in the down position, and 2 seconds to return to the starting position).

TUT, which is popular for improving hypertrophy, is beneficial for increasing strength in the ligaments and connective tissues, as well as smaller stabilizer muscles. These improvements may lead to greater overall gains in strength and power. The following are a few examples of how to use the TUT method. These can be applied to any of the dynamic Suspension Training (non-isometric exercises) in this text:

- *2-second descent*: 1-second hold, 2-second ascent (2-1-2 × 10-12 reps)
- *3-second descent*: 1-second hold, 3-second ascent (3-1-3 × 8 reps)
- *5-second descent*: 1-second hold, 5-second ascent (5-1-5 × 6 reps)
- *2-second descent:* 2-second hold, 2-second ascent (2-2-2 × 10-12 reps)
- *3-second descent:* 3-second hold, 3-second ascent (3-3-3 × 8 reps)
- *5-second descent:* 5-second hold, 5-second ascent (5-5-5 × 6 reps)
- *2-second descent:* 5-second hold, 2-second ascent (2-2-2 × 10 reps).

These are just a few suggestions on how to manipulate the tempos when using the TUT method. Remember, as the time that your muscles are under stress increases, muscular fatigue will also increase. If you are unable to perform the exercises with good form and technique for all of the desired repetitions, you may perform a cluster set in order to maintain overall training volume and good form.

Using the TUT method with Suspension Training increases both complexity and intensity while maintaining the safety of a lesser load. These methods are also good for improving motor learning, joint position sense, and body awareness, which translates to a greater ability to stabilize and support heavier training loads.

Integrating Suspension Training Into a Training Program

The following are two sample dynamic warm-ups using TUT training. They were designed for use with a split training program (i.e., upper body one day and lower body on another day). The first should be used prior to a heavy upper-body lifting session, and the second should be used prior to a heavy lower-body lifting session. These warm-ups should be performed just before the weight training session in the sequence listed for one or two sets. The feet can be adjusted to increase or decrease intensity. Because this is a warm-up, it should be moderately challenging but not overly difficult to avoid becoming fatigued prior to performing the working sets.

Upper-Body TUT Method Warm-Up

1. *Standing push-up plus*—10 reps at a 3:0:1 tempo (3 seconds down and 1 second to return to the starting position).
2. *Prone iron cross*—Lower and hold 10 seconds; then return to the starting position (5 reps).
3. Split fly—10 reps at a 3: 1: 3 tempo (3 seconds down, hold 1 second, then 3 seconds to return to the starting position).
4. *Suspended push-up*—10 reps at a 3:3 tempo with an isometric hold (3 seconds down, hold for 3 seconds at the bottom of the movement, and then 3 seconds to return to the starting position).
5. *Rear deltoid row*—5 reps at a 3:0:3 tempo (3 seconds down and 3 seconds to return to the starting position).
6. *Field goal*—5 reps at a 3:0:3 tempo (3 seconds down and 3 seconds to return to a starting position).

Lower-Body TUT Method Warm-Up

1. *Glute bridge*—5 reps at a 3:0:1 tempo (3 seconds down and 1 second to return to the starting position).
2. *Lying leg curl*—5 reps at a 3:0:3 tempo (3 seconds down and 3 seconds to return to the starting position).
3. *Iso squat*—Lower and hold 5 seconds; then return to the starting position for 5 reps.
4. *Iso lateral squat*—Lower and hold 5 seconds; then return to the starting position for 8 reps on each side.
5. *Overhead squat*—5 reps at a 3:3:3 tempo (3 seconds down, hold for 3 seconds, then seconds to return to the starting position).

Developing a Power Program Using Suspension Training

Plyometric exercises are commonly used to improve power. The term *plyometric* literally means to increase distance or measure. These exercises rely heavily on the stretch-shortening cycle, proprioceptors, and stored elastic energy to produce power. The following are the three phases of a plyometric movement:

1. Rapid and eccentric loading or descending portion of the movement
2. Concentric action (force production or the propulsive phase of the movement)
3. Amortization phase (the time between the eccentric loading and concentric force production portion of these movements).

Fully benefiting from this form of training requires reducing the time spent in the amortization phase, so the body can take full advantage of stored elastic energy. However, maintaining good form and technique when first learning these drills, or as fatigue builds, can be difficult. Two major reasons for this are poor technique and a lack of strength to maintain a proper body position when absorbing the force created by body weight at landing. For this reason, we recommend performing several weeks to months of resistance training prior to adding power training to an exercise program to build enough strength to maintain good form and technique. We also recommend learning how to absorb force at landing prior to performing jumping movements. This will ensure good technique at landing and reduce the risk of injury as the power training program progresses.

Sample Suspension Training Strength and Power Programs

The following are three sample strength and power programs using Suspension Training, starting with a beginner program. Those who can perform more than eight repetitions for four consecutive sets of an exercise can progress to the next level. Someone who can perform more than 8 repetitions of the exercises in the advanced column can increase the intensity by adding resistance in the form of dumbbells or a weighted vest.

Following the strength programs are three sample power programs using plyometrics. These programs should be performed prior to lifting sessions because they are quite fatiguing. Fatigue decreases the ability to maintain good form and technique, reducing both safety and effectiveness. Each drill should be performed with the best technique possible to ensure proper movement mechanics. The program choice should be based on the level of experience with the exercises; however, it is good to start with the beginner program and advance only after mastering both the form and technique of each exercise.

Beginner Suspension Training Strength Program

INSTRUCTIONS

Perform this program two or three days per week with a minimum of 48 hours between training sessions. For each exercise, perform three or four sets of six to eight repetitions with 60 to 90 seconds of rest between sets.

EXERCISES

1. Reverse lunge (pg. 107)
2. Inverted row (pg. 64)
3. Chest press (pg. 37)
4. Rear deltoid row (pg. 64)
5. Biceps curl (pg. 65)
6. Kneeling skull crusher (pg. 46)
7. Calf raise (pg. 100)
8. Reverse crunch (pg. 148)
9. Lying leg curl (pg. 102)

Intermediate Suspension Training Strength Program

INSTRUCTIONS

Perform this program two or three days per week with a minimum of 48 hours between training sessions. For each exercise, perform three or four sets of six to eight repetitions with 60 to 90 seconds of rest between sets.

EXERCISES

1. Pistol squat (pg. 119)
2. Low row (pg. 70)
3. Chest fly (pg. 45)
4. T fly (pg. 74)
5. Reverse biceps curl (pg. 75)
6. Standing skull crusher (pg. 61)
7. Single-leg calf raise (pg. 108)
8. Kneeling rollout (pg. 151)
9. Single-leg lying leg curl (pg. 129)

Advanced Suspension Training Strength Program

INSTRUCTIONS

Perform two or three days per week with a minimum of 48 hours between training sessions. For each exercise, perform for three or four sets of six to eight repetitions with 60 to 90 seconds of rest between sets.

EXERCISES

1. Rear foot elevated split squat with dumbbells
2. Single-arm inverted row (pg. 77)
3. Incline push-up (pg. 51)
4. Single-arm biceps curl (pg. 79)
5. Standing overhead triceps extension (pg. 38)
6. Single-leg calf raise (pg. 108)
7. Pike (pg. 158)
8. Single-leg lying leg curl (pg. 129)

Beginner Suspension Training Power Program

INSTRUCTIONS

Perform two or three sets of 8 to 10 repetitions per exercise. All single-leg exercises should be completed with 8 to 10 repetitions on each leg.

EXERCISES

1. Iso squat (pg. 92)
2. Iso lateral squat (pg. 96)
3. Drop squat (pg. 113)
4. Drop split squat (pg. 114)
5. Drop push-up (pg. 54)

Intermediate Suspension Training Power Program

INSTRUCTIONS

Perform two or three sets of five or six repetitions per exercise. All single-leg exercises should be completed with 5 to 6 repetitions on each leg.

EXERCISES

1. Drop split squat (pg. 114)
2. Squat jump (pg. 115)
3. Split squat jump to stick (pg. 118)
4. Lateral skater with stick (pg. 117)
5. Countermovement jump to stick (pg. 116)
6. Alternated split squat jump to stick (pg. 135)
7. Explosive push-up (pg. 56)

Advanced Suspension Training Power Program

INSTRUCTIONS

Perform two sets of five or six repetitions per exercise. All single-leg exercises should be completed with 5 to 6 repetitions on each leg.

EXERCISES

1. Squat jump (pg. 115)
2. Repeat countermovement jump (pg. 132)
3. Repeat lateral skater (pg. 133)
4. Alternated repeat split squat jump (pg. 135)
5. Plyo push-up (pg. 58)

CHAPTER 12

Speed and Agility

Speed is one of the most highly desirable attributes in sport. The need for speed is obvious in sprint events, such as in track and field. However, in field and court sports, speed is essential for creating space in relation to defenders when playing offensive positions. When playing defensive positons, speed is necessary for reducing space in relation to offensive players.

Suspension Training can improve speed by developing the underlying physical qualities that support speed development. Improving posture, mobility, and stability via Suspension Training can transfer directly to on-field performance, while also building injury resistance. This chapter addresses the speed attributes necessary for succeeding in sport, as well as how to use Suspension Training to develop specific muscles and abilities that can improve speed.

What Are Speed and Agility?

Although speed and agility have elements in common, they are different qualities. Improving them requires an understanding of their differences. Speed can be defined as the ability to cover a given distance in a certain amount of time. Generally, we think of speed as the ability to move between two points as fast as possible, especially in relation to sports like track and field. However, in most field- and court-based sports, these two points are rarely in a straight line for more than 5 to 10 yards or meters. For this reason, speed can be broken down into straight-line (linear) speed and change-of-direction speed (CODS). CODS is the ability to change direction with skill and efficiency without a visual, kinesthetic, or auditory stimulus signaling the need to do so. CODS is a critical aspect of agility as it represents a major physical attribute related to this skill. Agility combines CODS (a physical quality) and the ability to react and respond to a stimulus (a mental ability).

Physical Qualities That Contribute to Speed and Agility

From a physical standpoint, linear speed and agility depend on the ability to stabilize the trunk and specific joints to create, reduce, and transfer force during running and cutting movements. Mobility at other joints is also essential to promote proper reloading of the musculoskeletal system and to prepare the body to produce force at foot strike. Although the specifics of speed and agility technique are beyond the scope of this book, we present exercises for developing and preparing the musculature and joints to enhance speed technique.

Chu and Korchemny (1993) described two main phases associated with sprinting: the support phase and the flight phase. The support phase starts at foot strike and is where braking occurs. During this phase, the ankle, knee, and hip bend slightly to absorb the force of landing on one leg while the opposite leg ankle, knee and hip are flexed in preparation for the next foot strike. The flight phase is characterized by the rising and falling of the center of mass and the time during the sprint cycle in which the feet are not in contact with the ground. Figure 12.1 displays these phases.

Sample Suspension Training Speed and Agility Programs

Suspension Training can be used to improve three major areas of speed and agility: posture, arm action, and leg action. This section presents exercises for developing the muscles needed for making improvements in these areas.

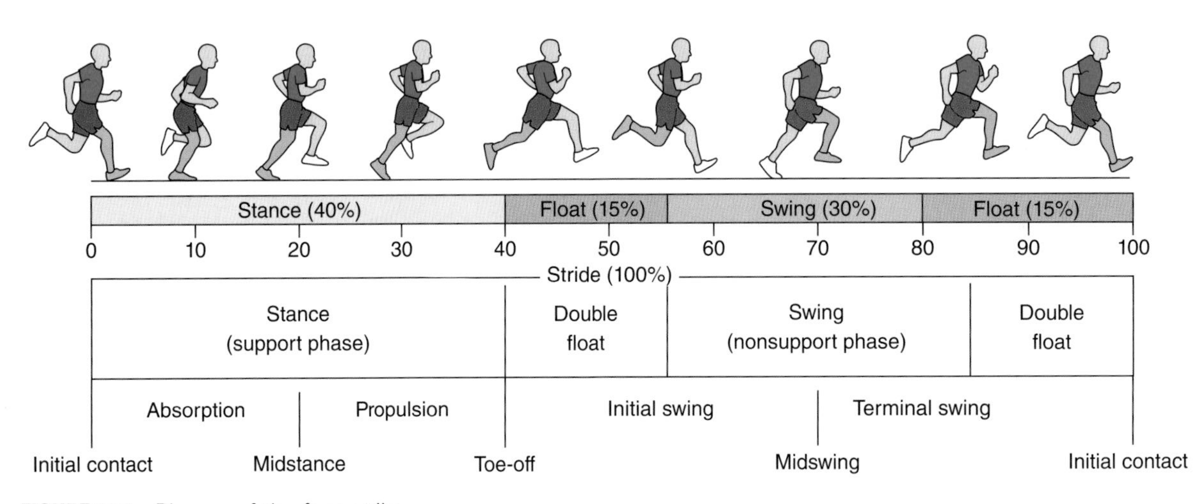

FIGURE 12.1 Phases of the foot strike.

Suspension Training Speed Posture Program

Proper posture is essential for proper sprinting mechanics and change-of-direction speed. Both the back extensors and the abdominal muscles, also known as the core, stabilize the pelvis while running. Therefore, a strong and stable core provides a solid platform, or base, for movement at the shoulder and hip joints. This platform is essential for maximizing stride length and stride frequency during sprinting and when accelerating. It is also essential for maintaining trunk integrity during agility movements, especially when an unexpected force is presented, such as getting hit by or colliding with an object or opponent. The following Suspension Training exercises can improve core stability and thus both speed and agility.

INSTRUCTIONS

Perform 2 or 3 rounds (one round is equivalent to performing one set of each exercise, preferably in order).

EXERCISES

1. Palov press (pg. 147): 5 times on each side at a 3:3 tempo
2. Side plank (pg. 145): 30 seconds on each side
3. Sprinter plank (pg. 144): 10 reps on each leg at a 1:3 tempo (drive the knee; then slowly return to the starting position)
4. Kneeling rollout (pg. 151): 10 reps
5. Reverse lunge with horizontal push (pg. 110): 10 reps

Suspension Training Arm Action Program

Arm speed governs leg speed: the faster the arms move and coordinate with lower-body actions, the greater the speed will be. Strength in the shoulders and arms is important for efficient arm action. The arms also help decelerate the body and maintain balance during all-out speed episodes and cutting movements. Therefore, strengthening the elbow extensors and flexors, in addition to increasing muscular endurance and joint stability, results in greater force generation and momentum during a hard cut or deceleration. Additionally, the muscles of the shoulders and back are essential for generating power and explosiveness for lower-body propulsion and leg turnover. The integrity of both the shoulder joint and the elbow joint is also important for remaining relaxed while running so that the postural muscles can stabilize the trunk and shoulders and thus maintain proper body positioning. The musculature also helps maintain speed endurance during longer track and field and endurance events, as well as during repeated sprints, by reducing fatigue during the latter stages of a competition.

A benefit of using Suspension Training is that when performing many traditional isolation exercises, (i.e., leg extension, leg curl) the core must work harder to stabilize the trunk. Many times, these exercises are performed with the trunk in contact with a pad, which acts to stabilize the spine and subsequently reduces the cores involvement in the exercise. Suspension Training shifts the emphasis form training muscle groups in isolation back to a total body integration to execute the exercise effectively. The following Suspension Training exercises can improve arm action while sprinting or changing directions, or both.

INSTRUCTIONS

Perform 2 or 3 rounds.

EXERCISES

1. Scapular retraction (pg. 62): 10 reps
2. Inverted row (pg. 63): 10 reps
3. Rear deltoid row (pg. 64): 10 reps
4. Supine iron cross (pg. 69): 5 reps
5. Sprinter chest press (pg. 42): 10 reps

Suspension Training Leg Action Programs

Speed is improved by increasing either stride length or stride frequency. Many drills develop these variables by improving balance, mobility, flexibility, power and strength, as addressed in chapter 10 and 12. This section uses a part-to-whole approach to look at muscles that may benefit from isolation work to improve stability and endurance while also enhancing power output for the larger-muscle-group exercises presented in chapter 10.

GLUTES

The gluteus maximus, gluteus medius, and gluteus minimus are critical for controlling motion at the hip joint and for hip extension during the propulsion phase of sprinting. They are also critical for preventing hip drop, which may lead to overuse injuries such as IT band syndrome, knee pain or injury, and low back issues. The following exercises can be used to target and strengthen the gluteal muscles and to develop controlled range of motion at the hip joint.

Instructions
Perform 2 or 3 rounds.

Exercises

1. Glute bridge (pg. 138): 30 to 60 seconds
2. Side plank (pg. 145): 30 seconds on each side
3. Deep squat (pg. 91): 10 reps
4. Reverse lunge with knee drive (pg. 90) or Sprinter lunge (pg. 98): 10 reps on each side
5. Lateral lunge (pg. 97): 10 reps on each side

HAMSTRINGS

The function of the hamstrings is to decelerate the leg during knee extension and to assist in knee flexion during running to position the leg for the next foot strike. Training the hamstrings is critical to reduce the risk of overuse injury and to prevent overstretching at the knee joint. Therefore, the hamstrings must be both strong and pliable to control high-speed stretching (eccentric muscle actions), yet strong enough to prevent knee hyperextension at ground contact. The following exercises develop hamstring strength and flexibility.

Instructions
Perform 2 or 3 rounds.

Exercises

1. Single-leg reaching Romanian deadlift (pg. 89): 10 reps on each side
2. Lying leg curl (pg. 102): 10 reps on each side
3. Single-leg lying leg curl (pg. 129): 5 reps on each side
4. Triangle squat (pg. 103): 10 reps
5. Figure-four stretch (pg. 105): 3 × 10-second hold on each side

(continued)

KNEE EXTENSORS

The quadriceps (the muscle at the front of the thigh) works as a knee extensor. Knee extension during running occurs when the leg straightens to prepare to make ground contact. The quadriceps consist of the rectus femoris, vastus medialis, vastus lateralis, and vastus intermedius of the upper portion of the thigh. The popliteus muscle helps stabilize the back of the knee during the extension and internal rotation of the tibia in relation to the femur to unlock it during knee extension. The plantaris muscle also assists with knee extension and ankle plantar flexion during running.

The biomechanics of running are complex: many muscle groups need to work in concert for efficient action. The following exercises can be used to isolate many of these muscle groups to strengthen them and reduce injury risk. The lower-body exercises in chapter 6 can be used to increase strength and power in these muscles.

Instructions

Perform 2 or 3 sets of exercise 1 and once you are able to perform 3 sets of this exercise for two workouts in a row, progress to exercise 2.

Exercises

1. Suspended knee extension (pg. 112): 10-12 reps
2. Single-leg suspended knee extension (pg. 130): 5 to 10 reps on each side

HIP FLEXION

Hip flexion is essential for generating power and forward propulsion during running. The iliopsoas, rectus femoris, tensor fasciae latae, pectineus, and gracilis muscles all contribute to hip flexion. Strong hip flexors are critical for loading the hip to generate force at foot strike. Hip mobility increases the amplitude of the hips' range of motion, which may assist in generating more force. The following exercises strengthen and stretch many of these muscle groups, while also developing the core.

Instructions

Perform 2 or 3 rounds.

Exercises

1. Push-up with reverse crunch (pg. 44): 10 reps
2. Bicycle crunch (pg. 149): 10 reps on each side
3. Reverse lunge with knee drive (pg. 90): 10 reps on each side
4. Pike (pg. 158): 10 reps

CALVES

The gastrocnemius and soleus muscles make up the calves. The gastrocnemius crosses both the knee and the ankle joint, whereas the soleus crosses only the ankle. The rapid eccentric loading of the gastrocnemius and soleus, combined with plantar flexion of the ankle, is responsible for the powerful push-off action that occurs at foot strike. Both are vital for locomotive movements such as walking and running.

Instructions

Perform 2 or 3 sets of exercise 1 and once you are able to perform 3 sets of this exercise for two workouts in a row, progress to exercise 2. Resistance can be added by adding weighted vests, or holding a dumbbell in one hand and using the suspension strap in the other hand to help maintain balance.

Exercises

1. Calf raise (pg. 100): 20 to 30 reps
2. Single-leg calf raise (pg. 108): 10 to 15 reps

FEET

The plantar surface (bottom) of the foot, in conjunction with the calf muscles, helps create a stable platform at foot strike. Strong plantar muscles are critical for stabilizing the foot joints during ground contact because of the extensive mobility of the foot. The following exercises target these muscle groups. It is recommended to perform these exercise barefoot when possible to reduce the stability created from athletic footwear and improves proprioceptive awareness.

Instructions

Perform 2 or 3 rounds.

Exercises

1. Single-leg reaching Romanian deadlift (pg. 89): 10 reps on each side
2. Leg sweep (pg. 99): 10 reps on each side

CHAPTER 13

Balance, Stability, and Flexibility

Movement is a complex process that requires harmonious interactions of the neural, muscular, and skeletal systems to produce, reduce, and resist forces. Unfortunately, muscle imbalances, poor posture, improper technique, previous injury, and repetitive physical stress can keep these systems from functioning properly.

Balance, stability, and flexibility are critical to athletic performance, good health, injury prevention, and most daily activities. Moreover, the natural aging process tends to result in a reduction in both balance and flexibility, which may impede function and the ability to live independently. For these reasons, it is extremely important to attain acceptable levels of these qualities and to maintain them throughout the life span. This chapter addresses factors that influence balance, stability, and flexibility, and explains how to develop them using Suspension Training.

What Are Balance, Stability, and Flexibility?

This section discusses the major differences between balance, stability, and flexibility. It also explains how they interact to foster efficient movement and neuromuscular activity.

Balance

Balance can be defined as the ability to maintain equilibrium. In terms of movement, balance is generally thought of as trying to maintain one's center of mass within the base of support. As weight shifts, numerous subtle adjustments are needed to remain in a balanced state and keep from falling. Although this seems to be a relatively simple concept, the ability to maintain balance, especially during activity, is a very complex process. The central nervous system must process information received from the balance mechanisms in the inner ear, the eyes, and the receptors in the joints and muscles (proprioceptors). It then sends this information back to the musculoskeletal system to create both static (in place) and dynamic (with movement) equilibrium.

Improving balance requires performing activities that challenge balance. Including Suspension Training exercises in a comprehensive training program is an excellent way to add progressive amounts of instability in a safe, controlled environment while also enhancing proprioception.

Stability

Stability, or motor control, is the ability to resist unwanted movements. Stabilizing joints and joint structures during movement is necessary for producing and reducing force, as well as for resisting unwanted forces on the body during sudden or unanticipated movements. For instance, during sprinting or jumping, it is important to stabilize the trunk to transfer the forces created from the ground up through the body to move either horizontally or vertically. An inability to stabilize the torso creates energy leaks within the body that result in unwanted and inefficient movements that may interfere with performance and increase the risk of injury.

One of the major benefits of using Suspension Training within a training program is that most Suspension Training exercises require and develop trunk stability. For example, a biceps curl or triceps extension exercise performed on a Suspension Trainer becomes a dynamic trunk stability workout as well as a way to work on aesthetic goals such as improving the tone or size of the upper arms. This is especially useful for those who want to develop the bicep and triceps, which is a goal often considered irrelevant to sport functioning. Incorporating these exercises into a workout can increase enthusiasm for training by meeting both aesthetic and training goals.

Flexibility

Flexibility is the ability to move freely throughout a wide range of purposeful movements without restriction. Some refer to it as the available range of motion around a joint. Technically, this describes mobility, because it relates to joint function rather than tissue (muscle) extensibility. Flexibility can be thought of as the muscles' range of motion, whereas mobility can be thought of as the joints' range of motion. However, the two are intimately related. Poor flexibility in the muscles that surround a joint can certainly impede joint range of motion, or mobility. Flexibility is affected by variables such as age, gender, joint structure, activity level, and heredity. Of these, the only modifiable factor is activity level. Performing exercises through joints' full safe ranges of motion can improve both flexibility and mobility.

Similar to balance, flexibility can be classified as both static and dynamic. Static flexibility exercises are best for improving long-term flexibility, whereas dynamic flexibility exercises improve short-term flexibility. Therefore, using dynamic flexibility exercises prior to a workout session is a great way to prepare the body for more vigorous activity. In contrast, static flexibility exercise is best used postworkout to reduce muscle imbalances and improve body symmetry.

Sample Balance, Stability, and Flexibility Programs

The following programs improve balance, stability, and flexibility. Depending on current fitness levels, they may be used as stand-alone workouts, as active recovery programs between more intense training sessions, or as part of a dynamic warm-up prior to traditional resistance training.

Suspension Training Balance Program

Holding the straps of the Suspension Trainer is an excellent beginning balance training exercise because it provides additional, yet slightly unstable, support. Performing floor exercises unilaterally or on an unstable surface (e.g., foam pad) can further challenge the proprioceptors. Although most exercises for balance involve the lower body, some upper-body floor exercises, such as planks, can also be used.

The progression of Suspension Training balance exercises should be from a two-point base to a one-point base. Next, a pillow or foam pad can be used to increase the instability of a one-point base.

The following are exercises that develop both static and dynamic balance. They are best performed as part of an integrated dynamic warm-up, as part of a superset during a traditional weight training session, or instead of a complete rest between sets. Using them in place of rests increases the density of a session by providing more work in the same time frame without detracting from the primary focus of training.

INSTRUCTIONS

Perform 2 or 3 rounds of the following circuit. If performing this as a stand-alone workout, use the higher end of the repetition range. If used as an active recovery or as part of a dynamic warm-up, perform the lower end of the repetition range.

EXERCISES

1. Reaching hip flexor stretch (pg. 106): 5 to 10 reps on each side
2. Single-leg reaching Romanian deadlift (pg. 89): 5 to 10 reps on each side
3. Leg sweep (pg. 99): 5 to 10 reps on each side
4. Single-leg chest press (pg. 39): 5 to 10 reps on each side
5. Single-leg chest fly (pg. 55): 5 to 10 reps on each side
6. Reverse lunge with chop and lift (pg. 109): 5 to 10 reps on each side
7. Reverse lunge with overhead press (pg. 124): 5 to 10 reps on each side
8. Reverse lunge with single-arm overhead press (pg. 125): 5 to 10 reps on each side
9. Overhead squat (pg. 94): 5 to 10 reps on each side
10. Drop squat (pg. 113): 5 reps
11. Drop split squat (pg. 114): 5 reps

Suspension Training Core Stability Program

Core strength stability is essential for optimal performance. The core provides a stable base of support that facilitates fluid and precise arm and leg movements. The following program emphasizes core stability and control. It can be used as a dynamic warm-up prior to a traditional resistance training session or as a stand-alone workout.

INSTRUCTIONS

Perform the exercises in order for 1 to 3 rounds with no more than 1 minute of rest between rounds.

EXERCISES

1. Glute bridge (pg. 138): 20 reps; hold at the top for two counts, then slowly lower the hips until they are approximately 3-6 inches off the ground, then return to the bridge position.
2. Rotational side plank (pg. 146): 10 reps on each side
3. Bicycle crunch (pg. 149): 20 reps
4. Pike (pg. 158): 10 reps
5. Extended-arm plank (pg. 143): 10 to 30 seconds on each side

Suspension Training Flexibility Programs

Suspension Training can be used to improve both static and dynamic flexibility. Performing purposeful dynamic movements at a low intensity improves the dynamic flexibility of muscles, tendons, and surrounding connective tissue. Using Suspension Training statically provides the advantage of gravity or resistance to increase range of motion. The following dynamic and static flexibility workouts can be used as part of a Suspension Training session before (dynamic) and after (static) a traditional strength training session to improve flexibility.

The exercises in these workouts progress in difficulty primarily through the angle of attack or the angle in relation to the anchor point. As in resistance training, an increased angle increases the difficulty of the stretch. Some exercises appear as both dynamic and static flexibility exercises; the main difference between these types of exercises is the amount of time spent holding the stretch (no more than a few seconds in dynamic versions, and longer in static versions).

DYNAMIC FLEXIBILITY PROGRAM

This workout should be performed as part of a warm-up prior to an exercise session. These exercises prepare the musculoskeletal system for more vigorous activity.

Instructions

Perform 10 to 20 reps per exercise. Hold the stretched position for 1 to 3 seconds before performing the next repetition.

Exercises

1. Deep squat (pg. 91)
2. Triangle squat (pg. 103)
3. Reaching hip flexor stretch (pg. 106)
4. Reverse lunge with knee drive (pg. 90)
5. Push-up plus (pg. 40)
6. Overhead squat (pg. 94)

STATIC FLEXIBILITY PROGRAM

This program should be performed at the end of a training session to improve flexibility.

Instructions

Choose at least 1 exercise for each body region. Hold the stretched position for 10 to 30 seconds. Perform 1 to 3 sets for each exercise for a duration of 30 to 60 seconds. The following is a sample static stretching program. These exercises can be replaced with more advanced exercises as the user progresses.

Exercises

1. Pec stretch (pg. 81)
2. Overhead lat stretch (pg. 84)
3. Rear deltoid stretch (pg. 85)
4. Deep squat (pg. 91)
5. Iso lateral squat (pg. 96)
6. Overhead squat (pg. 94)
7. Pigeon stretch (pg. 104)
8. Figure four stretch (pg. 105)

Balance, Stability, and Flexibility Suspension Program

The following is a dynamic warm-up routine that combines balance, stability, and flexibility.

INSTRUCTIONS

Perform 2 or 3 rounds of the following exercises.

EXERCISES

1. Glute bridge (pg. 138): 20 reps
2. Elbow plank (pg. 140): 20 seconds
3. Side plank (pg. 145): 20 seconds on each side
4. Reverse crunch (pg. 148): 10 reps
5. Push-up plus (pg. 40): 10 reps
6. Overhead squat (pg. 94): 10 reps
7. Lateral squat (pg. 95): 10 reps on each side
8. Reverse lunge with knee drive (pg. 90): 10 reps on each side
9. Excursions (pg. 88): 5 reps on each side
10. Drop squat (pg. 113): 5 reps
11. Leg sweep (pg. 99): 10 reps on each side

REFERENCES

Byrne, J.M., N.S. Bishop, A.M. Caines, K.A. Crane, A.M. Feaver, and G.E. Pearcey. 2014. Effect of using a suspension training system on muscle activation during the performance of a front plank exercise. *J. Strength Cond. Res.* 28 (11): 3049-3055.

Chu, D., and R. Korchemny. 1993. Sprinting stride actions: analysis and evaluations. *NSCA Journal* 11 (6): 48-53.

Garnacho-Castaño, M.V., Jiménez, P.J., Monroy, A.J., and Maté-Muñoz, J.L. 2014. Effects of instability versus traditional resistance training on strength, power and velocity in untrained men. *J. Sports Sci. Med.* 13: 460-468.

Janot, J., et al. 2013. Effects of TRX versus traditional resistance training programs on measures of muscular performance in adults. *Journal of Fitness Research.* 2 (2): 23-38.

Melrose D., and J. Dawes. 2015. Resistance characteristics of the TRX suspension training system at different angles and distances from the hanging point. *J. Athl. Enhancement.* 4:1.

Mok, N.W., E.W. Yeung, J.C. Cho, S.C. Hui, K.C. Liu, and C.H. Pang. 2015. Core muscle activity during suspension exercises. *J. Sci. Med. Sport.* 18 (2): 189-194.

Orr, R. 1999. The functional continuum. www.ptonthenet.com/articles/The-Functional-Continuum-557#sthash.zJ1KDQS3.dpuf.

Siff, M.C. 2003. *Supertraining,* 6th ed. Denver, CO: Supertraining Institute.

Snarr, R.L., and M.R. Esco. 2014. Electromyographical comparison of plank variations performed with and without instability devices. *J. Strength Cond. Res.* 28 (11): 3298-3305.

Snarr, R.L., M.R. Esco, E.V. Witte, C.T. Jenkins, and R.M. Brannan. 2013. Electromyographic Activity of rectus abdominis during a suspension push-up compared to traditional exercises. *J. Exerc. Physiol. Online.* 16 (3): 1-8.

ABOUT THE AUTHOR

Photo courtesy of Jay Dawes.

Jay Dawes PhD, CSCS,*D, NSCA-CPT,*D, FNSCA, ACSM-HFS ASCA-L2, is an assistant professor of strength and conditioning, coordinator for athletic performance, and head strength coach for women's soccer at the University of Colorado-Colorado Springs. He has worked as a strength and performance coach, educator, and post-rehabilitation specialist since 1997. He is a performance consultant for a wide variety of athletes, law enforcement officers, and those in physically demanding occupations.

Dawes is certified by the National Strength and Conditioning Association (NSCA) as a Certified Strength and Conditioning Specialist (CSCS) and as a certified personal trainer (NSCA-CPT); by the American College of Sports Medicine as a Health Fitness Specialist (ACSM-HFS); and by the Australian Strength and Conditioning Association as a Level 2 strength and conditioning coach. He was also recognized as a Fellow of the NSCA (FNSCA) in 2009.

Dawes is the coeditor of the NSCA's *Developing Agility and Quickness* (Human Kinetics, 2012) and coauthor of *Maximum Interval Training* (Human Kinetics, 2015). He has written numerous book chapters and articles on improving sports and tactical performance. His primary research interests are improving performance for sports and improving tactical performance among law enforcement officers. He lives in Colorado Springs, Colorado.